Ajax, the Dutch, the War

The Strange Tale of Soccer During Europe's Darkest Hour

Simon Kuper

NATION
BOOKS

A Member of the Perseus Books Group
New York

Copyright © 2012 by Simon Kuper

Published by
Nation Books, A Member of the Perseus Books Group
116 East 16th Street, 8th Floor
New York, NY 10003

Nation Books is a co-publishing venture of the Nation Institute
and the Perseus Books Group.

Books published by Nation Books are available at special discounts for
bulk purchases in the United States by corporations, institutions, and other
organizations. For more information, please contact the Special Markets
Department at the Perseus Books Group, 2300 Chestnut Street, Suite 200,
Philadelphia, PA 19103, or call (800) 255-1514, or e-mail
special.markets@perseusbooks.com.

Editorial production by the Book Factory.
Design by Cynthia Young at Sagecraft.

A CIP catalog record of this book is available from the Library of Congress.

ISBN-13: 978-1-56858-723-3 (paperback)
ISBN: 978-1-56858-724-0 (e-book)

10 9 8 7 6 5 4 3 2 1

PRAISE FOR
AJAX, THE DUTCH, THE WAR

"His fresh-eyed survey has a familiar theme but never
palls, crowded with a gallery of unlikely figures . . .
whose stories weave through the book."
—*Daily Telegraph*

"I have only bought one soccer book recently and
it's an absolute belter . . . heartily recommended."
—*The Times*

"Gripping and brilliant."—*Glasgow Herald*

"An intriguing social history, full of quirky anecdotes,
written with winning geniality and the dash of a
Brazilian forward . . . a beguiling book."
—*Financial Times*

"A fascinating tale, which Kuper describes
particularly well."—*Spectator*

"Kuper's poignant and perceptive account again proves
there can be more to soccer writing than fanzines
and pale Hornby imitations."—*GQ*

"A fascinating history, full of startling facts
and sobering detail."—*Telegraph*

"Kuper has fashioned a work which brilliantly juxtaposes
the everyday life of soccer clubs with the awful fate
suffered by so many of their Jewish players, officials,
and supporters."—*Time Out*

"An intriguing work."—*Independent*

Simon Kuper was born in Uganda in 1969 and spent most of his childhood in Holland. His first book, *Soccer Against the Enemy*, won the William Hill Sports Book of the Year and went on to become an international best seller. He now writes for the *Financial Times*.

ALSO BY
SIMON KUPER

Soccer Against the Enemy

Soccernomics

Soccer Men

To Adam, Jessica, Jeremy, and Hannah,
who shared the Dutch experience with me.

CONTENTS

ACKNOWLEDGMENTS

I received hundreds of hours of help in writing this book. Meijer Stad, Leon Greenman, Oscar Heisserer, Bennie Muller, Salo Muller, and many others spoke to me openly and at length. I cannot begin to imagine how difficult that was for some of them.

This book had an even more complicated genesis than most. Its ur-version appeared in March 2000 under the title *Ajax, de joden, Nederland* (or "Ajax, the Jews, the Netherlands"), as an entire issue of the fantastic Dutch literary soccer journal *Hard Gras*. It would never have been written but for the support of Holland's "Fonds voor Bijzondere Projekten," or Fund for Special Journalistic Projects. I am very grateful to the fund. Nor would the book ever have existed without the encouragement of the two founding editors of *Hard Gras*, Matthijs van Nieuwkerk and Henk Spaan. Over the last fifteen years they have become my friends and remained inspirations. I hope to work with them for decades more, as well as with other *Hard Gras* stalwarts and friends like Hugo Borst, Jimmy Burns, Jos de Putter, and Leo Verheul. Every writer needs a community like *Hard Gras*.

This book would never have appeared in English but for the Internet. I want to thank Menno Pot and his colleagues on the ajax-usa.com website for translating much of my Dutch book into English and posting it on the Web. There it was spotted by Mike Ticher of the *When Saturday Comes* fanzine who suggested I publish it in Britain. I remain very grateful to Mike and his colleague, Andy Lyons, and am sorry they were not involved in producing the English version.

In the mid-1990s I received a grant from the Society of Authors to help with my next book. It turned out to be this one. I am very grateful to the Society.

A number of excellent researchers worked with me on the book. Bart van Son was the ideal office mate in Amsterdam, collecting me from the hospital once as well as helping with the research. In England I want to thank Simon Martin, Duncan White, and my cousin, Dan Kuper.

My fellow journalists were surprisingly helpful. In our profession we are seldom generous with contacts or knowledge. Shaul Adar, Frits Barend, Tamarah Benima, Hugo Borst, Saggie Cohen, Gerhard Fischer, Shirley Haasnoot, Ulrich Lindner, Tara Spring, Jurryt van der Vooren, Evert de Vos, Tom Watt, and David Winner were. I am particularly grateful to the Ajax historian Evert Vermeer. I criticized Evert excessively in the Dutch version of this book, yet when I came to him for help in writing the second version, he was very kind—*een gentleman*, as the Dutch would say. I still disagree with him on one or two points, but no one can write about the history of Ajax without reading his work.

As a foreigner moving to Amsterdam for four months to write a book, I could easily have landed on the streets. That I did not is thanks to Willem Baars, Shirley Haasnoot, Hanno Huisjes, Muriel Rive, and Jeannette Kruseman. I wrote much of my Dutch book in the Baars Art Gallery on the Henri Polaklaan.

Much of what I know about the themes in this book I came to understand through conversations with friends and relatives. I may even have cribbed the odd idea. I am grateful to Shilpa Deshmukh, Adriaan Grijns, Raoul Heertje, Jeannette Kruseman, Adam and Jessica Kuper, the Levin family in Wassenaar, Rana Mitter, Will Pryce, Sharmila Rampeearee, Claudia Schnitzler, Hester, Jan Maarten and Rutger Slagter, and Philippe Wolgen.

Alex Bellos, Saggie Cohen, Adriaan Grijns, Jeannette Kruseman, Adam Kuper, Jan Maarten Slagter, and David Winner all read drafts of chapters and offered suggestions, most of which I used. It would probably be churlish to blame errors in this book on any of them.

For the time they gave me, I am grateful to David Barber of the Football Association, Victoria Barrett, Belia Brilleman, Wim Cassa, Uri Coronel, Phil Crossley, Remco van Dam, Simone Freeman, Karoline Fricke, Alex Fynn, Dick Gubbels, John Helliar, Chanan Hertzberger, Lex Hes, George Horn, Gerald Jacobs, Ann Jantzen, Olav Kes, Roechamma Koopman, Kuki Krol, Heiman de Leeuw, David Litterer, Guy Oliver, Rika Pais, Nico Salet, Thomas Schnitzler, Wim Schoevaart, Ger Schutte, Dror Shimson, Lennart Speijer, Mrs. Stad, Matthew Taylor, Margriet Valkman, Albert de Vries, Marcel ter Wal, Jacob van der Wijk, Harry van Wijnen, Marie-Ane van Wijnen, Jonathan Wilkinson of the British Council, Hans-Dieter Zimmermann, the Anne-Frankstichting, Amsterdam's Municipal Transport Company, the Nederlands Instituut voor Oorlogsdocumentatie, and the archivists of the *Nieuw Israelietisch Weekblad* and the municipal archives of Amsterdam and Rotterdam. Thanks also to Brian Oliver and the others at the *Observer* for remaining patient with me while I spent months locked in my room working on the book.

Many thanks to Ian Preece at Orion for agreeing to publish a book on the unpromising theme of Dutch soccer in World War II—although admittedly I did put in some English, German, and French soccer too. My previous agent Vivienne Schuster was a fierce supporter of this project despite knowing little about soccer and caring less. I am extremely grateful to Carl Bromley, my indefatigable editor at Nation Books, for being willing to risk this book in the United States. My agents at Curtis Brown, Gordon Wise and John Parton, fought my corner with their usual panache. Lori Hobkirk brilliantly managed the production of the American version, and Cynthia Young designed it. Thanks to all of them.

I thank everyone who is interviewed in the book.

A NOTE ON THE TEXT

Strictly speaking, the word "Holland" only refers to the two western provinces of the Netherlands. In this book I have often used it to mean the country as a whole. I have yet to meet a Dutch person who would be offended by this.

1

ORANGE SOLDIERS

In the Dutch movie *Soldier of Orange*, the main character, Erik (played by Rutger Hauer), is canoodling with a Jewish woman in a garden one night when they are startled by the sound of airplanes. "Germans, going to England," Erik reassures her, and they resume canoodling. Then the planes start firing their guns. It is the early morning of May 10, 1940, and the Germans are invading the Netherlands.

The unfamiliar sound of aircraft had awoken people all over the country. Few had expected the invasion because nothing much ever happened in the Netherlands. The Dutch had avoided the First World War, pretending not to notice when the German Army took a brief shortcut over their soil on its way into Flanders, and so had had no experience of war on their own land since Napoleon. So quiet was the Netherlands that after the Armistice in 1918 the Kaiser took gardening exile on a Dutch country estate. He was still there in 1940.

If the world's fires ever made it to the Netherlands, it was at a pretty low heat. A man named Pieter Troelstra had tried to proclaim a Dutch socialist republic in November 1918, but nobody paid much attention, and he was chastised in Parliament. Thirteen years later, while Stalin was executing hundreds of thousands of "Trotskyists" in the USSR, and street battles were raging in the Weimar Republic, the leading Dutch Trotskyist Henk Sneevliet was threatened by Stalinist thugs after a public meeting in Rotterdam. But he was escorted safely to the train station. Before World War II, that was about as hot as things got in Holland.

Waking in a Dutch hotel room on the night the Germans invaded in 1940 was a journalist named Ballantijn. He was traveling home from Rotterdam, where he had collected a Belgian visa to travel with Holland's soccer team to play Luxembourg on May 15. Hearing the planes, he raced outside to find German soldiers everywhere (this story is told by the Dutch historian Chris van der Heijden). Ballantijn asked one of the soldiers if he could return to his house near the German border, where his wife would be worrying about him. The German let him go. And so Ballantijn found himself ploughing eastward past a stream of German vehicles busy invading his country. "Strangely," he wrote later, "the drivers . . . gave all possible cooperation by making way for me."

Much of the Netherlands experienced something of a velvet invasion. In one spot, German soldiers needing planks to build a bridge over the river (one of the hazards of invading Holland) were looking for a wood mill. "The local people," recorded the author Anton Coolen, "argue among each other about whether the mill is still there, yes or no, and strain themselves to give the Germans the information they are asking for. . . . Some women have come out of their houses with trays of steaming coffee; they take these to the Germans, who fold up their maps and laugh."

The Dutch Army put up a brief fight, but on May 14 Luftwaffe bombs demolished central Rotterdam, and the next day the Netherlands capitulated. The first years of occupation passed calmly for most Dutch people. The few thousand Germans stationed in the country behaved themselves most of the time. The Nazi terror affected only a couple of hundred thousand people in the Netherlands: Resistance fighters, gypsies, and Jews. About three-quarters of the latter were murdered in the gas chambers; in all of Europe only Poland lost a larger proportion of its Jews.

On "Crazy Tuesday," September 5, 1944, there were sightings of Allied troops near the southern town of Breda. Premature celebrations of the Liberation began across the Netherlands. But the Allied landings at Arnhem failed ("a bridge too far"), and the part of the country north of the great rivers was doomed to a final winter of war. The *Hongerwinter*, in which people were reduced to eating tulip bulbs and about twenty thousand starved to death, remains a live memory in many Dutch families. Only on May 5, 1945, did the Germans surrender. Allied soldiers—mostly Canadians—drove through the country throwing emaciated people cigarettes and chocolate.

My family moved to the Netherlands just over thirty years later, in 1976. This was a fluke. My parents, Jews from South Africa, had spent the previous fifteen years traversing Cambridge, the Kalahari Desert, southern California, Uganda (where I was born), Jamaica, Sweden, and north London. My father, an anthropologist, had been hoping for a job in Ethiopia when he was unexpectedly offered one at the ancient Dutch university of Leiden. I was nearly seven years old at the time and had never heard of the Netherlands.

We moved into what I now know to be a typical Dutch street. The tiny terraced houses were fronted by large windows, through which passers-by could peer to make sure nothing untoward was happening inside. On one of our first Dutch evenings, my brother and I ventured outside to meet the other children, who greeted us by singing what were probably the only English words they knew: "Crazy boys, crazy boys!" But over the next few evenings relations improved, and soon we were regulars in the street's daily soccer match.

We integrated, more or less, learning Dutch and joining the local soccer club. But, without wishing to sound pathetic, we were never going to become entirely local. Our parents spoke Dutch with funny accents, and we were all too dark and too small to look Dutch. Nor were there many other Jews in Leiden, because they had almost all been killed in the war. My family was not religious, but I remember visiting the Leiden synagogue, an eighteenth-century building that was always virtually empty.

While I was at school the Dutch were just beginning to rediscover World War II, and particularly their resistance to the Germans. This was a thrilling topic if you were a boy in Leiden. *Soldier of Orange*, made in 1977 by the director Paul Verhoeven and nominated for the foreign-film Oscar of 1979, was set in our town. Watching the film again recently, I realized how cardboard it often is. The heroes are two-dimensional, and the British characters almost all speak like members of the royal family. Yet it remains probably the most popular Dutch film ever made, and it helped shape the Dutch memory of the war.

The film was based on the autobiography of Erik Hazelhoff Roelfzema, nicknamed the "Soldier of Orange." Born in 1917 into an upper-class Dutch family in Surabaya in the Dutch East Indies (now Indonesia), he had hitchhiked across the United States in the late 1930s and written *Rendezvous in San Francisco*, a book that would become a nonfiction best-seller in the Netherlands. Then he reverted to the classic path of posh Dutchmen, moving to Leiden, joining the student fraternity Minerva, and gently studying law. He was there when the Germans arrived.

The Leiden setting of *Soldier of Orange* was familiar to me. The city's ancient and beautiful center of brick houses along canals had barely changed since the war—in fact, it had barely changed since Rembrandt was born there in 1606. The Leiden I knew was still dominated by braying Minerva members dressed like nineteenth-century bankers, cycling from café to café, and intermittently diving drunk into canals. (Paul Verhoeven, inevitably, had been a Minerva fraternity brother.) *Soldier of Orange* was shown at Minerva every year, and many of the members knew the film by heart. They were carrying on the student life that Hazelhoff Roelfzema had known until that night of May 10, 1940. A few of them even inhabited his old student digs above a café on the magnificent Rapenburg canal street.

The film describes the war's effect on a group of Leiden students. One of the group, a Jew named Jan, is executed in the dunes while birds twitter and the wind howls. Another, the half-German Alex, joins the SS and is blown up on the Eastern Front while sitting on a toilet. A third, Robbie, initially operates a radio for the Resistance, but unbeknownst to his comrades is "turned" by the Germans. The Soldier of Orange himself, played by the extremely Aryan-looking Hauer, ends up fleeing with his friend Guus to England. There they meet Wilhelmina, the Dutch queen, in exile on London's Eaton Square. She sends them back to Holland on a Resistance mission.

Guus shoots the traitor Robbie and is then caught and executed, but the Soldier of Orange survives to escort the Queen back to Holland for the Liberation. In the final scene, he toasts the Liberation in the Leiden student digs of a friend who has sat out the war secretly taking exams. But the general impression the film gives is that half of Leiden was in the Resistance.

Hazelhoff Roelfzema moved to Hawaii in 1973 and died there in 2007 at age ninety. *Soldier of Orange* catapulted Verhoeven and Hauer into Hollywood where Hauer would build a career mostly playing Russian and Nazi villains. For me it confirmed Leiden as the home of the mighty Dutch Resistance.

Our town's other great Resistance story featured a dour law professor named Rudolf Cleveringa. In the first winter of the occupation, Cleveringa's former mentor, a brilliant professor named E. M. Meijers, received a standard stenciled letter informing him that as a Jew he was banned from teaching. On the morning of November 26, 1940, Cleveringa said farewell to his wife, and walked down the Rapenburg to the faculty building where Meijers had been scheduled to lecture. Cleveringa took his place.

The Great Auditorium was packed, and so the lecture was relayed by microphone to a second hall. Cleveringa's talk was a eulogy to Meijers's brilliance. Each time the audience tried to break into applause, he silenced it with a wave of his hand. The German dismissal of Meijers was illegal, he said. However, he advised his listeners against committing "pointless follies" (this was undoubtedly said to strengthen his case before the Germans after his inevitable arrest). Instead, he urged them to "always keep in our thoughts and our hearts the image of the figure and the personality of whom we cannot cease to believe ought to be standing here and, if God wills it, will return here."

There was silence, then a long ovation, and then a student began singing the national anthem. The audience took it up, many people in tears. Cleveringa handed the text of his speech to a colleague who had asked for it, and walked home.

That evening a student named Koch assembled some other students in his rooms, sat them down at typewriters, and made them type endless copies of Cleveringa's speech. "There were chaps there," Koch said later, "who could barely type. Many bottles of beer were pressed into use." By five the next morning he had nearly fifty copies. He then assembled ten girl students, "to whom I gave tea," and set them typing too. The copies were posted around the country, creating the impetus for the Dutch Resistance (or so the popular Leiden version had it). Leiden students went on strike, and in 1942 the Germans closed the university, which is why the Soldier of Orange's friend had to take his exams in secret.

Cleveringa had been arrested two days after his speech. After eight months in jail he was released unhurt. He and Meijers both survived the war. Discussing Cleveringa in the mid-1980s with a friend of my mother's, a local nurse, I asked her whether she knew if he were still alive. "He's dead," she said.

"Are you sure?" I asked peskily.

"He died in my arms," she said.

Even forty years on, the war was still all around us. As a child in Leiden I played soccer and cricket with a gangling, friendly boy whose grandfather, proprietor of a cigar shop, was known to have run the local Resistance. A colleague of my father's was the only survivor of a wartime raid by his Resistance group. Our Jewish next-door neighbor's father had lost his first family in the gas chambers. Everyone of the right age had a war story.

I got the sense that people had never forgiven the Germans, who, in those days before they began heading off to Spanish islands, still took their beach holidays in the chilly Dutch coastal villages a few miles from Leiden. The villagers hung signs in German in their front windows, saying "Room free with breakfast," and people in Leiden mocked them. One of our neighbors said that if he met a German asking directions he still sent him the wrong way, just as people had done in the war. One reason the occupation remained such an obsession was that no other great event had hit the Netherlands in living memory. "If the world comes to an end, I want to move to Holland, because everything happens there twenty years later," the German poet Heinrich Heine is supposed to have said (though no one can find the reference).

If Holland was a backwater of Europe, Leiden was a backwater of Holland. I remember spending many Sundays in the early 1980s looking out of my window (by now we had moved to a house on a main road) and marveling whenever a car drove past. On Heine's analogy, everything in Leiden happened about forty years later. Albert Einstein, a visiting professor at the university for more than a decade, had once considered moving there permanently. But while he was in Leiden agonizing over the decision, an expat German baroness had told him, "If you move here, you'll have a very pleasant life and no one will ever hear of you again." So he never came.

Half the Dutch novels I had to read at school were about the war (many of the others were about the main character's struggle to unshackle himself from the Calvinism of his parents, and a few combined both themes). Of course I read Anne Frank, who apart from everything else was a Jewish teenager of about my age living as a foreigner in the same country and writing better Dutch than most of the professional novelists. And in 1985, when I was fifteen, a flood of popular histories were published to mark the fortieth

anniversary of the Liberation. The general theme was of Dutch resistance to the Nazis.

At the time it was customary to use the words *goed* ("good")
or *fout* ("wrong") to classify the behavior of almost everybody in
the Netherlands in the war. Quite naturally, I came to believe that
the vast majority of Dutch people had been *goed*. I can see now
that this belief was an emotional necessity. My family did not belong in the Netherlands. I wanted to belong, and I also wanted my
parents (who belonged less than I did) to feel they belonged, and
so the thought that the Dutch had been good to the Jews was particularly attractive to me. (Once again, though, I do not want to
imply a tortured childhood lived under the shadow of the war. It
was not like that.)

Most of my generation, educated by the same films and books
and war stories, reached the same conclusion about Dutch goodness.
In my first book, *Soccer Against the Enemy*, I described the explosion
of these feelings when Holland beat West Germany 2–1 in the semi-
final of the European Championships of 1988. Millions of Dutch
people went on to the streets that night to celebrate. Though a Tuesday, it was the largest public gathering since the Liberation. "When
Holland scores I dance through the room," revealed Professor Lou
de Jong, the historian who had spent the previous forty years writing
the official history of the Netherlands in World War II in umpteen
volumes. "Of course it has to do with the war. Strange that people
deny that."

The general Dutch sentiment was best expressed in a book that
appeared a few months later called *Holland–Germany: Soccer Poetry*.
I quote a few representative extracts:

> *Ever since I can remember*
> *And before that*
> *The Germans wanted to be world champions*
> —A. J. Heerma van Vos

Dumb generalizations about a people
Or a nation, I despise.
A sense of proportion is very
Dear to me.

Sweet revenge, I thought, does not exist
Or lasts only briefly
And then there was that unbelievably beautiful
Tuesday evening in Hamburg.
   —HANS BOSKAMP

Those who fell
Rose cheering from their graves.
   —JULES DEELDER, IN A POEM TITLED "6-21-88"

(In *Soccer Against the Enemy* I also discussed the poems in the collection that were attributed to soccer players ["Jan Wouters" effort is the most sophisticated: blank verse with enjambements . . ." etc.], but when I later met the editor of the collection and said how good some of the players' poems were, he replied, "Thank you. I wrote them.")

The point is that the general Dutch feeling was that we were *goed* and the Germans were *fout*, and that our soccer victory proved it. For the next few years soccer matches between Holland and Germany remained ferocious affairs. Then, gradually, the feeling waned.

In part this was because in the 1990s the Dutch were starting to accept that they had not been so *goed* in the war after all. An Amsterdam historian named Hans Blom had been arguing since the late 1970s that the terms *goed* and *fout* were too simplistic to encapsulate the years of occupation. Most Dutch people, he said, had never made great moral choices. They had just gone on with their lives (like the student in the film taking his exams), and late in the war, when the occupation became more brutal, their main preoccupation had been "the question of how to incur as little damage as possible." They "retreated into a small familiar circle," going to the cinema, for in-stance, rather than engaging with the war.

Blom's view was very much a minority one and only became at all widely known in the early 1980s. But gradually more histories came to be written about the other side of the Dutch war: the worst survival rate among Jews outside Poland, the betrayal of Anne Frank, the second-largest Nazi movement in Europe outside Germany.

This is not to say the Dutch were actively anti-Semitic. They had welcomed Jews across the centuries, never showing the slightest impulse to kill them. A Dutch Jewish survivor of the Holocaust once told me that whatever else one says about the Dutch, one must always remember that it was the Germans who invaded Holland and deported the Jews, and not the Dutch who deported them from Germany. The Dutch could never have conceived of the Holocaust. (In Holland, if you really want to punish people you review their social-security benefits.)

I left Leiden for London in 1986, when I was sixteen. I visited Holland often in the years that followed, but didn't live there again until the winter of 1999, when I moved to Amsterdam to write a short book about Dutch soccer in World War II.

Although I was press-ganged into it by a friend and editor named Henk Spaan, I had various motives. Partly, I just wanted to live in Holland again and see what it was like, whether it was different from the country I remembered. I particularly wanted to get to know Am-sterdam, a lovely city. (Whenever foreigners tell me it is "tacky," I want to say, "Try leaving the red-light district.")

At the time, Ajax Amsterdam, Holland's biggest soccer club and probably the country's most popular institution after the royal family, was approaching its centenary. I was curious about the rumor (hotly denied by Ajax) that the club had been "Jewish" until the war. I had also heard fascinating snippets of other wartime soccer stories.

More than that, I have always thought that soccer is a good way into the daily life of a country. This is particularly true in the Nether-lands, where joining a soccer club is almost as fundamental a rite of male life as anything to do with girls. Most nations are described by their inhabitants as "soccer mad," but for much of the latter part of the twentieth century the country with the highest proportion of registered soccer players was the Netherlands. Those great Holland teams of 1974, 1978, 1988, and 1998 (and even the violent thugs of 2010) were the product of a culture.

A book about soccer and World War II would go to the heart of Holland. Soccer was a place where the Holocaust met daily life. What had happened in Dutch soccer clubs during the war would be a microcosm of what happened in the country. It might even produce wider truths about the war in the rest of occupied Western Europe. So I moved across and spent a winter lodging with various old school friends who had escaped Leiden for Amsterdam.

Even before beginning my research I had grasped that the Dutch had not been as *goed* in the war as I had once thought. In 1999 this realization was dawning on practically the whole country. The newspapers (many of them former Resistance news sheets) were full of official reports revealing how the Dutch had used the deportations to steal Jewish property. The *Groene Amsterdammer* magazine discovered that in the late 1960s civil servants at the Finance Ministry had held a sort of bring-and-buy at which jewels, gold, and silver belonging to dead Jews were sold. One former civil servant recalled, "My colleagues showed each other what they had bought. Someone came up to me with beautiful earrings. She was happy as I don't know what." I had long since ceased to be a starry-eyed schoolboy, but when I began researching the book I was still shocked by what I found. This was not the country I had imagined it to be.

My book (*Ajax, de Joden, Nederland*, or *Ajax, the Jews, the Netherlands*) appeared in Dutch in March 2000, in the week of Ajax's centenary. It told lots of stories about soccer in the war that I hope were new. The book's argument, however, was not. It read like a *J'accuse* against the Dutch nation. Soon after the book appeared, a Dutch friend told me she had found it ridiculously naïve, as everyone already knew that the country had not been *goed* in the war. I had wasted my time restating a case made by many people before me, she said. (The Dutch tend to be frank.)

She was exaggerating, but she had a point. All historians of the war in the Netherlands know that Dutch collaboration was at least as significant as Dutch resistance. This is not a country that hushes up its past. None of the reviews of my book objected to my criticism of the nation, and nor did anyone I meet rebuke me for spilling the family secrets. Only my old school friends became a bit irritated at being told every day how gray and cowardly their country had been.

Yet the Dutch seemed to know they had been gray and cowardly without wanting to think about it. There was a highbrow debate about the war full of breast-beating and remorse, and simultaneously a public sense that "we" had been *goed* regardless. Many people still consumed the war as a Resistance tale, like *Soldier of Orange*. Even at the Dutch Institute for War Documentation in Amsterdam, I found six and a half shelves of books on "Dutch Resistance" and just half a shelf on "Dutch Collaboration."

A year after finishing the book, driving through California with an English photographer, I told him about my discovery that Holland had not been *goed* in the war.

"Doesn't surprise me at all," he said.

"Why not?"

"It's always that way. All countries have myths about having been good, and they always turn out to be lies. I'm not shocked."

"It's probably more shocking if you grew up with the myth," I countered.

"Yeah, probably."

Meanwhile, I had decided that I wanted to rewrite my book. I had written the Dutch version too quickly (just under four months from start to finish including all the research; is this a record?) and wanted to expand and deepen the material. I wanted to write a book that did more than just accuse the Dutch of having been *fout*. I also wanted to reach foreign readers, because the myth of a tolerant country that was *goed* in the war is today believed most strongly outside the Netherlands.

Beyond Holland, I wanted to examine soccer in the war in other European countries: it astonished me that even while Stalingrad and Auschwitz were taking place, the ball had rolled on. World War II instantly takes on a different aspect when you know, for instance, that on June 22, 1941, the day the Germans invaded the Soviet Union, the decisive act of the entire conflict, ninety thousand spectators watched the German league final in Berlin. What were they thinking of? It recalled Kafka's famous diary entry for August 2, 1914: "Germany has declared war on Russia. Swimming in the afternoon."

And I wanted to go back to the years before the Second World War. The 1930s, root of all evil, had been a fascinating decade in soccer. There were the Nazis with their knack for propaganda, Mussolini's Italy winning two World Cups and the Berlin Olympics, and England still regarded as the untouchable masters. This was the epoch when the game became a political item.

I spent weeks in the excellent Football Association library, reading the minutes of old FA meetings, once running into England's then manager Sven Goran Eriksson at the front door (he said, "Hello"). I took trains from Paris to Munich to the Swiss lake resort of Lugano to meet a man who had played for Germany until 1942 and on the way back stopped in Strasbourg, France, to meet a man who had refused to do so. I read books and magazines from all over Europe (often with the help of a friend), and have tried to piece everything together to produce a sort of alternative history of World War II.

2

A SUNDAY BEFORE THE WAR

I wrote much of this book in the old Jewish Quarter of Amsterdam, sitting in a friend's art gallery amid stacks of Andy Warhol lithographs. The gallery hadn't always been a gallery. It was once the Dutch Communist Party's headquarters, and before that it had been a hospital for the Portuguese Jews of Amsterdam. Their symbol, a stone pelican, still marks the building's front door, but in 1943 the hospital's patients were deported to the death camps.

The gallery stands on the elegant little Henri Polaklaan, a street named after the Jewish trade-union leader who was regarded by Amsterdam's Jews as a species of Moses. Across the street from the gallery is the headquarters of Polak's *Bond*, his union: a people's palace with famous murals that his diamond cutters built, even though their trade was perennially in recession and they, like actresses waiting tables in Manhattan restaurants, were always "resting." Polak had these uneducated men reading Dickens and Zola from the *Bond*'s library.

The Henri Polaklaan is in the lovely, leafy Plantage neighborhood, which used to be the posh end of the Jewish Quarter. The poorer end, around the mammoth Portuguese synagogue, was where the Jewish rag merchants, banana sellers, and diamond cutters lived. On the day in 1940 that the Germans invaded, most of the eighty thousand Jews in Amsterdam inhabited the Quarter, or *Jodenbuurt*.

I once saw about thirty seconds of a film of the Quarter: people in rags selling rags to each other, a sort of cold Calcutta. This was Amsterdam's poorest and busiest neighborhood. Whole families lived in single rooms. Their internal feuds, and fights with the neighbors, would sometimes occupy the local police station for decades; but on the other hand there were hardly any drunks.

"In the poverty of the decayed Quarter," wrote its greatest memoirist, Meyer Sluyser, after the war, "they dreamed in detail of the unheard-of riches they would divide among their relatives, if only the orphans who drew the lottery numbers from the drum would ensure they won the hundred thousand guilders. . . . There is only one fairy tale: you do nothing and are rewarded with as much as possible."

On Friday evenings the Jewish vendors would turn their carts upside-down, sing socialist and Jewish psalms, and then, if they had enough money, go home for Friday-night chicken soup. On Saturday the streets were littered with chicken bones tossed out of windows. It was back to work on Sundays, when gentile shoppers from all over town thronged the Jewish market on the Quarter's Waterloo Square. Rembrandt, a resident of the Quarter, had shopped at one of its predecessors; the market that stands on the square today, selling junk to tourists, is its heir.

Dutch gentiles seldom gave the Jews any trouble. Many Christians lived in the Quarter themselves. There was some country-club racism (a few posh establishments like the rowing club De Hoop barred Jews as members), and every now and then a newspaper or a politician would have a dig at the "Israelites," but mostly the Jews felt at home in the Netherlands. They were tolerated. "At present [our] people live peacefully in Amsterdam," Rabbi Uziel wrote as early as 1616. Many of the families he had known were still there in 1940 when the German soldiers marched in.

The Germans turned the Quarter into a ghetto sealed with barbed wire. Jews were taken from their homes in alphabetical order, then collected and registered in the Hollandsche Schouwburg theater, which stands on the street that runs behind my friend's gallery. Almost every adult who entered the theater ended up dead in Poland, but some of their children survived. When a tram stopped outside the theater, blocking its entrance from sight, students would smuggle kids out of the building in rucksacks, boxes, potato sacks.

These children—one of whom became mayor of Amsterdam; another, legendary masseur of Ajax—would be hidden in a crèche on the other side of the road. Later they were moved to safe houses. Some of them passed through the room in which I worked.

So little does Amsterdam change that the trams stopping in front of the theater today bear the same numbers and run the same routes as they did sixty years ago. Writing this book in Amsterdam, I often felt as if I were living in a ghost town. Most of the buildings of the Quarter are still standing, and some of the old Jewish shop names, like Apotheek de Castro, are preserved on façades. The Portuguese synagogue from which the philosopher Spinoza was expelled by his orthodox co-religionists is still there, but other things have changed since World War II. The slums that surrounded the synagogue have made way for two-lane roads, which in this city of the bicycle have the feel of vast highways. Nearby, on the rubble of Jewish homes, stands the new City Opera. But the main thing that has changed in the Jewish Quarter is that the Jews are gone. Three-quarters of them were killed by Hitler. No other community of people in Western Europe suffered as much destruction in the twentieth century. The Quarter, with its Jewish monuments and virtually unused synagogue, is now a sort of open-air museum with through traffic.

That we know so much about the people who lived here—how they spoke, shopped, had fun—is thanks mainly to the innumerable memoirs of the survivors. That so many have been written is because of Jewish tradition: what happens to you when you die is vague and uncertain, there may not be a heaven or hell, and so the dead live on only in the memory of the living. Hence the dozens of memorial books, of which the most important is called, simply, the *Memorboek*. But in its 862 pages there is barely a word on soccer.

Before the war the Quarter supported five little Jewish soccer clubs, neighborhood teams, but most of the Quarter's inhabitants only dreamed of playing. Sometimes a pair of soccer boots all the way from England would hang outside the large Melhado store. Then passing kids would murmur, "If I'm ever allowed to play soccer. . . . "The game was expensive, and on Sundays many boys in the Quarter had to work in their fathers' market stalls.

All Dutch soccer was amateur until 1954, but even before the war Ajax was one of the clubs at the top of the tree. Its ground lay just a couple of miles east of the Jewish Quarter, but few inhabitants of the Quarter could imagine actually playing for Ajax. To do that you needed a soccer suitcase and clothes, which had to be washed every Sunday evening because you couldn't represent Ajax in muddy shorts. All that was unaffordable. The few Jews who were Ajax members before the war were wealthier people from merchant families rather like Anne Frank's, people who lived outside the Quarter in the richer neighborhoods of Amsterdam-South. But many people in the Quarter supported Ajax, whether they could get to the ground on Sundays or not.

Ajax usually denies any connection with Amsterdam's pre-war Jews. The club's historian Evert Vermeer told *Het Parool* newspaper in 1999, "The supporters of Ajax's opponents used to arrive at Weesperpoort Station, where there were a lot of Jewish street vendors. So they would say, 'We're going to the Jews.' But the club itself didn't have a Jewish culture at all before World War II."

If there were any institutions in Amsterdam that didn't have a Jewish culture before the war, they were the NSB (the Dutch Nazi Party) and the churches. The rest did. "Amsterdam is the city of the Jews and the cyclists," wrote the Prague journalist Egon Erwin Kisch shortly before the war. And the big soccer club nearest the Jewish Quarter was Ajax. Vermeer writes as if the Jews on one of those pre-war Sundays had stared dumbstruck at the gentile fans, thinking, "These Christians must be crazy," as if soccer were a goy pastime like eating the body of Christ or riding horses.

When Ajax men do concede the club had Jewish fans, they always give the same explanation. As Wim Schoevaart, the clubs nonagenarian archivist, told me, "Jew people like something good, and so they enjoyed going to Ajax." Joop Stoffelen, a former Ajax player who seemed ashamed of the club's Jewish links yet served soccer journalists as an unofficial historian of the Jewish Quarter, once said, "Whenever people called Ajax 'a Jew club,' I had my answer ready. I'd say, 'Do you know why Ajax has so much support among the Jews? Because they know what's good and tasty.'" Even Bennie Muller, Ajax's half-Jewish captain of the 1960s, told me, "Jews are people who like entertainment. They went to the theater, to the casino, gambled, and soccer was entertainment, too."

The moment you hear the explanation, you want to reject it. Do only Jews like what's good and tasty? Do gentiles prefer the bad and unappetizing? But when you reflect on the joyless Calvinism of the pre-war Netherlands, you see they might have a point.

Whenever Ajax denies its Jewish links, or tries to apologize for them, it is denying people who have been murdered. It is important to reconstruct a random Sunday in the Jewish Quarter before the war.

To find the few Jewish fans who remember those Sundays, you either have to fly to Israel or cycle south from Amsterdam's Museum Square. Riding out of town along the Beethovenstraat, you pass the neighborhoods where the remnants of Jewish Amsterdam live: here and there a menorah on a windowsill, a shop with a Jewish name, or a passer-by with olive skin and curly black hair. Not many, of course.

In a flat around the corner from the Hilton Hotel where John and Yoko held their bed-in for peace, eighty-seven-year-old Hans Reiss leads me to his office. There is a computer and videotapes (one of them of Ajax) and a Harvard University pennant that turns out to be more than a souvenir. Reiss has done well for a Jew from the wrong generation: born in 1912 in the Sint Antoniebreestraat, the street where Rembrandt went bankrupt in 1656 and Reiss's father later ran one of the many Jewish drapery stores. Reiss began going to Ajax with his father in 1921, when he was nine years old.

On Sunday mornings before the war, pretty girls would stand outside the Jewish textile shops to lure in the gentile customers. The wares were laid out on the street as if in an oriental bazaar. Reiss says, "Sundays were top days. So my father wanted to leave the shop as late as possible. He knew exactly when the tram came. My father had been going to Ajax since he was a boy. Soccer lovers. Passive, though. That generation didn't play, itself. The ground was unimaginably far away. All the way outside town. But there was an excellent connection to the Jewish Quarter."

At quarter past one in the afternoon, Reiss and his father and dozens of other people would cram into a little tram that trundled to the Weesperplein Square. Anyone wanting to cover that distance today would walk or cycle, but in the 1920s it felt like a long way: you were going to the very edge of the Quarter, and in those days people were not fit.

Reiss says, "On the Weesperplein there was a little steam tram called 'the Murderer from 't Gooi,' and it went to Ajax. It left every half-hour. So at the Weesperplein people would always storm it. They would be sticking out on all sides. Extremely dangerous. Almost all those people were Jews." At half-past one, Reiss and his father would fight their way on board.

"Amazing that you still remember it after seventy years," I remark.

"It was my youth, wasn't it? I lived in the middle of it all. Until 1931. The tram would puff along for a while, and then stop because the locomotive's water reservoir had to be refilled. And that tram often caused accidents, and so it was popularly known as 'the Murderer.' But there won't be many mouths left that can still tell you that."

At five to two Reiss and his father would join a cluster of Jews in the little covered stand of Ajax's "Wooden Stadium." On those Sunday afternoons in the 1920s Ajax would generally kick off with ten gentiles and a Jewish outside-right from New York. "Eddy Hamel," Reiss remembers. "Tall boy, black hair combed back. Not a product of the Jewish Quarter. He was what you might call an idol. Eddy Hamel, I can still see him before me. Quick, and he had a very good cross. Something like David Beckham now. *Ach*, it was all different then. The speed of Eddy Hamel is a snail's pace now."

After the match Reiss and his father would return to the Quarter by "Murderer." From beneath his Harvard pennant he says, "And you'd think we could then go home eh? But no. In the Old High Street there was a cigar shop, Swaap. On Sundays he had a big board hanging outside with all the soccer fixtures written in chalk. We'd be there at half-past four. The first results only began coming in from five o'clock. Every time a result came in, Mr. Swaap would walk outside with his piece of chalk and write it on the board. The place was black with people. If you went into the shop to buy a cigar you'd hear the result before the others, because Swaap was a good businessman.

"In the evenings, the first and only Sunday soccer paper would appear, the *Cetem*. 'Read the *Cetem!*' the vendor would shout, I can still hear him say it. 'Read the *Cetem!*' People would fight for the papers. There was a short report of each match. When you had the paper you took it home and the whole family would read it."

I remark that for at least some of its life the *Cetem* also printed regular news.

"That's possible," says Reiss, "but we were very narrow-minded."

As the *Cetem* was produced on Sunday, day of the Christian Sabbath, it was written, printed, and sold mainly by Jews. In the evening the vendors would stream out of the Quarter into the rest of the city. "Read the *Cetem*! All results!" Since the Dutch world for "results" is the same as the word for "rashes," "Get the *Cetem!*" became a popular curse.

Five issues of the *Cetem*—or bits of those issues, anyway—survive in a box in Amsterdam's city archive. Together the remnants tell the story of "the only newspaper on Sunday evening." Founded by Simon Weyl in 1923, it really did have all the results, as well as some rather perfunctory match reports: a Feyenoord–Ajax match on January 20, 1924, is covered in just 138 words, in which only one of the four goal scorers is named. Is this what people fought over?

That edition also includes a news report from Berlin: "20 Jan. (Own tel.) Stresemann yesterday received representatives of the foreign press. On this occasion he answered them concerning Poincaré's latest speech." At issue was a row between Germany and France and Belgium about reparation payments for the Great War.

The entire *Cetem* of November 25, 1928, survives. The front page has news ("The Fall of Stresemann") and inside there is a lot of sport. Holland has beaten Switzerland 4–1, and the *Cetem* publishes a picture of the Swiss team in their suits. *Yesterday we snapped the Swiss Eleven on their arrival at Amsterdam's Central Station*, announces the caption. And then the fantastically redundant addition: *Above you will see the result.*

But the *Cetem* was more than just results. On March 17, 1929, the newspaper reveals:

> FOR THE WOMAN:
> The Ideal Man
> Of whom the real woman
> Is in awe
> Need not be an
> Adonis.

No *Cetems* remain from the 1930s, but the very last issue of the newspaper, dated March 19, 1944, is in the box at the city archive. The *Cetem* has shrunk to tabloid size; Simon Weyl is no longer on the front page, nor is Stresemann. The main story is datelined "from the headquarters of the *Führer*," and headlined "Soviets Thrown Back in Various Places." There was still sports news (Amsterdam–Rotterdam 3–3), but they weren't fighting over it in the Jewish Quarter any more.

The paper continued as the *Zondagavondblad* (*Sunday Evening Newspaper*) and seems to have disappeared in 1950, by which time almost all the original journalists and vendors and many of the readers were dead. Reiss was lucky. The boy from the Jewish Quarter had left for Harvard on a scholarship in January 1939. He had known Europe was in danger since Jewish refugees from Germany had begun moving into Amsterdam-South telling terrible stories. Reiss studied economics at Harvard, enlisted in the U.S. Army, and returned to Amsterdam after the war to take over his murdered brother's firm. Some Jews still went to Ajax after 1945, but no longer on the Murderer from the Quarter.

What Ajax had meant to these people was best explained to me by Abraham Roet, a Jew who left Holland for Israel in 1946. I met him in his house outside Tel Aviv. On Sundays before the war Roet and his brothers, dressed in jackets, ties, and berets, would be taken to Ajax by their orthodox father. Roet, who still owned an Ajax season ticket in Tel Aviv told me he never saw Ajax as a Jewish club. That wasn't the point. Rather, Ajax was the place where Jews and gentiles met. At the stadium you found poor Jews, rich Jews, middling Jews, in a sea of gentiles all shouting for the same club. It was a melting pot, and that may have been one reason why Roet's father took his boys along. "I think it was part of our education, that we were part of the Dutch people."

A Jew at Ajax felt himself part of Amsterdam. He was protected there. When the swastika flag was raised above the stadium for a game against Admira Vienna in 1938, and the Viennese players gave the Hitler salute, the Ajax fans whistled furiously and some walked out of the stadium. Understanding pre-war Ajax helps make sense of Amsterdam's "February Strike," when for a day and a half in 1941 much of the city's working population downed tools in sympathy with the Jews. The gentiles knew Jews from school, from the market, from the stands at Ajax. The February Strike was the only gesture of its kind in Europe in World War II.

3

A FRIENDLY SALUTE
International Soccer in the 1930s

It was during the 1930s that soccer became politics. So much came together in that low, dishonest decade: the rise of Hitler and Mussolini, the brewing of war, the discovery of propaganda, and soccer's emergence as a mass passion on the Continent. All this gave international matches a meaning they had never had before.

It was the first decade to feature much international sport. Germany's tally of ninety-three internationals in the twenty-five years before Hitler remains low, even if you take into account their troubles finding opponents in the years after the Great War. Only in the run-up to the 1928 Olympics did the national team acquire a coach, Otto Nerz, and he was unpaid. As manager of Germany, Nerz continued his other pursuits, which included taking a medical degree. In the Weimar years, he presided over a shockingly bad team. A draw at home against Scotland in 1929 aroused euphoria, and two years later Germany was thumped 6–0 by the Austrian *Wunderteam.* The Austrians, unlike the Germans, were professionals.

Yet by the end of the 1920s soccer was ceasing to be a marginal activity for rich people. As the Continent recovered from the Great War, as transport improved and people continued moving to the cities, as the hours they worked in factories fell, they began playing soccer. In France the number of registered players trebled to about a hundred thousand between 1921 and 1926. In Germany and Italy big stadiums were built, and newspapers launched sports sections. Italian fans even began traveling to away matches. In 1929, Mussolini's government created a national league.

The Fascists had taken time to come to terms with soccer. Hitler, Mussolini, and their henchmen were born too early to have grown up with the game. It bothered them that soccer had been invented in England, and Mussolini's government initially tried to interest people in a new Italian ball game called *volata*. Many Fascists found the very idea of soccer offensive: eleven young men skipping around in shorts, kicking a ball in competition with eleven others, when they should have been working together at something more manly.

To the early Nazis, sport could have only one purpose: breeding soldiers. "Give the German nation six million bodies impeccably trained in sport," wrote Hitler in *Mein Kampf*, "all glowing with fanatical love of the Fatherland and raised in the highest spirit of attack, and a national state will make an army of them in less than two years, if necessary."

Using sport to train future soldiers seemed a particularly shrewd idea in a country where military service was forbidden under the Treaty of Versailles. The Nazis were not the first Germans to enthuse over *Wehrsport*, or "defense sport," a catchall label for pursuits like marching, man-to-man combat, and hand-grenade-throwing competitions. Hitler's government made PE the most important subject in schools, to be taught at least five hours a week. Pupils who showed "a lasting fear of body care" were to be expelled from school.

This was no time for fun and games. The Nazis in their early years took sport terrifically seriously. An SA man could write in the journal of the Eintracht Frankfurt sports club in December 1933:

In the spirit of the unknown SA man, who subordinates himself in a self-sacrificial and dutiful manner, who does not ask for acclaim or criticism, who always wants to *be* more than to seem, who in all his actions has his eye on just one thing: on Germany, nothing but Germany, I wish to assume my task as Führer of the sport community Eintracht. . . .

Heil Hitler.

But whatever Nazis and Italian Fascists thought about soccer, they failed to persuade people to give it up for grenade-throwing, and soon they stopped trying. The Fascists made a few Italian clubs drop their British names (AC Milan became Milano, and Internazionale was renamed Ambrosiana) and then embraced the game. By the time the Nazis seized power, on January 30, 1933, they were beginning to do the same.

Much has been written about how the dictators tried to manipulate soccer for their own purposes. Of course they tried, but that does not mean they succeeded. Soccer is a slippery tool. Raking through soccer of the 1930s spotting attempts to make propaganda is easy, but it is more interesting to study the decade's big matches for what they reveal about the feelings between the countries that would soon go to war. For all the tension in Europe at the time, citizens of different countries hardly ever met. The plane carrying the German team to Glasgow in 1936, for instance, was the first German aircraft of any kind to land at Renfrew Airport. The isolation of the era gave international soccer matches a piquancy they have never had since.

———

On the rainy Saturday afternoon of March 19, 1933, Germany played a friendly game against France in Berlin. It was only the second match between the two countries in history, and the first German soccer international of the Nazi era.

There had been some consternation in Europe when the war-mongering, anti-Semitic demagogue Hitler seized power in Berlin. The French had considered boycotting the coming exhibition game on moral grounds and were worried that their players and fans would be attacked in Berlin. But the Germans persuaded them everything would be fine. So it proved: supporters arriving at the train station were greeted with music, and the SA thugs outside the ground occupied themselves with rattling collection tins. Prices for terrace places were cut to 70 pfennigs, and eight thousand "unemployment tickets" were given out free. There was a sell-out crowd of fifty thousand, including Hermann Göring, and other people watched from a nearby oak tree.

The match passed off peacefully. After ten minutes Germany's Fischer thought he had scored, but the English referee Crew spotted that the shot had passed through a hole in the side netting, and mended the net with the help of French defenders. On the French bench the reserves smoked cigarettes.

Germany soon took a 3–1 lead, but in the second half they played so slowly that the crowd began chanting, "*Tempo, Tempo!*" and in the last ten minutes the French recovered to draw 3–3. The German keeper, Hans Jakob, was widely blamed for France's first and third goals, but the whole team had disappointed. "Soon Germany's international matches will be the best way to eradicate the love of the leather in soccer fans," commented the Munich magazine *Fußball*, which devoted almost its entire issue of March 21 to the match. Civilized, literate, and cosmopolitan, a relic from an older Germany, *Fußball* is one of my main sources for this account.

Soccer itself was the least interesting aspect of the match. The press at the time realized there was much else to say. It noted that the German crowd was well behaved and not even very partisan. The French paper *Le Journal* remarked on the "rather unenthusiastic masses, who hardly gave their own team more applause [than France] when it entered the field." *Paris Soir*, France's best-selling evening daily, praised the respect with which the crowd listened to the "Mar-seillaise," saying that the "Deutschland über Alles" anthem might have been treated differently at Colombes or Vincennes in Paris. *Fußball* said it was a shame an advertising plane over the ground had drowned out both anthems, "because it's not every day that you hear the 'Marseillaise' while the Reich and Swastika flags flutter in the wind."

So friendly was the mood that in a speech at the post-match ban-quet Jules Rimet, president of the French FA and inventor of the World Cup, promised to correct false impressions of Nazi Germany in France. In March 1933 no one, perhaps not even Hitler, could foresee the full horrors to come.

The mainstream German press was only just starting to be sub-jugated by the Nazis, and after the match it does not seem to have banged on about racial superiority. Quite the contrary: the *12-Uhr-Blatt* commented that if Germany could not produce a good team, it might be worth "letting good teachers, who have earned their rep-utation on international soil, hold training course after course." *Fußball* even risked the odd dig at the Nazis: "Hans Albers, the star of stage and screen, arrives and arouses more attention than the po-litical leaders in their uniforms beside him," noted the writer F. Richard in his diary of the day.

Only with hindsight is it possible to see the spirit of the "New Order" seeping into *Fußball*. The cover picture shows the German captain Hergert spattered in mud, and perhaps in blood too, glowering into the photographer's lens like a Great War soldier or ancient Teu-tonic warrior. And the main match report complains of the absence of a *Führer*, or leader, in the German team. German soccer required "a renewal by men!" added a Dr C. E. Laenge.

Yet the atmosphere around the game seems to have been more pleasant and calm than it might be for the same fixture today. In part, this was because the Nazis spent their early years charming foreign countries. This effort peaked at the 1936 Berlin Olympics, from which the future Fifa president João Havelange returned with the best impressions of Nazi Germany. "Everyone seemed happy, was my impression," he later told the author David Yallop. "There were no shortages, everyone was polite."

It is usually argued that the Nazis tried to use sport to demonstrate "racial" superiority, but often they used it just to make friends. For much of the 1930s they were obsessed with what the rest of the world thought about them. As long as Hitler was too weak to make war, he wanted foreigners to think he had no such intention. He needed time to rearm.

German soccer diplomacy must have assisted him. Millions of Europeans in the 1930s probably thought harder about the German soccer team than they did about the SS. In the weeks after the pogroms of *Reichskristallnacht* in 1938, when the Dutch were debating whether to allow Germany to visit Rotterdam for an international, Henri Polak, the Dutch diamond workers' Moses, guessed what his country's soccer fans would say: "Sport is sport, and murder of the Jews is murder of the Jews."

Few people in Europe seem to have spent much time thinking about the threat of Nazism until late in the 1930s. There was a general suspicion of Hitler, but this was insufficient to create much popular support for rearmament in Germany's neighboring countries. It took years for most people to understand that Germany was about to unleash a war. There were many reasons for their quiescence, but one of them was probably the friendly sports matches that Germany was always playing against its neighbors. Certainly *Paris Soir* was sufficiently impressed by the sporting diplomacy of the dictators to berate its own government for not taking games seriously enough.

The other reason for the friendly mood at Germany–France was the contemporary obsession with "*fair play.*" (Like many Europeans, the Germans used the English phrase.) Soccer had reached the Continent late, and with its Victorian wrapping intact. An Anglophile school of thought in 1930s' Europe even regarded sportsmanship as more important than winning matches.

To fair-play extremists, it was ungentlemanly even to support a particular side. Many of them were discomfited by the new phenomenon of vast crowds coming to internationals hoping to see their country win. F. Richard of *Fußball* lamented:

> Tens of thousands go to internationals who never otherwise attend a football match.
>
> Why do these tens of thousands not attend our league matches, not even the international matches of our clubs?
>
> Because they have not yet been raised to see good football.
>
> I would much rather that we had our record attendances at the big club matches, as they do in England, and not at internationals whose quality is often very questionable.
>
> In England not an international match can approach the Cup final or even the matches of the league leaders.
>
> In Berlin the stadium was filled to the last place, when France met Germany.

Herr Richard would turn out to have the temper of the times against him.

———

If the Nazis had been slow to see the point of soccer, they instinctively understood international sport. It was a way of both making friends and showing off the vigor of the "new Germany." In a speech in 1937 the *Reichssportführer* Hans von Tschammer und Osten said that "under no circumstances" did Hitler want to forfeit international sport, as it was "the fastest and most sustained means of confounding political troublemakers and rabble-rousers" who were out to blacken Nazi Germany's name.

The country was not ready yet to beat others at war, and it could not even reliably do so at soccer, but the latter problem was the easier to fix. With ever more Germans playing soccer, it was only a matter of time before the vast country produced a decent team. To speed things up, the Nazis ordered clubs and employees to release players for the national team whether they wanted to or not. The German team soon became a concept to millions. From 1933 to 1942 it played about twice as many internationals a year as it had in the Weimar period—seventeen matches in 1935 alone. The increase was even sharper for sport as a whole: in 1933 German sports teams competed in sixty-three international matches or contests; five years later the figure had nearly trebled.

Two memoirs published on cheap paper soon after the war memorably evoked German soccer of the 1930s. Paul Janes, the German full-back and captain for much of the 1930s, wrote *Ein Leben für den Fußball* (*A Life for Football*) in 1948, and a year later Hans Jakob, the keeper accused of the two mistakes against France, produced *Durch ganz Europa von Tor zu Tor* (*Through all of Europe from Goal to Goal*). Though both books bear the mark of the immediate postwar years, contriving almost to pretend that the Nazis never happened, both nonetheless give fascinating accounts of the Hitler era.

The books are written in a peculiar mix of soccer clichés and Nazi jargon, which the players (and their ghost-writers) had presumably assimilated subconsciously. This passage from Janes is a good example:

> Much had happened up to the autumn of the year 1933. . . . A whole new national team, sealed beside the Rhine at home, arises and in October, in a Duisburg stadium illuminated by the autumn sun, celebrates a triumphant 8–1 victory over Belgium. In frenzied enthusiasm the masses go along . . . we have recovered the faith in our national football team. . . . A new spirit began working in the hearts of the old and the new players.

The tone was not entirely Janes's fault. The German language itself had been contaminated. Yet the triumphant victories and the frenzied enthusiasm of masses were not his main points. Both his book and Jakob's are chiefly concerned with establishing that the German team of the Nazi era was well liked abroad. Jakob in particular at times descends into simply listing endless friendly meetings with foreigners. A picture of unsmiling men in trilby hats watching the players emerge from a hotel is captioned *Wherever we showed ourselves, hundreds of sports friends surrounded us*, and in other pictures Jakob laughs with Peruvian soccer players at the Berlin Olympics, or throws his arm around the black American athlete Jesse Owens ("a unique sprinter"). The French, the English, the Spaniards were all wonderful people with passionate fans who applauded the German players. The keeper has had a happy career with "sports comrades" everywhere. (On the other hand, Jakob once said that eight German international players of his era were Nazi Party members.)

Similarly, writing the afterword to Janes's memoir, Sepp Herberger, German manager from 1937 to 1964, would claim that every match in which the full-back captained Germany was "*ein Sieg des 'fair play,'*" a victory for fair play.

Obviously this is how the Germans liked to remember things in the late 1940s, when they were the world's pariahs. But Herberger, Janes, and Jakob did have a point—for most of the 1930s, Nazi Germany was far from being a pariah in Europe. Hitler's early years in power were relatively quiet in terms of foreign policy. The German team was indeed welcomed throughout Europe by all but a few antifascist demonstrators.

At least fourteen of these were arrested before the England–Germany game at White Hart Lane in London in December 1935. Yet by all accounts the match was otherwise a peaceful affair, with as many as ten thousand Germans in the crowd. Germany was thrashed 3–0, but Jakob recalls on the second page of his book:

"After the game we received ovations and cheers as seldom before abroad. This was London, this was the people of the motherland of football." Janes remembers the match with equal fondness ("in London, sportsmen shook hands"), and British press reports seem to bear out these happy recollections. "Whatever the result, all of us hope Germany will have a nice enjoyable match and find at the end of it that their education has been suitably enriched," wrote Frank Throgood in the *News Chronicle* on December 4, 1935. According to the next day's London *Times*,

> The afternoon was a great success for at least two reasons. First the game was played throughout in the friendliest of spirit; secondly . . . the sun came out . . .
>
> The ground seemed to be packed long before the teams came out and when they did the sight was an impressive one. Both teams were given a tremendous reception . . . the two national anthems were played, and the Germans gave their salute to both.

The *Sporting Life* mentioned the demonstrators: "Greater than the game—a thoroughly enjoyable game—was the atmosphere of good fellowship in which it was played. . . . The huge crowd . . . was managed without a hitch . . . seven individuals tried to upset the serenity of the plans—they are now under lock and key."

A police officer told the *News Chronicle* "that in his twenty years' experience of crowds he had never dealt with such an orderly and well-managed crowd as the visitors."

And at the post-match banquet, speakers from both nations condemned the demonstrators' attempts to get the game canceled.

———

The mixing of soccer with politics was then considered an exciting novelty. The *News Chronicle* even called the encounter "the most discussed match in the history of Association Football." No continental countries had ever previously been interested enough in the sport for it to matter so much. Certainly Mussolini had done his best to help Italy win the previous year's World Cup on home turf, but it is doubtful how many Italians noticed: the Giro d'Italia bicycle race overshadowed the early rounds, and the average crowd per game in the World Cup was only twenty-three thousand.

In fact, the first modern sporting event whose political significance was generally understood was the Berlin Olympics of 1936. Enough has been said already about Hitler storming out of the stadium to avoid giving Jesse Owens his gold medal. Less well known is that Hitler also walked out of a soccer match. Apparently he had never seen the sport played until Albert Forster, the Gauleiter of Danzig, persuaded him to watch Germany thrash little Norway instead of going to see the rowing at Grünau. Goebbels, who watched the match with him, would write, "The Führer is very excited, I can barely contain myself. A real bath of nerves. The crowd rages. A battle like never before. The game as mass suggestion."

But, to Forster's mortification, Germany lost 2–0. "Not fully deserved," Goebbels noted in his diary. The German forward Willy Simetsreiter would later blame the defeat on Hitler's visit to the changing-room just before kick-off. None of the players had apparently met the legendary figure before, and after shaking his hand they were still "all muddled up" when the match began, Simetsreiter claimed. Hitler would never see a soccer match again. To him, as to most senior Nazis, motor racing and boxing remained the sports that mattered.

Italy won the Olympic soccer gold by beating Austria 2–1 in the final. This was particularly impressive since the Italians, in the name of "fair play," had selected a team of students in order to show up other countries who were said to be fielding covert professionals. Surviving footage of the final focuses on the Italian fans in the ground. There are soldiers, and a mustachioed figure holding his head in anguish who looks like a caricature of the hot-blooded Latin, but most remarkable is the young man in a T-shirt with the number 20 on the back, who seems to have parachuted in from another decade.

———

"I've played for England before 110,000 screaming, yelling, heiling Germans at the Berlin Olympic Stadium, the day we humbled the pride of Nazidom on the world's most luxurious ground," reminisced the Arsenal and England captain Eddie Hapgood in his 1945 memoir *Football Ambassador.*

> I've kicked a football into Mussolini's lap in Rome, and experienced the worst refereeing of my life at Milan; I've been to Switzerland, Rumania, Hungary, Czecho-Slovakia, Holland, Austria, Belgium, Finland, France, Norway, Denmark, Sweden and Yugo-Slavia. I've eaten garlic until I've never wanted to eat another thing in my life. . . . I've been in a shipwreck, a train crash, and inches short of a 'plane accident . . . but the worst moment of my life, and one I would not willingly go through again, was giving the Nazi salute in Berlin.

The England team's salute before the match against Germany at Berlin's Olympic Stadium on May 14, 1938, remains, for Britons, the nadir of England's soccer history.

Reading the Football Association's minutes of the late 1930s in the comfort of the FA's library at Soho Square, you get no sense of gathering war, or even of an outside world at all. The tone is placid throughout. Much space is taken up with mourning the deaths of ancient officials. The association's president Sir Charles Clegg died in 1937 at the age of eighty-eight, after holding the post for forty-seven years. His successor, William Pickford, who had become a member of the FA in 1888, would die a year later.

The curious nature of minutes is that all items seem to acquire equal importance. Take the meeting of the FA's International

Selection Committee at the Royal Hotel in Great Yarmouth on Saturday June 26, 1937. Item five on the agenda was a letter from the Jersey FA asking for a team to be sent to the British island. The committee deferred the decision to "a later date." Then came item six: "Letter from the German FA requesting the Football Association to send a Representative team to play a match in Berlin on 14th May, 1938." Again, "consideration was deferred." Item eight was an invitation from Fifa to send a Great Britain team to the "World's Cup Competition" in June 1938. The committee did not even defer, rejecting the offer immediately.

On November 11, 1937, the same committee met at the Lion Hotel in Cambridge. Here is the last item on the agenda: "Continental Tour, 1938. It was decided that Representative Matches be arranged with Germany and Switzerland on the 14th and 21st (or 22nd) May, 1938, respectively."

The FA had just made perhaps its worst ever decision. Choosing Nazi Germany as the opponent for one of its rare foreign friendlies was an implicit vote of support, and the association would not even make any money out of the match. The Germans were to keep all the gate receipts while the English paid their own travel expenses. Then, when a German team visited England in 1939 or 1940, the Germans would pay and the English collect. You would almost think the German FA knew a world war was going to forestall the return. In the event, receipts from the 110,000 spectators in Berlin would reach £23,000—"a colossal total," said the *News Chronicle*.

On May 11, the Wednesday night before the Berlin match, the English tour party met at Liverpool Street Station. They took a train to Harwich, a ferry to Hook of Holland, and another train to Berlin. The journey took nearly twenty-four hours. On arrival in the German capital, Hapgood recalls in *Football Ambassador*, "We all got down to a bit of sightseeing . . . but I think the majority of the party were a little disappointed there was no fighting or lorry-loads of Stormwehr rushing hither and yon!"

Meanwhile British officials were trying to work out whether the team was going to give the Hitler salute. This was a common diplomatic problem in the 1930s, a decision every sports team playing Germany had to make. In 1936, the kickoff of a Spain–Germany soccer match had been delayed for over half an hour as both sides argued over whether "Deutschland über Alles" would be played and whether the Germans would salute.

The English in Berlin could have avoided saluting. But war between Germany and Britain seemed very possible just then. A few weeks earlier the Germans had annexed Austria (the Rapid Vienna player Hans Pesser would appear for his new country in the match against England) and now they were planning to take the Sudetenland. In the phrase of the day, "It needed only a spark to set Europe alight." If it took a salute to avoid that, well . . .

The Football Association's secretary Stanley Rous favored a salute for different reasons. Two years before, at the march-past at the Berlin Olympics, Rous had seen the German crowd jeer the British team for only giving Hitler the "eyes right." He thought a salute would put the crowd in good temper.

So on the morning of the match the *News Chronicle* reported in a paragraph on the front page, "It has been decided that since in Italy the English team greeted the Italians with the Fascist salute [presumably in Rome in 1933], and in London the German team gave three cheers to the English, there is no reason why in Berlin they should not do as the Berliners do."

England's salute has become a symbol of prime minister Neville Chamberlain's appeasement of Germany. It has also dominated the British memory of the Berlin match. "The photograph of the England team giving the Nazi salute appeared in newspapers throughout the world the next day to the eternal shame of every player and Britain as a whole," wrote England's great outside-right Stanley Matthews in *The Way It Was*. (Oddly, both Matthews and his captain Eddie Hapgood reprinted the photograph in their autobiographies.)

For decades, whenever the match was recalled, on radio or television or in print, the testimony of the England players was sought. The problem is that they were unreliable witnesses. Members of a very patriotic generation, who after 1945 knew the horrors of Nazi Germany as they could not have in 1938, they were aghast at what they had done. Their version of salute and match was invented after the fact.

Both Hapgood and Matthews described the match at some length in their autobiographies. Both took the classic English line: the England players had fought not to have to salute, saluting had been a blunder, the Olympic Stadium was like a lion's den, and the German players were arrogant, Aryan monsters who felt certain of victory.

One of the few differences in their accounts concerns the negotiations over the salute. Hapgood, the captain, recalls FA officials telling him at a meeting well before the game that the players would have to salute. He claims to have replied, "We are of the British Empire and I do not see any reason why we should give the Nazi salute." But then he gave in and went to tell the other players. Matthews, by contrast, suggests the players were first told by an FA official in the dressing room shortly before kick-off, "All the England players were livid and totally opposed to this, myself included. Everyone was shouting at once. Eddie Hapgood, normally a respectful and devoted captain, wagged his finger at the official and told him what he could do with the Nazi salute, which involved putting it where the sun doesn't shine."

The players then had to walk down four flights of stairs from their changing room to the field. Hapgood and Matthews agree on their reception by the crowd. Hapgood writes, "You could feel the jubilant, triumphant tone of the 110,000 crowd when the German team ran on to the field. A terrific roar greeted them, then a roaring crescendo of 'Sieg Heil' and 'Heil Hitler.'" And Matthews, "If ever men in the cause of sport felt isolated and so very far from their homes, it was the England team that day in Berlin. . . . It seemed every supporter on the massed terraces had a smaller version of the swastika and they held them aloft in a silent show of collective defiance as the England team ran out."

Then the English saluted. "The only humorous thing about the whole affair," wrote Hapgood, "was that while we gave the salute only one way, the German team gave it to the four corners of the ground." In Matthews's memory, England's gesture did nothing to pacify the crowd, which he remembers as remaining hostile throughout. After England's Len Goulden scored a brilliant, volleyed goal from long range, Matthews recounts, "The terraces of the packed Olympic Stadium were as lifeless as a string of dead fish. 'Let them salute that one,' Len yelled as he carried on running, arms aloft."

The German players and fans, as Hapgood and Matthews tell it, showed the same single-mindedness that their nation would soon apply to conquering Europe. They were desperate to win, an attitude that the English thought was not fair play. Hapgood claimed that the German team, "a bunch of arrogant, sun-bronzed giants," had been picked "with as much thoroughness as if . . . destined to be Hitler's personal bodyguard." "For months past [Hapgood explained] the Nazi soccer chiefs had been holding trials, had searched and tapped the soccer resources of the Reich, had discarded this player and that, and had even gone into over-run Austria for the pick of their talent, in an endeavor to discover a combination capable of taking on England's best."

But, as both Hapgood and Matthews recall with relish and at length, England thumped the Germans 6–3.

So much for memories. On almost every score they clash with contemporary accounts, or with facts, or both. The truth is that the official German attitude to Britain in May 1938 was fairly friendly. The Nazis, still preparing for war, had no desire to quarrel just yet. The *Reichssportführer* Von Tschammer und Osten, who never quite understood soccer but had come to like it regardless, opened the match program with a "Greeting to England!" in which he said the

English have "a great name as a sporting people." Later in the program, another article recalled English fans at Tottenham in 1935
cheering the German team bus: "People of the same race stretched
out their hands to one another. . . ." Even an advertisement in the
program for Café Aschinger in Berlin was in this vein: German and
English fans with identical faces, all smiling and wearing the same
cloth caps and Panama hats, standing side by side in a crowd waving
swastika flags and Union Jacks. Beneath this drawing was a smaller
one of an Englishman and a German with arms linked. "And now?"
the Englishman is asking in English. *Zu Aschinger!* his friend replies.

The second error is that the German players had not been hand-
picked for months like Hitler's personal bodyguard. The eleven that
faced England was the regular German team that emerged after the
fiasco of the Berlin Olympics: nine of them had faced Norway the year
before, and seven had played Scotland in Glasgow in October 1936.

Thirdly, the German fans do not seem to have been hostile at all.
Hapgood himself wrote that on the morning of the match "there
was a crowd to see us leave our hotel for the Stadium, and they even
raised a cheer." The *Manchester Guardian* reported that after the final
whistle "the crowd invaded the pitch, loudly cheering the players of
both sides for their splendid game." And *The Times* said the Goulden
goal "drew gasps of admiration from the crowd and is the talk of the
town to-day." Germany's keeper Jakob, a biased witness in his own
way, remembered the goal differently but equally respectfully: "Thun-
derous applause erupted—it was as if *our* attack had scored a goal,
so inspiring was the achievement." Jakob describes the goal at length
and with relish, as if he were proud to have conceded it.

Far from being arrogant, the German players were in awe of the
English. (In the 1930s they were even in awe of the Scots and Irish.)
Jakob writes, in the course of a long paean to English forwards, that
Matthews could have been stopped in Berlin only with a lasso. The
Italians really were desperate to beat England in the 1930s, partly
to prove that they would have won their two World Cups, even had

the English deigned to enter, but the Germans knew they were just not good enough. No German side would beat England until West Germany won 1–0 in Hannover in 1968.

In short, the German players, fans, and press in Berlin were much friendlier and more humble than the collective British memory of today admits. To believe that they were machine-made monsters, bent on victory, cheered on by a sort of Nuremberg rally, accords with our postwar knowledge of Nazism. But it is only possible to believe this if you forget the main features of soccer in the 1930s: the Nazis were out to charm as much as to win, and fair play carried almost as much prestige as victory.

The crowd was not partisan in the way a modern one would be. Watching a soccer international in the 1930s was almost an impartial experience, like going to the theatre. I have seen footage of a Germany–Italy game in Berlin in November 1936 that shows the home spectators cheering and waving their hats even when Italy scores. Observing the etiquette was particularly important when England came to visit, because the Germans admired English soccer almost as much for its sportsmanship as for its quality. The match program in 1938 admitted that though German fans were as enthusiastic as the English, "The general acquisition of the sporting attitude has not yet been achieved." But in time, it promised, the Germans would catch up.

British observers of the match also fastened on fair play. "The Game and Not One Foul" was the front-page headline in the *News Chronicle* on the Monday after the match. The FA's International Selection Committee would later note that "every member of the English team, even though determined to win, realized that his play must be consistent with the best British sporting tradition," and recommended a gift for each player. For both England and Nazi Germany, prestige lay not just in playing well but in playing fair.

It's also crucial to remember that German fans of the Nazi era loved and respected British soccer, which is why Aston Villa could draw a crowd of a hundred thousand playing on the same ground the next day. Odes to the British game were *de rigueur* in German soccer books of the time. Introducing Janes's memoir, the journalist Richard Kirn actually refers to English soccer players of the early years of the century as "a sort of *Übermenschen*."

Nerz, the German manager until 1937, was an Anglophile who often traveled to Britain to study the game, but even humble fans knew their English soccer. *Fußball* magazine seems to have carried a regular page from England, headlined "At the Source of the World's Game." On March 21, 1933, "Williams," the magazine's London correspondent, provides detailed reports of matches like Arsenal–Leicester and Everton–West Ham, and heralds the coming FA Cup final as "the all-dominating event of English soccer." The Nazis liked the FA Cup so much they started one of their own, which survives to this day.

Hapgood himself once received a fan letter from Germany addressed to "Herr Hapgood, *Beruffußballspielführer*, England, London." In short, when his England team took the field in Berlin it could count on far more sympathy than he and Matthews would later recall. Many of the 110,000 in the ground would have paid their money to see England as much as the home team. *Fußball Woche*, the German FA's official organ, judged in a special eighteen-page edition the next week, "The English showed how soccer should be played. . . . It was perfect soccer."

Lastly, that salute. We now find it hard to imagine that it was ever regarded as anything but an embarrassment. In fact, *The Times* reported on the Monday after the match that "the English team immediately made a good impression by raising their arms in the German salute," and none of the other mainstream newspapers seems to have been particularly bothered by it either. The FA Council meeting at Lancaster Gate sixteen days later did not mention the continental tour, let alone the salute.

When the International Selection Committee did consider the tour a month later, at the Prince of Wales Hotel in Scarborough, there was only one hint of unease at having visited Germany. The committee recommended that a special committee assess future tours, considering among other things "any other circumstances, which might militate against the prestige of the Football Association as a sports controlling body. Particular consideration should be given to these questions, especially during times of tension, when more than the playing of a match is at stake, and when it is particularly necessary for English prestige in sport to be maintained."

But the committee also recorded that the salute "did much to ensure the friendly reception by the huge crowd present," and it seems too have stuck to this view. A year later, before kickoff against Italy in Milan, the England team would give the Fascist salute to all four corners of the ground, and then salute again after the match—gestures that have long since been forgotten.

———

At the time of the 1938 match, the great preoccupation of the Nazis was not Britain at all. It was Austria. Thousands of Austrians had lined the streets when Hitler had returned to the country of his birth a few weeks before, but it was unclear whether they really wanted to surrender their independence. Trying to win them over, the Germans turned to soccer.

On April 3, 1938, a week before the Austrians voted on the Anschluss, the two countries played an "*Anschluss* match" in Vienna. It was probably meant to end in a draw, but Austria won 2–0, and the sixty thousand Viennese spectators celebrated with such abandon that the *Reichssportführer* expressed surprise at their "nationalism." A week later, nonetheless, 99.75 percent of Austrians voted for *Anschluss*.

Then, on June 4, the 1938 World Cup kicked off in France. The Nazis had intended the event as a celebration of the *Anschluss*. Sepp Herberger was under orders to field six Germans and five Austrians or vice versa in every match. Surely combining two of the best teams of the era would guarantee victory in the World Cup and help justify Hitler's incursion?

"Sixty million Germans will play in Paris!" trumpeted the Nazi *Völkischer Beobachter*, a slogan spookily like that of Argentina's military leaders when they hosted the World Cup forty years later: "Twenty-five million Argentinians will play in the World Cup!" The Argentine slogan was soon popularly adapted to "Twenty-five million Argentinians will pay for the World Cup," and the Nazi one would be altered when it turned out Germany could not even beat Switzerland.

The Swiss and Germans drew 1–1 in the World Cup's opening match in the Parc des Princes in Paris. By 1938 the French had started to cotton on to the truth about Nazi Germany, and the crowd jeered the German salute and pelted the players with bottles, eggs, and tomatoes throughout the match. The Italian team had also been met on arrival in Marseille by a barrage of abuse from French anti-Fascists and Italian exiles, but Italy went on to win the World Cup. Germany lost their replay with Switzerland 4–2 and went home. "So 60 million Germans were playing," teased *Zürich Sport*. "We only needed eleven soccer players." It summed up the bad luck the Nazis had had with soccer. The game was just too unreliable for them. In Nerz's phrase, later made legendary by Herberger, "The ball is round."

The World Cup probably disenchanted some Austrian fans with the *Anschluss*. Their *Wunderteam* was gone, and the defeat in Paris contained an obvious moral about the difficulties of merging two countries. The German and Austrian players had failed to gel: the Germans thought the Austrians were arrogant, partly because the Austrians had negotiated professional terms while the Germans remained amateur. (Later, much to Viennese chagrin, the Austrians were "reamateurized," because the Nazis considered professionalism a "Jewishization" of sport.)

But perhaps the greatest symbol of Austrian defiance to Germany, whether in soccer or outside, was Matthias Sindelar. A simple working-class boy from the Viennese neighborhood of Favoriten, Sindelar had been probably the best soccer player of the 1930s. He was a lanky and intelligent forward, known as the "Man of Paper."

Sindelar inspired the Austrian *Wunderteam* that in 1931 thrashed mighty Scotland 5–0, beat Germany 6–0 and 5–0, and Hungary 8–2. The *Daily Mail* called him "a genius." Manchester United reportedly tried to buy him from Austria Vienna for £40,000.

Sindelar scored one of the Austrian goals in the "*Anschluss* match" against Germany. But, asked by the German manager Herberger to play in the World Cup, the Man of Paper refused, claiming that at thirty-five he was too old. Ulrich Lindner and Gerhard Fischer argue in *Stürmer für Hitler*, their excellent account of soccer under Nazism, that although it may be unreasonable to expect soccer players to have resisted the Nazis when hardly any other Germans did, others could surely have followed Sindelar in not representing Nazi Germany.

A few months after the World Cup, in January 1939, the Man of Paper was found dead in bed with his girlfriend, the former prostitute Camilla Castagnola. "Death by carbon monoxide," said the police report. The official story was that the apartment's oven had been blocked, driving the poisonous gas back into the room. This was a common form of death in the neighborhood, and the verdict was plausible.

However, few believed it. A national hero in his prime simply did not die like that. It was rumored that there was nothing wrong with the oven, that when the bodies were found there had been no smell of gas; in short that Sindelar and Castagnola had either killed themselves in protest against Nazism or been murdered by the Nazis. Fifteen thousand attended his funeral, and annual pilgrimages to his grave continued throughout the war.

No one knows for certain how Sindelar died. The documents in the case reportedly went missing in the war years. But whatever the truth, many Austrians came to regard the country's best soccer player as a martyr to Nazism. His death undoubtedly influenced public opinion against Germany—not that that would achieve anything.

4

THE WARM BACK OF EDDY HAMEL
An American in Amsterdam and Birkenau

We know that Eddy Hamel was born in New York in 1902 and that he later moved to the Netherlands. He was Jewish, probably of Dutch descent.

Hamel played outside-right for Ajax from 1922 to 1930, scoring only eight goals in 125 league matches but gaining a reputation as a good sport who never hacked opponents. Rob van Zoest, compiler of the jubilee book for the club's centenary in 2000, told me he thought Hamel had died before the war. All he could offer me was the small binder with a hard green cover and blue pages that a long-dead Ajax chairman had used to record membership details. Van Zoest had found it lying around in the old club stadium. There it was:

> Name: Hamel
> Initial: E
> Address: Amstelkade 69, Amsterdam
> Joined: the 1/9/1922
> Working member

The Amstelkade, where Hamel must have spent his bachelor years, is not in the old Jewish Quarter but in the smarter streets of Amsterdam-South. The outside-right was probably number 69's first inhabitant, because the curves in the brick, the balconies with bent iron railings, and the stained glass above the front door are characteristic of the art-deco-like "Amsterdam School" architecture of the 1920s. When I visited the address there was a doll's house in the front window, but otherwise, like much of Amsterdam, it seemed barely to have changed since Hamel's day.

In 1928 Hamel married Johanna Wijnberg, and on April 19, 1938, she gave birth to twins called Paul and Robert, names that could work in either English or Dutch. Hamel seems to have lingered at Ajax after his glory days—a club journal of December 1939 mentions a "Hamel" playing for the veterans—and he also became a coach in local soccer. When the Germans invaded the Netherlands, he was probably in charge of the Amsterdam Jewish club HEDW. At the time of the invasion the Hamels inhabited a second-floor flat in Amsterdam's Rijnstraat, a couple of streets from the square where Anne Frank's family lived.

Evert Vermeer's book *90 Jaar Ajax* (*Ninety Years of Ajax*) contains a photograph of Hamel: a handsome dark man with a quiff from an early gangster movie. Beside the picture is an anecdote from his teenage years at neighboring Amsterdamsche Football Club, or AFC:

> The AFC ground was then behind that of Ajax, and in mischievous moods at training boys would often aim "accidentally" at the windows of the Ajax changing-room. After one such well-aimed shot, Hamel had failed to make a timely getaway, and became acquainted with the paws of the Ajax groundsman. A thorough immersion in the stream that bordered the grounds apparently had the desired effect.

We know hardly anything about Hamel the player. The very old Ajax fan Deetje van Minden told me what he could remember.

"Nothing. That he was a terrifically nice, popular soccer player." Wim Andriessen, the Amsterdam policeman and former Ajax center-half, published a memoir in 1944 in which he named Hamel in his all-time best Ajax side. And in 1965 the Dutch Jewish weekly *Nieuw Israelietisch Weekblad* recalled that in the 1930s "Eddie Hassel" had been on the fringe of the Dutch national team.

Hamel must have been a good soccer player and a man of some social standing, as AFC and Ajax were clubs of standing. Much more than this we do not know. By 1999, when I began searching for Hamel, the living person who knew most about him was probably Leon Greenman. Every Sunday Greenman sat at a table in the Jewish Museum in Finchley, waiting to guide visitors through an exhibition of his life. "You ask, I tell," as he had written on a piece of paper. However, in the three hours that we talked nobody came to ask.

Greenman was in his nineties, a shade over five feet tall, and beneath his thick jacket appeared to be swaddled in clothes. "It's warm here, but I'm very cold," he said. Or as he pronounced it, "ferry colt," for there was a Dutch tinge to his English. At his request I had brought two Dutch honey cakes from Amsterdam. They had been dented on the way, but Greenman said that of course that didn't bother him.

He was born in Whitechapel in London's East End in 1910, but when he was five years old his Dutch-Jewish grandparents (his grandfather had been born in Rotterdam in 1828) decided they wanted to spend their last years in the Netherlands. In those days the entire family would accompany aging parents. The Greenmans crossed the North Sea and took a house in the almost entirely Jewish Helmersstraat, near the Rotterdam train station. The house number, Greenman emphasizes, was 10-A.

"It's gone now, it was bombarded, it's over," he says. Rotterdam's Jewish Quarter disappeared in 1940. The guest now staying in a certain room in the Hilton near the train station finds himself, as it were, above the Greenmans' old front room. But when Greenman walks through modern Rotterdam, he sees a city that no longer exists.

Greenman wants to tell me everything, in a mixture of Dutch and English, using a bureaucratic, almost stenographic tone that reveals no emotion. It is his duty: Greenman is no longer a participant in life but a witness. It is a version of the promise he made God on his first night in the Birkenau camp: if He let Greenman and his wife and child survive, Greenman would try to tell the world about the camps.

Sometimes he closes his eyes to help himself think. He had a nice youth in Rotterdam. He still sees himself lying in the grass of Kattenburg and accidentally stopping a certain goal that his brother Morry had shot. Greenman himself played soccer sometimes, but preferred boxing (he almost turned pro) and singing. It was at a musical evening of the Jewish Circle of Friends in Rotterdam that he met Esther van Dam, a Jewish girl over from England to visit her Dutch relatives. Esther, also known as Else, later told him, "When I heard you sing, I knew that you would be my husband."

They were married at Stepney Green Synagogue, London, in 1935. On their wedding photograph in the exhibition, he has a thin moustache and she towers over him. They went on honeymoon to Rotterdam, where Else's aging grandmother asked them to stay and keep an eye on her. They agreed. Greenman began commuting between Rotterdam and London, trading in second-hand books.

In 1938 he emerged from a London auction house to see people on the street digging trenches and handing out gas masks. He hurried back to Rotterdam to fetch Else. If there was going to be a war, they would be safer in Britain.

Back in Rotterdam, he heard Neville Chamberlain on the wireless saying there would not be a war. "So there was no hurry to return to England," says Greenman. "In those days you believed the Prime Minister. No war, no war." Despite Greenman's misgivings about the future they even went ahead and had a child, Barney, born in Rotterdam on March 17, 1940. The boy was registered a British subject like his parents. The British Consul in Rotterdam promised to tell Greenman when the time came to leave the Netherlands.

Fifty-four days after Barney's birth, the Germans invaded Holland. "I don't think you were there already?" Greenman asks me. "No, I wasn't," I say.

Fearing that the Germans would confiscate the family's British passports, Greenman gave them and his fortune of £758 to gentile friends for safekeeping. He knew the Nazis hated Jews, but he did not believe the British government would allow anything to happen to its own subjects. Furthermore, the Germans would presumably want to swap any captive Britons for German POWs. It was essential to prove that he was British. So he visited the British Consulate, only to find the gate locked and the building deserted. Then he went to his friends' house to fetch the family passports. But the friends, not wanting to be caught with enemy passports, had burned them. Greenman tried to tell the chief of Rotterdam's alien police, a man named Roos, that his family was British, but Roos hissed at him, "You're a Dutchman!"

Greenman says now, "He could have saved me. Why didn't the man say, 'You have English parents, so you must be an Englishman'? But he said something like, 'I'm not going to break my neck for you.' So there were good, and there were Dutch." He corrects himself. "I mean, there were good and there were bad."

On the evening of October 8, 1942, two Dutch policemen rang at the Greenmans' house on the Harddraverstraat. They took the family to Hangar 24, a glorified shed at Rotterdam Harbor where Jews were assembled for deportation. After the war Greenman visited Hangar 24 again. "But nobody I spoke to there seemed to know what had happened. Yes, they knew, but they didn't talk about it."

From Hangar 24 the Greenmans were taken to Westerbork, the Dutch internment camp where the trains left for Poland. In the English Barrack at Westerbork, Greenman met Eddy Hamel. The American had no documents either—in those days people didn't bother much with passports. While in Westerbork, the two men barely spoke because Greenman was too busy trying to prove that his family was British.

One morning in January 1943 the crucial documents proving their nationality finally arrived at Westerbork. Kurt Schlesinger, the German Jew who was the camp's chief administrator, found them in his mail after breakfast. He immediately had the Greenmans paged: they were now to be treated not as Jews but as British subjects.

It was too late. Earlier that morning, a trainload of about seven hundred Dutch Jews, including the Greenmans and the Hamel family, had departed for Birkenau, near Auschwitz.

"Have you ever been to Birkenau?" Greenman asks. "You should do it, it's interesting. Because all the proof is there. At least it's there at the moment. Two years ago it was certainly there." Greenman himself is proof. He rolls up the sleeves of some of his clothes to reveal the green number 98288 on his wrist, and makes me rub it.

At Birkenau the women and children were taken away. Else blew Greenman a kiss and held up Barney for his father to see. Greenman later reflected in his autobiography, "What was going through her mind, I will never know. Perhaps she was pleased that the journey had come to an end. We had been promised that we could meet at the weekends. . . . "

He watched as Else, her grandmother and Barney were driven away in an open truck. Else and Barney were wearing capes with peaked hoods that she had made from red velvet curtains. Greenman saw two splashes of red. He called out to them, but they didn't turn around.

Greenman and about fifty other men were selected for work. When these men asked other prisoners where their wives and children were, the other prisoners would point at the sky. But Greenman says, "We didn't believe that healthy women and children would be killed by gassing." German records show that Else and Barney Greenman and Johanna Hamel-Weinberg and her twin sons were all murdered in Auschwitz on February 1, 1943.

Over the next few weeks, Greenman and Hamel grew close. Speaking Dutch mingled with the odd word of English, the former Ajax player told Greenman he was an American citizen. Hamel had been unlucky on all counts. Had he been able to prove his nationality, or had he been a better outside-right, or had he played for the Ajax first team more recently than 1930, he might have been sent not to Birkenau but to Theresienstadt, the show camp for protected Jews.

Greenman says, "It's strange how things went. It could have been anybody, but it happened to be Eddy and myself. We shared the top bunk. There was more fresh air at the top, and if the *Kapo* passed you were lying out of his sight. In the beginning there were eight of us lying on the planks of the top bunk. But more and more people were selected, and then there were only three of us left. Two had to lie with a leg over the edge. So it was hard to sleep. Eddy and I often rubbed our backs against each other. His body was very warm, you see. And we were very cold."

I ask Greenman whether the reason he and Hamel survived so long was that as athletes they were both unusually strong. "No. I think it was luck."

They had been at Birkenau about three months when the day of the Big Selection came. "From early in the morning until late in the evening: just looking at your body. We had to take our clothes off and stand in the queue. Eddy Hamel was standing behind me—his name begins with an H and mine with a G. He said to me, 'Leon, what is going to happen to me? I have an abscess in my mouth.' It did look swollen."

Greenman slaps the table at which we are sitting. "We had to pass between two tables. There was an SS man sitting at each table. If you weren't fit you went to the left, and if you were fit you went to the right. When I passed between the tables they pointed to the right." Greenman points vigorously to the right. "And when Eddy passed, I looked round: he was sent to the left." He points again. "That unfortunate moment. I thought he was going to the hospital. But I never saw him again. It took a few months before I realized that they really did gas people. It's not a lot that I know about Eddy. It was very cold in the camps. We only had a jacket and trousers. And his back was warm, you know?"

Greenman's book *An Englishman in Auschwitz*, which he published in 2001 at the age of ninety, adds a snippet, "Our conditions were turning some of us into different people; not all of us, some remained almost the same as when they arrived. Eddie Hamel was always a gentleman."

In Memoriam, the register of the 104,000 Dutch Jews who were murdered in the war, records that Hamel, Edward, born in New York on October 21, 1902, died in Auschwitz on April 30, 1943. Greenman thinks Hamel was killed slightly earlier than that.

The Germans performed medical experiments on Greenman, but he survived the camps. Liberated by the Americans from Buchenwald on April 11, 1945, he took some human bones with him as a token of remembrance. He was interviewed by the BBC in a French hospital, but the material was considered too awful to broadcast.

Back in Rotterdam, he heard that Else and Barney had been gassed. She was thirty-two years old; he was two. "There was no point in staying," says Greenman. On November 22, 1945, he took the boat from the Netherlands to Gravesend in England, where he was collected by his mother, his stepfather, and his brothers Charles and Morry. (Fifteen days later Morry suddenly died.)

Greenman worked at markets all over England for more than forty years and sang in England and Holland under the stage-name Leon Mauré. He never remarried. Through the Red Cross he discovered that of the seven hundred people who boarded the train at Westerbork that January morning, only he and his friend Leon Borstrock had survived the war.

A few years ago, talking to an Amsterdam tailor who had saved Greenman's life in the camp by taking him to the sickbay, Greenman happened to mention Hamel. The tailor, an Ajax supporter, said, "You should tell Ajax!"

"I'm sure they wouldn't be interested," said Greenman. But he wrote the club a letter in Dutch, a copy of which is now in his museum. It ends,

Apologies that these facts were not forthcoming, not everybody is interested in what once was. Yet I hope to have done something good out of respect for Eddy Hamel and your mighty soccer club.

With friendly regards, and wishing Ajax success.

In reply, Ajax's ancient archivist Wim Schoevaart sent Greenman an old Ajax booklet and team photographs from the 1920s. Greenman wrote back,

I read your letter first, then page 44 and looked straight at the photo of Eddy Hamel, the face that I cannot forget, of calm friendliness and body warmth. Eddy had a good circulation and was truly warm.

In October 1998 the *Ajax Magazine* published Greenman's letters as part of a feature on Hamel. "So it *was* important for them," Greenman concludes. "Eddy Hamel was gassed because he had an abscess in his mouth. I have had this in my head since 1943. Hamel was a gentleman; he had a quiet voice. I am just sorry that I didn't tell this before."

Telling had become ever more urgent to Greenman. His friend Borstrock had died in South Africa a few years earlier. By 1999 only Greenman knew the story of those seven hundred people. Greenman said, "It's not a nice story. I've been telling it for thirty years or more."

5

THE LOST MEMORIES OF MEIJER STAD

There is a lot Meijer Stad can't remember. It has nothing to do with his age, he says, "It's because I was shot to pieces."

Stad spent the last weeks of World War II working in a salt mine in Germany. Just before the Liberation, the Dutchman and his fellow miners were thrown into a goods van and told they were going to Buchenwald concentration camp. A couple of hours later, however, the train stopped, and soldiers opened the doors to reveal a peaceful spring landscape with rolling fields. Then they opened fire. Stad jumped from the train, and the last thing he remembered was a burning pain.

When we meet, he is old and pot-bellied, but he looks healthy. "Obviously I don't play soccer anymore, but I still play golf three times a week." That he walks with a slight limp is solely due to rheumatism, he insists. He doesn't like it when people at the golf club hold doors open for him, because he doesn't need it.

But he knows he has forgotten things, and this has taught him to collect documents. It is crucial to him to prove his story. In his cellar and in his glittering white office, he keeps an archive of his life. Here in his living room, on the arm of his leather chair, he has laid out a few documents: a 1941 team photograph of Xerxes, his Dutch soccer club; a testimony from a psychologist, arguing that he should be allowed to carry a gun; and an old Christmas card from Argentina. "It just goes to show what private individuals have lying around the house!" says Stad.

We are sitting in his villa in Wassenaar, the wealthiest dormitory town of The Hague. The garden is so large that you can't see the neighboring houses. Stad, who grew up in the poor Jewish quarter of Rotterdam, now has a posh Hague accent. When he isn't playing golf (he is the oldest member of the club) or watching soccer on television (a Holland Under-21s match is enough to keep him off the streets), he is busy writing a novel. He seems to have turned out all right. However, he has trouble sleeping.

Born in Rotterdam in 1919, Stad was raised in the Jewish Quarter. On the street he was sometimes called "rotten Jew," or "Moos" (for Moses), and when he applied for a job in a Catholic department store after leaving school, he was rejected.

He did better as an athlete. Stad was an excellent runner and a good soccer player. In his teens he joined Xerxes, then one of the best Rotterdam soccer clubs. He made his first-team debut soon after the Germans invaded.

By then the Stad family had already left Rotterdam. Stad's stepfather, a Christian who traveled regularly to the United States on business, had come home one day in 1939 with surprising news. The family was moving to The Hague, he said, because there was a war coming in which Rotterdam would be bombed. The notion seemed absurd, because surely Holland would always be neutral in war? "The good man never said how he got the idea!" exclaims Stad.

But the Germans came, and in a few minutes around lunchtime on May 14 Rotterdam city center was duly flattened by Luftwaffe bombs. Twenty-five of Stad's relatives were made homeless and came to stay with them in The Hague.

Stad had resolved not to wear the yellow star. But to get a ration card he had to register with the new authorities. Arriving for registration at the Hague Zoo, he recognized one of the clerks as a fan of his soccer team. They chatted about soccer, and when the clerk produced the stamp with the hated "J," Stad whispered, "What are you doing? No 'Jew' on it! I want a normal food stamp." The clerk put the stamp aside, and Stad left the zoo as one of the few dozen Dutch Jews not to register as a Jew.

At home, his relatives begged him to wear the star for safety's sake. Stad ignored them. "Jerks," he writes in his memoirs. For the next five years he would live as a gentile named Bouwens, his stepfather's surname.

Stad was never a great soccer player, but with Xerxes he played in the highest Dutch division. A few moments have stayed with him. He remembers Puck van Heel, the Feyenoord captain, standing on his foot as they awaited a corner kick in a full Feyenoord stadium. Stad shouted, "Hey, what are you doing?" and Van Heel replied, "Boy, when you're as old as I am, you'll do that to another."

And he remembers playing against a one-armed outside-left in Delft. Stad kept leaning against the man, who kept falling over, to the rage of the Delft crowd. After Stad scored the winning goal from a corner, he had to be escorted to the train station by the police.

Stad suspects these were good times. "The strange thing is that I can't remember much from my career in '40, and why? Because I was executed, I lost a little of my memory." He taps the side of his head.

He does recall a cup match against a fourth-division side in the village of Geertruidenberg. When the Xerxes team arrived in the village café, they found an honor guard of the Dutch Nazi Party's Youth Storm assembled to lead them to the ground. The Xerxes captain Wim Lagendaal, a legendary soccer player known as "the Cannon," later police commissioner of Rotterdam, said, "The Youth Storm has to go." Stad, who lived in fear of being unmasked as a Jew, said, "Don't be crazy, they'll check us out, you never know." But in Stad's memory Lagendaal held firm and the Youth Storm disappeared.

Before the game Lagendaal told his teammates, "We're going to beat this lot by double figures." So they did, and when Xerxes had scored about sixteen goals, Lagendaal was awarded a free kick thirty-five yards from the Geertruidenberg goal. In Stad's memory, the Cannon fired the ball at the head of a tubby Dutch Nazi standing beside the goal. The Nazi dropped to the ground, his cap fell off, and there were cheers.

This is one of the standard war stories the Dutch tell: a small symbolic humiliation of Evil by Good, always recounted by the goodies. It would be interesting to hear what the Youth Storm members, now mostly in their eighties, remember of that day. In Holland their story is rarely heard.

Stad says Lagendaal was one of the very few at Xerxes who knew he was Jewish. "The coach also knew and, very bizarre, there was a Dutch Nazi Party man who took care of the team, and he knew it too, and he protected me in a special way."

But eventually Stad had to leave the club. Taking the train from The Hague to Rotterdam for training sessions four times a week had become too dangerous, so he joined his local third-division team of Scheveningen. On his debut he scored a hat-trick, but a Dutch Nazi playing for the opposition recognized him from schooldays in Rotterdam. After the third goal, the man threatened to turn him in as a Jew. In Stad's account, a teammate of his then cracked the Nazi's knee and jumped on the man while the referee looked the other way. The Nazi was taken to the hospital where he died of "complications." "They finished him off," explains Stad.

Meanwhile Stad had joined an athletics club named Celebes, founded in 1940 and recruited largely from Resistance members. Running as Bouwens, in a field consisting mainly of Germans, he won the Dutch 3,000-meter championship of 1942 in the

Amsterdam Olympic Stadium. He disappeared before the awards ceremony but later read about his victory in the Dutch Nazi newspaper *Volk en Vaderland*. One evening we had dinner in a yuppie restaurant inside the Olympic Stadium, overlooking the track, and he told me the story again.

Stad was young in the war, and remembers the time with a mix of horror and thrill. There were German soldiers and deportations, but also sport and lots of girls. He remembers lying on the beach outside The Hague with friends, burgling storehouses at the harbor, selling cigarettes on the black market and, more than once, killing people. A militiaman, for instance, who had caught him with a sack of wood, or two drunken German soldiers whom Stad and a friend drowned in a canal.

No one carried a card saying, "Resistance member," but Stad seems to have done his share. He told me he hid Albert Einstein's great-nephews in a Hague typhoid barracks and then smuggled them to a safe house in the countryside. (They survived the war, but to Stad's dismay one of them later converted to Christianity.) He remembers helping a wounded British pilot, but he says the man had eventually been caught trying to cross into Spain.

"It was a nasty time," Stad says. "My grandmother, a sweet, civilized woman, who didn't want to go, who was pulled by her hair out of her house in Scheveningen! It was a disaster."

Over the months I became very fond of Stad. He would phone me in England, overjoyed at having sold his company, or to say he had just remembered a wartime match in which the players had been asked to bring their own shirts. He and his wife took me out for Chinese food. But although I never for a second doubted that he had survived a concentration camp and had been shot, I wasn't sure of all the detail of his war stories. With an addled memory, how could he possibly remember? I was depressed when he called one day to say that he had suddenly remembered meeting Anne Frank in Bergen-Belsen, and that he had been struck by her "ethereal" air. It was just about feasible (anything was feasible in World War II), but it seemed improbable given that Anne Frank was in the Belsen women's camp. I don't think Stad meant to embroider. But a man who has lost part of his memory makes frantic efforts to remember, which are doomed by definition.

What happened to Stad—and to millions of other people—in the Second World War will never be fully ascertained. But I was immensely relieved to find a 1976 report on the Jewish turncoat Weinreb, published by the Dutch state, which confirmed that Stad had been very active in the Resistance. Tragically, though, one of his patrons had been Weinreb. The report says Stad worked for him as a courier and strong-arm man, hiding Jews and dropping warnings into the mailboxes of people who were scheduled to be deported the next day.

The report recounts the time that Stad, escorting a Jewish woman and her child to a hiding place in Amsterdam, was asked by a stranger in the street if he was heading for a certain house.

"Yes," said Stad.

"Don't go there. It's been betrayed," said the stranger.

Stad turned tail with the woman and child and took the train back to The Hague. But when he walked into Weinreb's office to tell him what had happened, Weinreb stared at him as if he were a ghost. That was when it began to dawn on Stad that Weinreb often made money betraying the Jews he hid.

The authors of the state report seem to accept Stad's testimony without question. This is reassuring, even if Weinreb's story itself illustrates the confusion and manifold identities of Jews and Resistance men in wartime. Interestingly, the report describes Stad as a "half-Jew." Lord knows whether this was accurate. But it is a crucial question, because the Nazis did not deport half-Jews for fear their gentile relatives would protest.

In the spring of 1944 the Germans caught up with Stad. However, they only knew that he was a Resistance man, not that he was Jewish—if indeed he was. He was interrogated in Scheveningen

Prison, beaten up, and sent to an internment camp in the town of Vught. There he was drafted into a team of prisoners captained by a former German international. Early in his first game, he scored a great solo goal and promptly fainted from fatigue.

To catalogue the rest of Stad's war, I quote another document from his archive, a medical declaration from the Jelgersma Clinic in Leiden dated November 4, 1980: "On 6.3.1944 he was transferred to the Westerbork camp and from there on 9.13.1944 as a prisoner to the Bergen Belsen camp. From there he was sent to the Buchenwald camp on 12.19.1944 as a political prisoner. On 4.16.1945 he was liberated there, to be repatriated to Eindhoven on 5.24.1945."

Stad shows me the letter he received while in the Dutch transit camp of Westerbork from some of his Celebes friends. A man named Henk writes, "It's going well with Celebes, especially with the girls and women, oh well you'll hear that more fully from the others. Only this: when you are in our midst again, you will have to train hard so as not to fall too far behind Xenia." At the London Olympics of 1948, Stad would watch Xenia de Jong, by then his wife, win gold in the relay with Fanny Blankers-Koen. Later, when Stad and Xenia divorced, she destroyed many of his documents.

On the same piece of paper another Henk adds, "For a change I'll tell you about Celebes. Our ladies' team is excellent and up till now still unbeaten. . . . In Veenstra we have found a worthy replacement for you, especially on the 800 meters. . . . I too am doing OK: in Leiden 11.5 ahead of Schouten." And on the back of the same sheet of paper, Aat concludes, "Meij we miss you, especially this afternoon when the 3,000 meters was run. . . ."

I have brought Stad a picture from the time he was in Westerbork: a team photograph of Xerxes from a tournament in Rotterdam in 1944. They had all kept playing. Stad studies the photograph closely. "In that period everybody lived alone. I myself always had the feeling that I was being followed." But he does remark that while imprisoned in Scheveningen and Vught he never once received a Red Cross parcel.

———

After jumping from the German train and feeling the burning pain, Stad had come to in the sickbay at Buchenwald with about ten bullets in his body. It turned out that the murdered miners had been returned to the camp, where the nurses charged with taking the bodies to the incinerator had found Stad alive. They had swapped him for a corpse from the camp, and in the sickbay had dressed his wounds with rags.

A French prisoner, a former professor of medicine, had removed the bullets with a pen-knife: six from his right arm, one from his left hand, two from his left leg, and one from his right leg. One bullet had glanced off his head. Stad rolls up his sleeves to display a bump on his arm, takes off his glasses to show a skewed right eye, and lifts a trouser-leg to reveal a scarred dent above the knee. He says, "But it was OK. I can't make a fist any more. And after the war I had to play soccer very carefully. I lost a couple of years from my memory, and I've tried to get them back. I think about it, but. . . ."

In 1946 he ran a 3,000-meter race in The Hague and finished third. Otherwise, especially in the first few years after the war, he had a hard time. At first he could not find work. Then he got a job examining camp survivors, which made him ill. Subsequently, like many other survivors, he turned into a workaholic. Stad opened an advertising agency and became a millionaire.

"You did it alone," I say.

Stad slaps himself angrily on the knee and starts shouting. "Don't forget! Don't forget! As a Jew and a former Resistance fighter, you didn't get a chance to work anywhere. I'd been too prominent, I'd done too much in the war, I'd been world news! I'd run the three thousand meters when I was barely out of plaster. I made it myself, I came back from the camp with nothing! With nothing at all!"

A Belgian in the bed beside him in the Buchenwald sickbay had told him, "I'll die in this camp, but you are going to pull through. And remember, when you get out of here, no one will ever frighten you again. Everyone will only make you happy."

"I'll always remember that," Stad says. But as the decades passed he realized that the Belgian had been wrong. At some point in the 1990s, finding that he could no longer sleep, Stad was advised by his GP to write his memoirs. "But there are dozens of stories I haven't written." He tells me one about a fellow prisoner who ate human flesh; after the war, back in Holland, he once saw the man in the street. "Can you imagine that? I'll tell you: it's terrible. If you hear the stories of survivors; you can't imagine it. . . ."

"It's unimaginable," I agree.

"Don't you believe me?" asks Stad, shocked. A common fear among Holocaust survivors is that their stories are so awful and bizarre that no one will believe them.

This story would have ended here, had Stad not met an Argentine wine dealer at a congress in Copenhagen soon after the Dutch team had shone at the World Cup of 1974. "In those days, if you were a Dutchman abroad, you felt as proud as if you played for Holland yourself," Stad says.

The Argentine happened to be the director of a soccer club. He made a proposal, which Stad repeats to me in his most posh Hague accent. "Listen here," said the Argentinian. "We have a boy, a very young boy, and he is a marvelous soccer player. Couldn't you place this boy with a Dutch club?" The boy was not yet ready for professional soccer, the wine dealer said, but would be suitable for the youth team of a big Dutch club.

At the time Stad trained a women's athletics club in the grounds of FC Den Haag. He asked the club if it was interested in a young Argentinian. It was not. Stad had done business with a director of the Rotterdam club Sparta. The director told him, "I'll have a word. You'll hear from me." Stad never did. Stad called Feyenoord, where a soccer player answered the phone, and later Ajax, but no one wanted the young Argentinian, whose name, of course, was Diego Maradona.

From the documents by his side Stad picks up the Christmas card from Maradona. It originally contained a short note in English, purportedly written by Maradona himself, asking whether Stad was still thinking of him. The boy would then have been about fifteen.

I have just one more question for Stad: Who was the Sparta director who didn't want Maradona?

Stad sighs—something else he can't remember.

"Cor van Rijn?" I ask.

No.

"Jos Coler?"

No.

"Hans Sonneveld?"

"Yes! Sonneveld. Incredibly nice guy he was! And once a feared outside-right."

———

A few weeks later I visited Sonneveld in his flat in Rotterdam.

He led me to a little room where we sat in chairs diagonally opposite each other like Communist leaders. On the walls were pictures of dead soccer and cricket teams, a certificate confirming that Sonneveld had visited the Dead Sea in Israel, and a photograph of his twin sons, who had succeeded him as Sparta scouts. It was an impressive room. "But," Sonneveld, who was in his late seventies, said, "there are a lot of boys who play for Sparta now who don't know who Sonneveld is—who was a member for sixty years, captain of the cricket first eleven and of the soccer first eleven!"

He told me about the players he had discovered in his twenty-five years as a Sparta scout. They had later been sold, he said, for a total of 25 million guilders (about $10 million). He had given up a lot of holidays, but had seen every soccer field in Holland. Sonneveld had discovered the future Ajax libero Danny Blind, the greatest ever Dutch keeper Jan van Beveren, the Austrian Willy Kreuz, the English center-forward Ray Clarke. . . .

I had to tell him. When at last I could get a word in edgeways, I explained how he had missed Diego Maradona. There was a silence. Then Sonneveld shouted, "It can't be true! Good Lord, Maradona!" He shook his head. "But well, he was an Argentinian, and I don't think the Sparta board. . . . But I did comb through all of Holland. Maradona! Is it really true? If only I'd seen him. If that man had said he played in Belgium or Norway, I'd have gone to have a look."

Within seconds Sonneveld made a full recovery. Telling me about his discovery of Clarke at Mansfield Town in England, he built a wonderful detective story out of the trail of tips, false leads, and informers. "Without having seen him, just by asking a few Englishmen here and there about him. . . ."

Later I told Stad I had spoken to Sonneveld.

"Sonneveld?" asked Stad, surprised. "Is he still alive?"

6

SPARTA
A Soccer Club in Wartime

I.

You can usually tell the oldest Dutch sports clubs by their names. Their late nineteenth-century founders tended to be wealthy students, versed in the classics, who favored names from Greek history.

One of these clubs is Sparta Rotterdam. Almost every Dutch soccer fan has a weakness for Sparta, founded in 1888 and now playing in the second tier of Dutch professional soccer. People often call Sparta an "English" club, meaning that it is very old, was once posh, and has never discarded its traditional shirts with the red and white stripes. Sparta used to produce talented soccer players, like Ed de Goey or Danny Blind or the legendary Van Beveren, but it no longer does very often.

As a boy I played cricket and soccer for another old Dutch club. Ajax Leiden was founded in 1892 and went into decline soon afterward. Today it is remembered chiefly for a decision it made in 1900, to allow a new club in Amsterdam to call itself Ajax too. But, like many of the old Dutch clubs, Ajax Leiden still plays cricket, and in the early 1980s I regularly traveled to Rotterdam to play Sparta's mix of Dutchmen, English expats, and the odd Pakistani who worked in the harbor. It was a thrill, partly because I always hoped I might meet a real professional soccer player (albeit not a very good one), and partly because it was so rare to leave Leiden. Rotterdam was nearly an hour away by car.

I had never expected Sparta to figure in this book. I had begun my research by trying to dig up the war history of Ajax, Feyenoord, and the Dutch FA, but soon found that there was almost nothing there. Little bits of Ajax's and Feyenoord's archives are spread over various addresses—the Ajax historian Evert Vermeer lives in a small flat crammed floor-to-ceiling with old club papers. The Dutch FA's documents for the period 1940–1945 seem to have disappeared entirely. Who did that?

Then, in Rotterdam's municipal archive, I chanced upon the Sparta files. No other big Dutch club has anything like it for the war years. Not a scrap of paper at Sparta seemed to have been thrown away, or edited, or retold in a different way decades later. The neat files contain the oddest documents: almost every letter Sparta sent in the war, as well as club journals, scattered memos, and painstakingly typed minutes of board meetings. It gives a sense of daily life in occupied Holland like nothing else I had encountered.

Much of what follows in this chapter are scraps from club documents and my conversations with surviving Spartans. A baffling number of different names are mentioned. There is no need to remember most of them. The point is that the experiences of these hundreds of Spartans—collaborators, Jews, and everyday folk muddling along—add up to a microcosm of the Dutch war.

II.

By the time the Germans entered Holland on May 10, 1940, Sparta's British members had already gone home, but the war truly reached Rotterdam four days later. A little after one o'clock on the afternoon of Tuesday the 14th, a crowd of German Heinkel planes discharged their bombs over a stunned city. Up to nine hundred people died, and the spreading fires devoured most of central Rotterdam. The Netherlands surrendered the next day. In a temporary hospital at the Sparta ground, bomb victims were cared for in the cricketers' deckchairs. The cricket season would have just begun.

On July 25, 1940, a Sparta member named J. Pino writes one of the first letters in the club archive relating to the war. Complaining that "my entire sports clothing was lost as a result of the bombard-ment," he asks the board for help.

Nowhere in the records is there a mention of Sparta members dying in the bombardment. But someone called A. Blitz is dead. On October 25 the club writes to his father to commiserate, and adds, "Regarding his expulsion from the club, recorded in our previous club journal, this occurred in accordance with the regulations, which how-ever does not mean that—had we known the circumstances—pub-lication might better have been omitted." Sparta promises to rehabilitate Blitz in the next issue of the club journal.

Meanwhile German soldiers are camping under the Sparta ter-races and playing on the pitches. On October 20 the Sparta board asks Robert Koch, a German living in Rotterdam, to ask the Wehrmacht to stay off the main field. Koch immediately translates Sparta's letter into German and sends it to the local German head-quarters. In an accompanying letter, he informs the occupiers that his son is probably Sparta's only German (or as he puts it, *Reichs-deutsches*) member.

A letter from Bulgaria reaches Sparta: Franz Köhler has heard that the club is looking for a coach. Köhler writes that he is Viennese, a soldier, "free of children," and that he has coached in many countries including Italy, France, and Greece. Now he is working for Slavia Sofia and the Bulgarian FA. "With German sporting greetings, *Heil Hitler*," Köhler concludes politely. Someone at Sparta has indicated on the letter that it has been answered, probably with "No thanks," because the Dutchman Koonings remains club coach.

Today, any mention of World War II tends to evoke thoughts of Auschwitz, Dunkirk, or Stalingrad, but the experience of most people in Western Europe was very different. Particularly in Holland, the German occupation was relatively mild. The Dutch journalist Frits Barend goes so far as to argue that there wasn't a Second World War in the Netherlands. He says there was a war in Amsterdam, there was a war if you were Jewish, and in the "Hunger Winter" of 1944–1945 there was a war in the part of the country north of the great rivers, but otherwise people lived much as they had before, though with slightly less food. Reading the Sparta archive, one sees what he means. When the Hermes DVS player A. v. d. Tuijn shouts, "*Boerenlul*" (literally "farmer's penis") during a game against Sparta on February 16, 1941, a disciplinary case ensues. On February 28 Sparta tells the Dutch FA "that only our player J. Seton heard the expression *boerenlul*, but he does not know with certainty whether the referee or Hermes's own linesman was meant by this."

The date is striking: in the week of Sparta's letter, hundreds of thousands of workers in Amsterdam went on strike to protest against the deportation of four hundred Jews from the city's Jewish Quarter. Today the February Strike is considered perhaps the proudest moment of the Dutch war, but it seems to have passed Sparta by.

III.

"Sparta was the club with the most Jewish members in Rotterdam," Hans Sonneveld, the man who turned down Maradona, told me. That would cease forever in 1941. That summer, Sparta received a letter from the authorities ordering "Forbidden for Jews" signs to be hung above all food and drink stalls on its grounds. At the bottom of the letter, a Spartan has noted in pen that the signs need only be hung in public places. Triumphantly, "Our clubhouse, if clearly indicated and reserved for members and donors, does not fall under this order."

But it is the first step. Sparta's board reports that Jews are hesitant to remain members. On June 28, L. Querido cancels his membership. J. Posner, another Jew, writes on July 8, "Due to the circumstances of the time I see myself compelled to withdraw as donor. If times change I hope speedily to become a member again." He never would. M. Brandel, also most probably Jewish, informs the club on August 28 that he is resigning from the club journal *De Spartaan*: "Various worries for now and the future, which occupy me constantly, are such that 'my head is not right' to pen humorously tinged pieces for the organ, as has been my custom until now. Maybe a time will come, however, that I can rescind my decision."

But there are also other kinds of Spartans. On September 8 a member of the Sparta board writes to the chairman of Ajax in Amsterdam:

My dear Koolhaas,

As you probably know our youthful member Haro Koch is currently living in Amsterdam (Deurloostraat 86). He would like to train a little once a week, and now I make the friendly request as to whether that could happen at Ajax.

Harro Koch (as his name is properly spelled) is Robert's son, Sparta's only German member. Later events suggest that he has come to Amsterdam in Hitler's name. Ajax replies that Koch will be welcome at practice.

On September 9, a club called HVV 't Gooi sends a circular to Sparta and all other clubs in District 2. Having told them that it will no longer provide towels for visiting teams, 't Gooi raises "another very important question." The state commissioner for the Hilversum area has banned Jews from playing soccer, refereeing, or acting as linesmen. "We would therefore like to request you emphatically, if there are Jews in your team *not* to let them play in Hilversum. Considering our chairman, Mr. G. v. d. Poel, is personally responsible for the potential participation of these people."

On September 15, 1941, the Germans impose the ban nationwide: Jews can no longer play sport in public in the Netherlands. Only on October 23 will Jews be barred from sports clubs, but Sparta does not wait for that. Anxious to be on the safe side, it sends a circular to its Jewish members on September 23, saying the German order of September 15 "must be understood to mean that entry to our grounds is forbidden under any circumstances, that is, also for playing in or attending training sessions. Anyone who wants his membership fee for the current season returned should send us his certificate."

The Jews had long expected this. They react laconically. M. Leefman replies, "Your letter received, and taken good note of. I request you politely to return my paid fees to the address below." His certificate of membership is enclosed.

IV.

Nonetheless, on Saturday, September 27, a special board meeting rages beyond control. Sparta's chairman from 1913 to 1946, Mary Overeijnder (who despite the name was a man), would later say that "the show then performed will fill an ugly page in our minute-book and in the history of Sparta." He might have added that the page would also be unique in the Netherlands. The sports historian André Swijtink says that at no other Dutch sports club or association did board minutes capture reactions to the expulsion of the Jews.

The meeting of volunteers on their free Saturday afternoon is a typical Dutch scene. The Netherlands is a country of clubs: charity clubs, reading clubs, tae kwon do clubs, anything. Today one in every fourteen Dutch people is a member of a soccer club, and playing soccer is only half of it. The Dutch mostly work short hours, and many of them think their real job is chairing their soccer club, or editing its journal, or coaching the fifteenth team.

Sparta's board meeting of September 27 was prompted by complaints about the administrator Jan Wolff, a Spartan since 1890. The minutes explain that he had hung "an extravagantly large sign" in front of the ground saying "Forbidden for Jews." Wolff had also apparently treated the Jewish member Van Lier and another couple of young members "in a most discourteous manner."

A director named Jos Cohen is "incensed" and requests that the board meets first without Wolff. The administrator leaves the room.

Decades after the war Jos Cohen would find a measure of international fame as treasurer of UEFA, the European soccer association, by which time he had renamed himself Jos Coler. He had joined Sparta as a boy, and by the 1930s had become known as the best-dressed keeper in the Netherlands. The proprietor of a clothes shop, Cohen wore a new outfit for almost every match. People remember him keeping goal in a blazer. He chaired Sparta's Ballot Committee ("What does your father do?" he would ask prospective members) and wrote poems in the club journal under the Anglophone pseudonym "Glance." Cohen was half Jewish, a category of people the Nazis were sparing for the while.

Cohen tells the board meeting that he himself saw Wolff insult Van Lier. He had wanted to chastise Wolff, "but the presence of staff restrained him." The perfectly typed minutes continue: "The crowning folly, however, is the installation of an enormously large sign with the text, 'Forbidden for Jews,' above the entire width of the main entrance on the occasion of the 'youth day' of Saturday, 27 September"—the day of the board meeting, in fact.

After Cohen had complained about the sign, Wolff replaced it with "the already existing small lengths of cardboard." However, the sign had already been seen. "An inestimable number of people has thus been grieved and hurt, and great disadvantage brought upon Sparta." The chairman of Hermes DVS had told Cohen he was "astonished that Sparta had taken the measure," since Hermes had yet to do anything of the kind.

Enough is enough, Cohen concludes. There have already been many complaints that Wolff "addresses the members sharply and rudely." Wolff must stand down as director of materials.

Other directors agree. One of them, Lieftinck, notes that "Mr. Wolff is also said to treat the boys of better background more properly than others," and says that he himself has "repeatedly been treated discourteously."

Then Bok de Korver speaks. Captain of Holland until he stopped playing for his country in 1913 because he didn't feel like it any more, in 1941 he was still considered probably the best soccer player in Dutch history. So famous was he that a club in Amsterdam, BDK, had been named after him. De Korver's first contribution is to say that they have known Wolff for decades and know him to be "brusque," but that the man doesn't mean it badly.

Then Overeijnder (still warmly remembered at Sparta today) discusses the German measure of September 15. Wolff had taken the order to mean that Jews weren't allowed into the ground at all. Overeijnder had then "pointed out emphatically to Mr. Wolff that we must do or omit to do nothing that could create the impression that we were trifling with this ban, and . . . that [Mr. Wolff] in the first place and the directors would be held responsible for any transgressions and would be punished." Overeijnder adds, "On the other hand he urged him to avoid anything that could hurt or grieve the Jewish members."

Overeijnder says the other directors should stop complaining. De Korver himself had offered to fetch the "Forbidden for Jews" signs, and Lieftinck had expelled from the ground a Jewish member called Jokelson (who would soon be dead). In any case, Overeijnder has heard from the Dutch FA that Jews have indeed been barred from sports grounds.

Then Wolff, who has been allowed back into the room, defends himself: "It is far from him to hold any antipathy toward Jews, on the contrary, he has many friends among them and he is sorry they must suffer from the ban. He was only doing his work. He is sorry. As regards Van Lier, he only told him he couldn't enter the ground any more, without, as Mr. Cohen claims, making a hand gesture."

But Cohen says he remains deeply shocked. Wolff repels many people, he adds. Other board members confirm this.

It could be, Wolff says, that he is not always friendly, that may be in his character, but he never deliberately intends to treat anyone rudely; he knows that among the Spartans there are many who enjoy associating with him.

Overeijnder orders him "in future to act with more tact, in the first place to dress up any refusals in a more friendly manner."

Overeijnder warns against exaggerating the affair. Reduced to its true proportions, all it amounts to is that instead of a sign of modest size a far too blatant sign has been hung up, but it is certain that some sort of sign was required. It would have created a fuss anyway, simply because Sparta happened to be the first club with such a sign. "That the chairman of Hermes DVS more or less mocks us because we got so worried about the ban leaves the speaker cold, and if he re-marks that his own club has done nothing in that direction, that is his business." Then the meeting ends.

In one of the files in the archive there is a cardboard sign about twenty inches long. The pinholes are still in it. You unfold it, and it says, in fat black capitals, "FORBIDDEN FOR JEWS (regulation no. 20—1941)." This is probably not the big sign that Wolff hung above the entrance, but one of the smaller "Jew signs" (to use a Dutch phrase of the era). After the war, someone must have put it in the file for safekeeping.

The board sends the Jewish member Van Lier a letter apologizing for his treatment, expressing "the wish that the pleasant understanding between you and our Club will continue to exist, albeit at a distance."

The day after the meeting, on Sunday, September 28, Sparta plays VSV at home. The October 1941 issue of *De Spartaan* (by then re-duced through a shortage of paper to a couple of sheets in purple ink hung in the clubhouse) includes a match report by Cohen. It does not refer to the expelled Jews, not even in a hint. Instead Cohen ponders whether under-fed soccer players can last ninety minutes, and writes, "An equally typical problem of this time is the passing of aeroplanes during a match. . . . But Sunday it stayed calm, up there in the sky."

However, the Wolff affair refuses to die. On October 18 the board reconvenes. Overeijnder tells his directors that he tried to forget what had happened but couldn't and eventually decided to put a long account on paper. He calls the previous meeting "an ugly page" in the minute-book and even in Sparta's history. It is his "first duty" to repel the danger of division (a comment that explains much of the Dutch Second World War). Overeijnder wants to discuss the matter "in a calmer atmosphere. . . . As for Wolff's one mistake, the hanging-up of the big sign, the indignation of the public has turned out to be rather modest, and the speaker thinks the meeting should be grateful it didn't reach an ill-considered decision."

Cohen says he is sorry that Overeijnder has returned to the affair. "It was indeed of an unpalatable nature and he would prefer to see it forgotten." But as regards the big sign, "he has repeatedly seen what displeasure it has aroused." Other clubs have applied the German order far less coarsely and hurtfully, says Cohen.

Overeijnder considers that opinion "extremely unseemly." Other clubs have been much less obliging than Sparta, he insists, for example retaining a quarter of the fees the Jews had paid. He even mentions a case in which Jewish members had to pay the full fee. But he wants to calm things down. "The speaker considers it of the greatest importance that all deal with each other in a well-meaning manner." Salters agrees. This conversation has cleared the air, he says, and Wolff is already behaving better. The matter is declared closed.

In 2001 I asked Jacques Frenkel, who before the war had been a Jewish member of Sparta, whether reading about the board's deliberations in my Dutch book had made him angry. He replied, "I always have to laugh about these sorts of stories. I think it's quite funny."

<hr />

V.

In October 1941 the last Jewish members resign from Sparta. They do so in the formal manner that characterizes all Spartan correspondence of the era. One letter states, "On the grounds of the order of the *Rijkscommissaris* regarding the membership of Jews of associations without economic goals, the below-mentioned, L. M. and M. S. Schaap, politely request you to scratch them as members of your club." Only the letterheads reveal the odd personal detail: M. van Gelderen is a cattle trader, and M. van Leer deals in "All Musical Instruments." Both will die in the war.

On October 27 H. Rippe and his son resign with great formality, and J. Stad returns his Sparta certificate, wishing the club good luck in the league. Stad and the Rippes will also be killed. Cohen reports in his chronicle of Sparta at war, published in the summer 1945 issue of *De Spartaan*, that about eighty Jews had to leave the club.

Sparta moves on to more pressing matters. On October 20 it writes to the State Bureau for Rubber, asking to be allowed to keep its old car tires. "For many years now running in tires has been one of the main exercises for the game of soccer at our club, as you will see from the enclosed photograph." And Cohen's postwar report for November 1941, the month after the expulsions, merely says, "After seven games Sparta unbeaten at the top of the table. We owe this success to our strong attack; the mediocre defense will soon bring great disappointment. Public interest in our matches grows strongly." For sport blossomed in the war: the archive contains an undated, unsigned memo saying that, "given the flood of boys into the soccer clubs," Sparta should introduce a selection procedure.

Even after 1941 Jews occasionally pop up in the correspondence. M. Katan writes on May 22, 1942, "Some years ago my membership seems to have lapsed due to an oversight on my part. I would like to see my membership restored." But an alert Spartan has typed beneath the letter, "From Katan's answer to my question I heard that he falls under the order regarding the Jews, so that I had to tell him we could not admit him as a member."

On March 19, 1943, the Jewish ex-member Hans Frenkel sends a postcard to say he is working for the Jewish Council as a courier between Amsterdam and the camp in Westerbork. Six months later Frenkel writes again from the "Jewish Home" in Barneveld, a country estate where seven hundred "protected" Jews were staying. When he wrote this letter he must have known that within a few days the Barneveld Jews would be moved to the Westerbork internment camp, and that trains left Westerbork for the camps in the east. But he does not mention that. Instead, he writes:

Dear Spartans,

First of all my sincere thanks for the *Announcements* you sent me,
which gave me a lot of pleasure! Particularly the Cricket section
had my interest, and I noted that it's still the same team of 2,
3 years ago! Congratulations especially to Lou for his century. . . .
I heard from Sonneveld that you had an enjoyable season!

I also hope the soccer season will be favorable, although the
beginning isn't promising. I still remember the last game I played
for Sparta, exactly 2 years ago in the streaming rain somewhere
deep in Charlois with the Twelfth Eleven against Spartaan 4!
The score was 11–7 in our favor!! I had the pleasure of scoring
the eleventh goal with a ricochet off my left leg. We came home
dripping wet! Those are all nice and good memories.

Mr. Wolff, I thank you in particular for the trouble I have given
you and hope I'm not being cheeky, if I ask if in the future you
would like to send me the *Announcements*.

Frenkel has enclosed a visiting card on which a Rotterdam address
has been crossed out and replaced with a handwritten *Barrack 35,
Jewish Council, dept. Westerbork.*

On April 23, 1943, Rotterdam is officially declared "cleansed" of
Jews. However, Cohen appears in the board minutes almost throughout the war. If he felt like a walking *memento mori*, he gave no sign
of it. "He wasn't the man to be weighed down by that. He was extremely self-confident," Jacques Frenkel told me.

Indeed, Cohen proceeds as if World War II were not happening.
On June 24, 1942, he tells the board "that Sparta has entered the
Dutch Baseball Association and that the costs of this are 12.50
guilders." At the board meeting of July 31, 1943, by which time most
Dutch Jews have been gassed, he is upset when the board fires him
as *leider* (a sort of general manager) of the soccer first eleven. The

chairman is insistent: "If Mr. Cohen wants a clear answer to his question whether or not he is suited to be *leider*, he roundly says *no*." And at the board meeting of October 30, 1943, Cohen reveals the marks he has given to Sparta players of all elevens, based on reports from their *leiders*. The minutes record, "It is advised against publishing this list at club evenings."

VI.

In Sparta's files in the Municipal Archive, the letters from Jews canceling their memberships mingle with resignation letters from other members. Each departure has its own story. Someone called Schram writes on May 28, 1941, that "my parents are against me still staying at Sparta." A father resigns for his son with a lengthy explanation of how long it takes them to get to the ground on Wednesday afternoons, and anyway, the boy seems to lack "the right spirit."

However, a new trend emerges: some Spartans resign because they are going into hiding to avoid being sent to work in Germany. They can hardly write this, so they use euphemisms. A remarkable number of members resign citing "studies." Others drop hints: someone resigns in a letter in which he gives only his "previous address," while another quits "due to stay outside the city." On June 18, 1942, A. M. Veltenaar "isn't interested in soccer any more after all."

In September 1943, several Spartans join another Dutch club. This club, which Cohen does not name in his postwar report, can apparently obtain passes absolving players from work in Germany. Cohen writes, "When several of the disloyal members want to return [to Sparta] later, they are told that their membership is no longer desired." Better to remain a Spartan and make munitions in the Third Reich than betray the club and stay home.

While some Spartans leave and others hide, a few seem to have no idea where they are at all any more. On November 10, 1942, someone with almost illegible handwriting (De Vlaag? De Vlaming?) writes to the board, "I hereby politely request permission to fly a glide plane I have built myself in your stadium, since Rotterdam does not offer much opportunity to practice this sport. Preferably on Saturday afternoon or Sunday morning."

VII.

From 1943 the greater violence begins to emerge in the files. On the last day of March, Rotterdam suffers its "Forgotten Bombardment": 341 people are killed by Allied bombs, an event that has never received a prominent place in the city's memory. Among the dead are several Spartans, including the club doctor Vader and his sons, Wim and Jan. M. G. Gelens goes to Berlin, where he dies of heart failure while swimming.

A. Kaptein dies in a bombardment in Germany.

Some Spartans can only turn out for the club occasionally. On September 24, 1943, G. C. den Hartog writes from the Dutch island of Texel, "As I am now very far removed from Rotterdam, it is possible that I can't play this coming Sunday." In October a telegram follows: "Nothing on Sunday? Answer please—Hartog." And on February 23, 1944, Sparta receives notice of the death of Mr. Cor den Hartog, who has died at the age of twenty-eight "in a fatal accident." Was he executed as a Resistance man?

After the war it became known that at least two Spartans, both army colonels, had died in the Resistance. The first, Reinder Boomsma, was a Dutch international who had played for Sparta until 1908. He had become an expert in code work in World War I.

During the second war, a young man planning to fly to England in a few days came to see him to discuss the British code. The young man took notes, these fell into the hands of the Gestapo, and Boomsma was sent to a concentration camp. On his way there he wrote a message on a scrap of paper, carried back to Holland in a matchbox by a released fellow prisoner, saying he was "going to Neuengamme in the best of spirits, not doubting a happy reunion after the war." He also boasted that he had slimmed down to the weight at which he had played outside-right for Sparta. In the camp Boomsma was initially allowed to peel potatoes, but was later assigned to stone carrying. He collapsed on May 26, 1943, and died that evening.

His fellow colonel and contemporary, Willem van der Nieuwenhuizen, keeper of the championship team of 1909, was arrested by the Gestapo in the last year of the occupation. "A few weeks later," reported his postwar death notice, "some objects belonging to him were returned to his house, among them a fountain-pen, watch and wallet from which all the money—circa 1,200 guilders—had disappeared."

Robert Koch writes to inform Sparta that his son, Harro, the only *Reichsdeutscher* in the club, died on November 4, 1943, as a German soldier on the Eastern Front. "I would be grateful if you could make this news known to Harro's fellow club members," Koch requests. The board replies, "We deeply feel this loss, so heavy for you to bear . . . your son, at Sparta and among Spartans, will live on as a pleasant sporting mate in everyone's memory." It promises to inform the members.

On April 16, 1944, at a playoff between HVV and Neptunus at the Sparta stadium, the club experiences its only *razzia* (or German raid) of the war. Cohen writes in his postwar chronicle, "Only a few incautious people, who though without ID cards cannot seem to do without soccer, fall victim. A few uneasy Spartans are guided to safety through an unguarded exit."

Sparta would have been shocked to hear there was a Jew at the ground that day. Simon de Winter, then a twelve-year-old in hiding, told me in Israel fifty-six years later that he had risked going to the match because he was a Neptunus fan, the game was crucial, and children didn't need ID cards. When the stands were suddenly sealed off, De Winter took fright, climbed the fence, and ran across the pitch to the changing rooms. "Of course they still knew me at Neptunus, and I left the ground in the players' bus," he told me. De Winter, who when I met him lived in the Israeli desert town of Beersheva, was the only member of his family to survive the war.

D-Day landings or not, the Sparta board never wavers from its duty. In July 1944 the club decides, after some debate, to repay P. Marron his membership fees, even though he has resigned too late as "candidate member." Marron has quit chiefly "because my bicycle tires are in such bad condition that I can no longer make use of my bicycle." On October 4, 1944, Mrs. Sagius writes to say "that since the beginning of the year my husband has been in the concentration camp of Dachau, in Germany. Mr. Moeliker, who awards the certificates, has been informed of this."

Around this time Cohen seems finally to have gone into hiding. Shortly before her death, Rietje Kleingeld, widow of a Sparta member, showed me a letter Cohen had sent her fiancé on January 4, 1945, upon hearing of their engagement: "Man, I had no idea that anything like this was in the works, and had never encountered you in female company. . . ." Cohen wishes Kleingeld all the best and hopes he will remain involved with Sparta despite the encumbrance of a wife (as indeed happened: Kleingeld would serve as club secretary from 1945 to 1970). The letter ends, "It is a shame, though, that such a festive event should happen in a time when we all have to play hide-and-seek to remain free of forced service to the new Europe."

That last season, 1944–1945, the Allied armies are stuck just a couple of dozen miles from Rotterdam, on the south banks of the great rivers. North of the rivers the *Hongerwinter* begins, and soccer ceases. Freezing and starving local residents steal wood from the fence around the Sparta ground. Although the club installs guards (one of whom is beaten up by thieves), the fence gradually disappears. Then the clubhouses, trees, a changing room, and even Sparta's tennis courts are carted off for firewood.

Wolff's reaction could have been imagined. But in May 1944 he had resigned "in the most honorable way" on grounds of age and ill-health. He died on March 2, 1945, a day before his seventieth birthday.

VIII. AFTER THE WAR

Club journals and letters in wartime tell a censored story. However, even after the war the Sparta files make no mention of help given to Jews or other acts of resistance.

Nor is there any discussion of suffering. When I asked Sonneveld what Cohen's state of mind might have been at the end of the war, with many of his relatives presumably dead, he raised his hands and said, "You know what it was? We came back after the war and didn't talk about it." In those early postwar years, most Jews in particular could not speak of what had happened. All the old Spartans I met had known Cohen for decades, yet none had any idea how the war affected him or his family.

Cohen later changed his name to Coler, explaining to friends that he didn't want his daughter to have to bear a Jewish name. And later still he would become treasurer of UEFA. He lived until 1986, but he never again experienced a meeting like that of September 27, 1941.

A few Spartan Jews return from the war. S. Presser, who like so many other Jews had found a hiding place in the northern province of Friesland, sends a letter that starts, "It is a pleasure to be able to inform you. . . ." Sparta replies, "Little by little we are seeing all our friends emerge above water again, although, sadly, several of our comrades are missing because of the violence of war and the inhuman behavior of members of the *Herrenvolk*." However, those Jews who had been expelled as members in 1941 and want to rejoin the club after the war have to pass through the Ballot Committee again. At least one Jew leaves Sparta rather than doing this.

Hans Frenkel, who had previously written to Sparta from the country estate at Barneveld, is among the survivors. On June 1, 1945, he reports from Switzerland:

> Dear people,
>
> After much roving, through Barneveld, Westerbork, and Theresienstadt, I have arrived here.
>
> I hope you are all well and that I will hear something from you soon! My whole family, except my eldest brother Jacques, is here! He is probably in The Hague.
>
> With affectionate greetings

In the Dutch version of this book I suggested that Frenkel's missing brother Jacques might in fact be the A. Frenkel who would later appear in Sparta's list of war dead. A few months after my Dutch book appeared, one of the bookcases in my flat fell over, and amid the rubble I found a letter that I had previously overlooked. The author of it had read my Dutch book, and wrote:

> May I introduce myself? My name is Jacques André Frenkel, 81 years old, born in Rotterdam and still a participating inhabitant of the city. I am the Jacques Frenkel you mention. . . .
>
> My father and mother (dentist) were deported to [Camp] Vught with seven children in the spring of 1943, son Hans was then working for the Jewish Council in Amsterdam and later joined the family when shortly afterward it was transferred to Barneveld [on the list of protected Jews]. . . . Of the nine

children, I was the only one who stayed behind in hiding,
initially in Rotterdam, later in The Hague. . . .

It was a surprise to me and my family to discover the letter you
printed from my brother from Barneveld and the visiting card
from Westerbork, on which the address appeared of our
temporary house in Rotterdam. . . .

I subsequently visited Jacques Frenkel in his flat in Rotterdam.
He turned out to be a retired film critic, a convert to the Dutch Reformed Church, and a sports fan. "I still love cricket, I can watch the
BBC for hours when there's a Test match on," he told me. Indeed,
his late brother, Hans (the author of the wartime letters), had become
an international cricket umpire after the war.

Frenkel said it was statistically amazing (and possibly unique)
for nine children and both parents from one Dutch Jewish family
to survive the war. People sometimes told him, "Well, you must
have had to do something for that." There was a great deal of nasty
gossip, he said. It was true that for a while during the war he had
had a job making registration cards for the Jewish Council. "Those
cards were used by the Germans for deportations. And you worked
on that. Not so good, of course. Oh well." And he chuckled.

In early October 1945 Sparta receives a letter from The Hague
engineer C. Hordijk. He has bad news: his brother, recently released
from a Japanese POW camp in Thailand, has told him that the Spartan John de Korver died there on August 22, 1943. Hordijk expresses
his sympathy with Sparta and remembers "the son of Bok de Korver
as one who fell for our freedom." Hordijk asks the board to tell John's
parents.

Fortunately Bok and his wife had already heard the news, Overeijnder later writes to Hordijk. "It is a sad tiding for the parents who
on August 16, 1943, just a week before his death, had first received

a sign of life from him, namely that he was a prisoner of war." Bok de Korver lapsed into a long depression after hearing of his son's death. The New Year's postcard that John sent from his ship journey to the east is still in the Sparta archive.

IX.

Like the rest of the Netherlands, Sparta is purged of a few of its collaborators. At the end of September 1945 L. Ehrbecker is summoned to the chairman to discuss "the rumors that are circulating about you." On November 16, Sparta writes to the Political Investigation Department, Rotterdam, "Many complaints are reaching us about the behavior during the war of our member L. Ehrbecker, born 5–8–1913. We would like to hear from you whether a certificate of political reliability would be conferred upon him were he to ask for one."

The department is clear:

> Regarding your request, I hereby inform you that
>
> L. Ehrbecker
> d.o.b.: 5–8–1913
> resident: Delftweg 77, Overschie
>
> is considered by me to be politically unreliable.

On November 29, Sparta writes to Ehrbecker "that we no longer value your membership." Ehrbecker's lawyer responds expressing his surprise: he cannot imagine the department would give the club such information, nor does he understand how Sparta can simply dismiss a member. But it does.

P. van Kuijk is also told, on applying for a club certificate for 1945–1946, that he can't have one. "Complaints have reached us about your behavior during the war," Sparta informs him on December 3. The club advises him to request a certificate of political reliability. Van Kuijk, too, replies "with astonishment":

> Firstly: that you suspend a member without informing him of such;
>
> Secondly: that you take this measure on the grounds of politics, which after all is totally incompatible with sport and its exercise;
>
> Thirdly: that neither during the war, nor immediately thereafter, did you inform him of the complaints made against him nor of the names of the complainants;

etc., etc. "You owe me an explanation," concludes Van Kuijk. But Sparta neglects to apologize for not having raised the subject during the war. In all, the club seems to have purged three members.

X.

In the years after the war, the club's surviving Jews are generally mentioned in their absence. For instance, in a 1946 issue of the club journal, the "Sparta-Cocktail" column reports,

> Johnny Weitmann, freed from a concentration camp after the German capitulation, has proved to be far from recovered since his return to Holland. A course of rest has been prescribed, and so he has been living for some months in the region of Haarlem. May we see you under the crossbar again soon, John! And with the old spirit of before.

(In an intriguing item beneath, K. T. Lo, "follower of Chiang Kai-Shek," is congratulated upon his graduation from university.)

From a "Sparta-Cocktail" of 1947, "Max Mogendorff, one of our few Jewish members to have survived the war, sends his hearty greetings from Tjibinang (Java) where he forms part of the [Dutch] 7-December-division."

From a "Cocktail" of January 1948, "In recent days Max Mogendorff has returned to Holland after an absence of five years because of concentration camps and voluntary service in the Indies. Welcome home, Max."

Above this is a jolly item about the lowered ceiling and improved lighting in the main hall.

On October 14, 1950, a bronze plaque is unveiled in a niche of the club hall to commemorate the Spartans who died in the war. After a moment's silence, Henk Lagendaal (presumably a relative of the P. J. Lagendaal whose name is on the plaque) plays a Bach *sarabande*. The former Resistance lays a wreath for its dead. Several Spartans, among them the De Korvers, lay flowers. Then there is tea.

The great majority of the sixty-nine names on the plaque are Jewish. Many surnames appear twice, presumably denoting a dead father and son, or two brothers. One family apparently committed suicide together. Seeing the list again fifty years later, Mrs. Kleingeld remarked how long it was.

Not everyone is on the plaque. A. Blitz, who died in 1940 after he had already been expelled from Sparta, did not make it. Nor did Harro Koch or the Cor den Hartog who may have been executed. There were probably also Jews who were forgotten before they were gassed in Auschwitz.

7

BOOM
The Rise of Soccer in the Occupied Netherlands

Every other Sunday afternoon in the autumn of 1942, five men set off from a house in Rotterdam-South on the hour's walk to the Feyenoord Stadium. They moved in a phalanx: a dockworker and former Dutch international soccer player named De Bruin, his three sons, and sandwiched between them a seventeen-year-old boy with peroxided hair and a cap: Herman Menco, a Jew in hiding. On the corner of their street, the five would fall casually into step with the tens of thousands of men walking to the stadium.

"The road was a sea of people. It was a people's walk," the white-haired Menco recalled for me in 2001. Born the son of a pious cattle trader (who died in the war), Menco rose to be chairman of a publishing conglomerate whose stable included the formerly illegal papers *Vrij Nederland* and *Het Parool*. When I met him he was retired and living in a villa in Amsterdam-South, but he still remained a Feyenoord fan.

Wasn't watching soccer matches in the middle of the Holocaust a terrible risk? "Yes and no. Of course I didn't go outside otherwise. This was my only bit of air." The rest of the week Menco spent hidden in the De Bruins' house, milling grain, playing billiards on the table in his room, and pretending to study industrial bookkeeping. The radical socialist De Bruins also taught him to sing the "Internationale." Menco can still remember the words.

On their way back from the stadium, the five men would try to slip through their front door without anyone noticing that there was a De Bruin too many. "I gathered later that the neighbors knew there was someone in the house," said Menco.

His visits to Feyenoord ended in 1943, when German soldiers knocked on the door of the De Bruin house. They were thinking of requisitioning it and wanted to have a look around. "Since I was the one who spoke the best German, I showed them around. They were very polite. All they wanted was housing."

Was he nervous?

"Of course."

The Germans commandeered the house, and Menco found a new hiding place in an old-age home run by the Dutch Reformed Church. In 1944 he was betrayed and sent to Auschwitz. He remembers arriving back in Holland by train after the Liberation, and the Dutch officials on the platform screaming at him, "In the queue! Don't jump out of the train!"

On those Sunday afternoons in 1942 Menco and the De Bruins had been participating in an improbable boom. Rather than merely survive in the face of tremendous difficulties, soccer flourished in the Netherlands in World War II. Only a decade or two after the game had spread through the country, in a terrible time when many young men were working in Germany and others were in hiding for fear of being sent there, the numbers of people playing and watching soccer soared. It was then that the game became the Dutch mass passion it remains today.

In the Netherlands, as in most of Europe, soccer had long been considered something of a quirky pursuit, rather like table tennis is now. Many of the soccer matches at the Amsterdam Olympics in 1928 had drawn just one or two thousand fans. Much of the credit for finally bringing the game into the Dutch mainstream in the 1930s belongs to a radio commentator named Han Hollander.

Hollander, a Jew from the eastern town of Deventer, had become an icon quite by accident. As a young army conscript in the early years of the century, he had sat on the edge of his barracks bed telling his fellow soldiers spellbinding stories of soccer matches past. One of those soldiers, Willem Vogt, later became a big fish at AVRO radio. When live soccer reports became possible, he remembered Hollander. On March 11, 1928, Hollander covered his first Holland–Belgium match. Soon he was a phenomenon.

He was a temperamental man, and Vogt acted as his hand-holder, generally opening the broadcast with a "Nice weather, Mr. Hollander." A photograph shows the two together on the roof of a stadium: Vogt is thick-set, with wavy hair blowing in the wind, while the smiling, pencil-thin Hollander, in his panama hat, suit, and white socks, a handkerchief in his breast pocket, could be a tap dancer from vaudeville.

His commentaries on Holland matches were often a bit fictitious, but in the 1930s they helped turn soccer into an institution among hushed families gathered around the wireless in the living room. When the national team played, the streets were, if not quite deserted, certainly emptier than usual. Holland was the only country to buy the broadcast rights to the 1934 World Cup in Italy.

In 1938, at a reception in Hollander's honor, the Dutch world chess champion Max Euwe said that often after a soccer match, particularly when the Dutch had won, "One has the feeling that we would like to put Mr. Hollander on our shoulders and carry him from the field." Vogt concluded the speeches for his old army buddy "by expressing the heartfelt wish that thou shalt perform the sport broadcasts for our AVRO for many long years."

Then the Germans came, and for five days in May 1940 Dutch sport ceased. But after the Netherlands capitulated, a sports magazine summed up the new mood: "The May sun is shining over the Low

Countries; the sports fields and the water call." They did indeed. In the year of the invasion, a little over four million tickets to sports events were sold. In 1943, the figure exceeded eight million. Sports clubs could not cope with the flood of new members. During the war the Dutch read more books and attended more plays, films, concerts, and probably church services than before, but no other form of entertainment grew as quickly as sport.

The occupiers were delighted. "He who plays sport does not sin," was a motto of Arthur Seyss-Inquart, government commissioner of the Netherlands. The Nazis often talked during the war about arranging internationals between Germany and Holland. In fact this never happened, largely because they sensed things might go wrong. The *Reichssportführer* Von Tschammer und Osten said no games should be played on Dutch soil "that are suited to raising the temperament of large local spectator masses such that the limit of political demonstrations is reached."

But apart from banning Jews, the Germans left Dutch sport largely alone. They encouraged the various Dutch soccer federations—the Catholics, the Protestants, the workers, the "general," etc.—to merge into one FA that exists to this day, but otherwise they stuck to cleaning up the language of sport. The cricketers were charged with finding Dutch equivalents for English terms like "wickets" and "overs," but the main linguistic assault was on tennis, where keeping score in English was banned. At a match in 1941 the tennis player Hans van Swol earned himself an ovation lasting several minutes by repeating in English the score that the umpire had just announced in Dutch. The umpire warned the crowd.

However, even in the marginal field of sporting language the occupiers were circumspect. Stalin had removed English words like *futbol*, *gandbol*, and *bootsy* from Soviet soccer, but the Germans kept their paws off Holland's most popular sport. Corners and penalties remained *corners* and *penalties*, notes the historian Swijtink. Only soccer clubs named after members of the exiled Dutch royal family, like

Wilhelmina or Juliana, had to change their names. Juliana became Spekholzerheide, and the ball rolled on.

The scenes that ensued astonished contemporaries. Before a crucial game between the Amsterdam club De Volewijckers and Heerenveen on Whit Monday of 1944, the Volewijckers director Ph. K. Corsten wrote, "Certain foodstuffs are hard to obtain. However, people don't go to the Beemster [an agricultural region] for themselves, but solely with the intention of exchanging the vegetables and potatoes they obtain for . . . match tickets."

The biggest sports fans of all were the half a million or so Dutchmen sent to work in Germany. Homesick and bored, they flocked to "internationals" staged in the "Reich" between "Holland" (a team of Dutch workers in Germany) and teams like "Flanders" (their Flemish counterparts). Thousands of Dutchmen joined German clubs. The Dutch international Bram Appel became something of a sensation at Hertha Berlin, and would also return home with one of the war's most bizarre stories. In 1979 he told *Vrij Nederland* that after helping extinguish a fire started by a bomb falling in the next-door garden, he was rewarded with a drink poured by his grateful neighbor, Heinrich Himmler.

People in the strangest places followed the game. At the end of the war the former Ajax member Karel van der Lee, just released from a Japanese POW camp in the Dutch East Indies, wrote to the Ajax chairman, "In the camp, where there were a great many former soccer players, I was often asked how things were going with Ajax. I would then answer: well—[we] have become champions of the great Third Reich."

Contemporaries all gave the same explanations for the sudden mania for sport. As the editor of the *Feyenoord* journal wrote in 1944, "Oh well, what more does a person have to entertain himself with at the moment than the sport on the green field? For all of us in the club, the league will be a good interruption of the daily grind and pressure, which these war years have brought us. In a time like this we need a stimulant."

Sport was an escape, but it is important to specify what it was an escape from. "Stimulant" is the operative word. The occupied Dutch were fleeing not terror but tedium. For most people in the occupied Netherlands until late 1944, danger was not an issue. Tellingly, the sports historian Jurryt van der Vooren has discovered only one Dutch soccer match abandoned because of an air-raid alert. Safe and dull before the war, the Netherlands remained mostly safe and dull during it too.

The Nazis regarded the Dutch as fellow Germans who had left the tribe due to a historical error and were to be brought back gently. As long as they weren't Jews or in the Resistance (and about 98 percent of Dutch people were neither), they were treated fairly respectfully until the last months of the war. The German soldiers who were barracked in the Ajax Stadium, for instance, would always ask Ajax's chairman for permission to use a pitch. When it was granted, they would say, "*Jawohl, Herr Koolhaas.*" The Dutch seldom gave them much cause to crack down.

In smaller Dutch towns it was rare even to see a German. The worst that could happen to most families was that the son or father was sent to perform paid work in Germany.

Dutch historians rightly tend to describe the 1940–1945 period in the Netherlands as "the occupation" rather than "the war." Of course the years of occupation were somewhat miserable. People watched what they said and did and were subject to a curfew. Food, initially abundant, later grew scarce. The newspapers and radio lied. The royal family was in exile in London. The bombing of Rotterdam (though nowhere near as bad as in London or Berlin or Dresden) shocked everyone. There was a general grimness, as in an economic depression.

But there was little of the death and fear and great moral choices that we associate with war. "For a large number of Dutch people," writes the historian Chris van der Heijden, "the occupation was limited to signs on the street, notices in the newspaper, stories and sounds on the radio."

———

It was different for Jews. On May 21, 1940, two years after Willem Vogt had expressed the wish that Hollander might commentate on sport for "many more years," he sacked his friend along with the rest of the AVRO's Jewish staff. It was six days after the capitulation, and long before the first German measures against Jews.

But the Dutch Jews knew that more was to come. One of them, Ben Bril, who had become Dutch boxing champion with a Star of David embroidered on his shorts, entered the ring at the national championships of 1940 and announced, "Ladies and gentlemen, I hereby say farewell to boxing." Then he bowed and walked off, having beaten the Germans to it.

Measure by measure throughout 1941, Dutch Jews were removed from their jobs, schools, cafés, and sports clubs. They became a separate community, exiled from Dutch life. Pressured by the Germans, they founded a Jewish Council, which in impossible circumstances would do everything wrong. It ended up helping the Germans arrange the deportations. David Cohen, a Jew from Deventer (like Hollander, and of about the same age), a professor of ancient history who became co-chairman of the Council, would later liken himself to a general who had had to sacrifice part of his army. Cohen lived on as a pariah until 1967.

Holland's Jews—depressed, fearful, prone to heart attacks—read of their approaching fate each week in the Council's newspaper, the *Joodsche Weekblad*. The publication was a mishmash. There were many obituaries, some of young people but also one of a woman who died in the village of Borculo at the age of ninety-three. There were notices of bar mitzvahs, and there were advertisements: a perfumery sought "proper girls, 15/16 yrs." Ecuador and Palestine were assessed as potential destinations for emigration; there was an "announcement regarding bathing places etc."; and there were theological debates ("Enduring the Fall," Jeremiah).

And there was sport. On May 16, 1941, the *Joodsche Weekblad* had good news for the soccer players: "It is most probable that one of their dearest wishes, namely training under the direction of a coach, will be fulfilled. . . . The first and second teams will participate in the Amsterdam Football Association's series of evening matches. The ground is part of the Voorland complex on the Middenweg, a little past the Ajax Stadium."

They would never play in the evening series. But notions of muscular Judaism persisted almost until the end. On June 27, 1941, the paper reported on the opening of a Maccabi hockey wing: "The players were summoned to the side of the field at the first training session. And there the chairman of the Federal Board of Maccabi, Mr. E. Spier, addressed them all in a cordial manner and pointed out the value of sport for young Jews in these times. A hearty applause from the circle of youths proved that his words had been well understood."

As 1941 wore on, the sports notices disappeared from the *Weekblad,* and the people in the death notices grew younger. However, it was also announced (in the issue of August 15) that Elly Irene Leuw had been born, that Louis Blok had married Marianne van Aals, and that Liny van Straten and Ben van Gelder had become engaged in the village of Rumpt. The next week it was reported that the famous Jewish club De Ooievaars had held a sports day in The Hague.

But the axe was falling. In August 1941, before the Germans had ordered anything of the kind, the Dutch FA decided to stop appointing Jewish referees in places where the local Dutch authorities had banned them. Quickly a shortage of referees arose. The task seems to have attracted many Jews, perhaps because the most famous Dutch referee of the pre-war years, Hans Boekman, was Jewish.

After the Germans banned Jews from sport in September 1941, Amsterdam's five predominantly Jewish soccer clubs withdrew from the city's league. Otherwise, however, there were only squeaks of protest. A few Amsterdam clubs told the FA they wouldn't play league games while Jews were banned; some swimming pools avoided installing the compulsory "Forbidden for Jews" signs for a few months;

and the chaplain of the soccer club VVZ is supposed to have taken down his club's sign, saying, "Whatever the directors want, or whether it is the federation's or VVZ's, that sign is going." But these were exceptions. For almost everyone, the ball rolled on.

If people don't stop playing sport when their country is occupied by Nazis during World War II, when do they? This was what the illegal newspaper *Het Parool* wanted to know. In the autumn of 1941, after a sports magazine had urged its readers to apply as referees in place of the banned Jews, warning that otherwise the league might stagnate, *Het Parool* erupted:

> Yes, imagine that! Stagnation in the soccer league. It is true: the Netherlands is at war. . . . And it is true that meanwhile thousands of people are dying each day in the battle with the German conqueror of the world . . . while not a day passes without the German firing ranges or barrack squares shuddering to the boom of the execution squads. All that may be. But what a disaster would happen if meanwhile the soccer league were to stagnate.

The newspaper called for the league to be abandoned. This was never going to happen. Though the Dutch Protestant *korfball* union organized no matches in the 1941 season "due to the circumstances of the age," hardly a man in Dutch soccer seems even to have wondered whether the fate of the Jews should deter him from carrying on just as before. Since its recent invention the game seemed to have become a basic human need, almost like eating and sex. The Dutch weren't about to give it up just because of a genocide. Outside Amsterdam, anyway, few of them even realized what was happening: one Jew looking for a hiding place in the countryside found he first had to explain to people what Jews were, and then explain that they were being persecuted.

The general attitude of the Dutch was captured in an anecdote by the Jewish writer Abel Herzberg after the war: "One of the collection points during the *razzia* was the Olympiaplein. The weather was good that day and so on the sports field people were playing tennis. The waiting Jews heard the balls ticking on the ground and the players calling, 'Ready-game-deuce.' It wasn't NSB-ers who were playing. It wasn't Resistance men. It was the majority of the Dutch people."The most surprising fact in the paragraph is that the tennis players still kept score in English. That they played on is exactly what one would expect. Why stop? Life for them was continuing much as ever.

There is a second story that expresses the Dutch wartime attitude better than a hundred books. Ad van Emmenes, secretary of the Dutch Union of Sports Journalists under Herman Levy at the outbreak of war, told the former Resistance newspaper *Vrij Nederland* in 1979, "In 1942 we met in Hotel Riche. Frans Otten, who worked for the *Avondpost* newspaper and was in the Dutch National Socialist Party, said, 'Levy has to step down because he is a Jew.' 'That is not going to happen,' the others said, 'unless the Germans order it.'"

By 1942 the Jews were beginning to sense they were on their way to their deaths in the east, but they were still upset at being excluded from sport. Some of them risked continuing to play—fourteen Jews had been arrested for this by June 1942—while others watched. In the northern town of Groningen, a woman wrote to the chairman of the local soccer club Be Quick: "The ban on Jews at sports fields, does that also go for me at the Be Quick ground? Could it be that I am requiring an extra permit? Who should I apply to then? I would like to have notice of this from you. As you know we have been there a good 40 years and not ever had any problems. With polite greetings. Respectful widow J. Drielsma."

Even after the deportations began, Hollander felt safe. Didn't he have a certificate signed by Hitler honoring his radio reports from the Berlin Olympics? He waved away friends who offered to find him a hiding place. Gradually, however, it became clear that the Germans were serious. In March 1943 the Dutch FA wrote to the authorities to request that if Hollander, Boekman, and J. Gosschalk, former chairman of the Amsterdam FA, had to be deported, they be sent to the "Jewish Home" at Barneveld with other "protected" Jews. The request was denied.

Hollander was sent to the transit camp of Westerbork. He got a relatively cushy job serving in the canteen, and as a celebrity could have expected to stay for a while at least, but something went wrong. It seems that either his wife made a nasty comment about Germans to a German Jew, or Hollander himself boasted publicly about his protected status, or both. After ten months in Westerbork, the couple was deported and killed.

In 1968 AVRO published a booklet to mark the fortieth anniversary of Hollander's first match commentary on the radio. The introduction by his friend Vogt sketched Hollander fondly, if warts and all. "How terrible and incomprehensibly unjust that this man, good through and through, somewhat childish, kind and noble, was taken by the Germans to Westerbork," wrote Vogt. "Then to Theresienstadt, which we were assured was—relatively—mild. But there he nevertheless died." (In fact Hollander seems to have died in Sobibor, a camp of which almost nothing is known as hardly any selections of able-bodied workers were ever made there.) And Vogt concluded, "His fate became a contribution to a guilt that can never be extinguished."

What more is there to say? Dutch Jews continued playing sport to the end. There were matches in Westerbork, the antechamber of death, from where the Haarlem keeper Juda de Vries wrote to his wife, "Jenny, please send me my soccer boots." De Vries expected to end up playing for a factory team somewhere in Germany. In Amsterdam, the Jewish Council organized some sport virtually until the last trains had left for Poland. Even in the concentration camps there was soccer.

A few Jews returned from the war. Amsterdam's five Jewish clubs tried to re-form (though one of them had lost 95 percent of its members), but when they applied to rejoin the Dutch FA they were told they couldn't automatically return to the division of the local Amsterdam league they had left in 1941. HEDW also asked to be forgiven an old debt, on the grounds that it had no money now that more than two hundred of its members were dead. The FA refused, perhaps fearful of setting a precedent for future genocides, though it did allow the debt to be rescheduled.

The five Jewish clubs never recovered from the war. All that remains of them today is the Amsterdam amateur club WV-HEDW, product of a merger between the decimated Jewish clubs Wilhelmina Vooruit and HEDW. Almost no Jews play for WV-HEDW any more, though a monument outside the club's ground honors the hundreds of Jewish members killed in the war.

On November 4, 1945, a man named J. Kleerekooper wrote to the board of the Amsterdam soccer club Neerlandia:

Honorable gentlemen,

I am aware that in many areas there are great shortages, which on occasion force us to take all sorts of emergency measures.

However, what I observed at your ground today seems to me somewhat to exceed the common term of "boundaries." The question to which I refer is the corner flags that mark your ground.

These consist of parts of prayer clothing as used by Israelites.

Personally I regard myself as a free thinker yet I none the less find the solution that you have found at the least inappropriate, certainly when one considers where this clothing comes from and why it is no longer where it ought to be.

Kleerekooper asked Neerlandia to return the clothing, apologizing for "having interfered in your internal affairs." The club replied "that we obviously did not know that our corner flags were composed of Israelite prayer clothing. We shall immediately attempt to replace them with others."

8

STRANGE LIES
Ajax, World War II, and P. G. Wodehouse

I.

One summer afternoon soon after starting work on this book, I went to visit an octogenarian named Wim Schoevaart in the flying-saucer-like Amsterdam Arena. It was the third Ajax stadium he had known. Schoevaart joined Ajax in 1930 and is now the club's archivist and guardian of its wartime secrets.

He turned out to be an extremely amiable character, in a blazer and Ajax tie (I promised to bring him a Liverpool one for his collection, but to my shame I never did). He told me that the family connection with the club pre-dated even him: his father had made his first-team debut in 1904, just four years after Ajax's foundation. That two generations of one family can almost span the life of a venerable club shows how new soccer is on the Continent.

I told Schoevaart I was writing a book about Ajax, the Jews, and the war, and he kindly told me I was wasting my time, because I would soon find out there wasn't enough to say. Like every other Ajax official

I spoke to, he instantly denied my suggestion that the club had ever had many Jewish members. How could he be so sure? Because there were few "Jewish-sounding names" on pre-war membership lists—certainly no more than at other Amsterdam clubs.

In a city that was about 13 percent Jewish until the war, this was a double-edged claim: other Amsterdam clubs had many Jewish members. But nobody from Ajax wanted to say anything at all about the war. One of the club directors barred me from seeing the club's archive on the grounds that there was "nothing interesting in it for you."

Everyone trying to write about Ajax in the war receives the same treatment. The Ajax historian Evert Vermeer, though a club member himself, spent years just trying to find out whether anyone from Ajax had died in the war. "I asked various people, including Schoevaart," Vermeer told the former Resistance newspaper *Het Parool*. "They shrug their shoulders and mumble something, and never give a real answer. They're really very mysterious about it."

When *Het Parool* asked Schoevaart why Ajax didn't have a war memorial, in contrast to many other Dutch clubs, he explained that it would be "too painful for the surviving relatives." Asked about the fate of Jewish members in the war, he said he didn't like "raking up the past"—an unusual attitude for an archivist.

On the rare occasions when Ajax men do talk about the war, usually under duress, they explain that nothing much happened. Schoevaart claimed, ludicrously, in the club's centennial book in 2000, that the club had silently "ignored" the German ban on Jews. Often, when the question of Ajax's Jewish members is raised in the Dutch press, it is killed off with a 1979 quote from Jaap Hordijk, an Ajax player in the war: "There wasn't much going on yet at Ajax. Until 1942 no players had disappeared. In a sense we didn't even have very many Jewish soccer players. Jaap van Praag and Jopie Schelvis were in hiding, really Jopie de Haan and Eddy Hamel were the only ones I missed after the war."

Even Vermeer has a tendency to sketch the club's war as a bit of a lark. In his book *95 Jaar Ajax* he plays up the club's refusal to let German soldiers barracked in the stadium play soccer on the main field. "Treasurer Volkers even had the insolence to demand a sum in rent from the German commander . . . a sum to which the latter agreed without difficulty, to Volkers's amazement." The glorious Ajax Resistance. Vermeer then proceeds to an apparent contradiction, "Ajax always refused to play soccer against the soldiers, although in the first days of the occupation a veterans' team did play a game against the occupiers, resulting in a most satisfactory scoreline of 14–1." They sure did teach those Germans a lesson! Not a small symbolic victory, but a thirteen-goal one. And that was not all: "They stole freely from the German stock of coals and potatoes for the benefit of Ajax members."

All we have from Ajax, then, is the standard Dutch account of risk-free symbolic humiliations of Germans: the war as comic book. The fear of discussing the occupation properly suggests that Ajax has something to hide. It does. However, what it is hiding is not what you might expect. Ajax's war was both braver and darker than it admits today.

Certainly there was greyness and cowardice at Ajax as at every other Dutch institution, and the ball rolled on whatever happened: in October 1941, as Jews were being expelled from Dutch sports clubs, women and children were trampled in the crush in the trams on the way to Ajax–Feyenoord. However, Ajax also had more than its fair share of heroism.

II.

"The misery of war remained relatively limited, in the sense that at the end of the occupation there were no deaths to mourn among the Ajax members," writes Vermeer in *95 Jaar Ajax*.

This is a truism. If there were no deaths to mourn among Ajax members, it was because the Jews had been expelled from the club in 1941 and thus were no longer Ajax members by the time they were gassed in the concentration camps. It is scandalous that a club like Ajax allows such hurtful nonsense to be recounted in its name.

Ajax used to be more honest. In the annual report for 1944–1945 the board remembered "with sorrow the passing" of eight named members, although even then several other victims were not mentioned.

In fact, until 1941 Ajax was much more Jewish than most Dutch clubs. Vermeer, who no longer believes there were no deaths to mourn, recently discovered that in the autumn of 1941 twelve Jews were expelled from the club. Others may have resigned before the Germans banned them, as happened at Sparta.

And yet, despite everything, what distinguishes Ajax from most other Dutch clubs is the support and help it gave its Jews in the war. Its annual report for 1941–1942 contains these remarkable lines:

> [We are] in the fearful expectation that many more of our members will be taken away, among them those who have stood loyally by our side for 35 years or longer and of whom we have yet to hear anything. Many among us have already left, and we regard the coming times with anxious fear, because we live in an age in which no one can say for sure whom we will see again.

This is unmistakably a reference to Jews. The lines cannot refer to men sent to work in Germany, because people who had been members "for thirty-five years or longer" were too old for that. In any case, workers in Germany could write home and were reasonably sure of their lives. Ajax, however cautiously, was standing up for its Jews. Susan Smit, author of a marvelous university thesis on Ajax and Amsterdam soccer in the war, says that at no other club did she find a similar text. Certainly Sparta would never have risked it. Why does

Ajax never talk about this? Boasting about minor acts of wartime re-sistance is a Dutch custom, so why doesn't the club join in?

It wasn't the only brave comment either. In the *Ajax-Nieuws* of November 30, 1940, a contributor calling himself "James" wrote a review of the year that reads like something out of an underground newspaper. Claiming to speak for all at Ajax, "James" says that never, writing in the journal at the end of a year, had he felt so "sad and down." He concluded with a wish: "That 1941 be not only a better year, but that it be the year in which that may happen for which we all yearn 100 percent." The reference to liberation is plain. No wonder an Ajax donor informed the occupiers that both club and board were "anti-German."

And Ajax went further than words. One of the Jewish members who resurfaced after the war was Jaap van Praag, owner of the Am-sterdam music store His Master's Voice. He would later become the club's legendary chairman (and the subject of Johan Cruijff's leg-endary barb, "I have never been able to catch Jaap van Praag telling the truth").

Van Praag sat out the last two and a half years of the war in a flat above an Amsterdam photography shop. Because the shopkeeper did not know he was there, he had to spend shop hours sitting motionless on a chair. Horrified at the loss of dignity, he vowed that after the war he would wear impeccable suits every day.

In Ajax's shriveled postwar journal of November 10, 1945, Van Praag wrote a note of thanks "to all Ajax friends who have treated me with such friendliness after my long period in hiding. I would particularly like to thank Cor and Jan Schoevaart again in our Club Journal from the bottom of my heart for the place I was granted in their hospitable home in the weeks in which the danger for me was greatest." Van Praag must have hidden at Wim Schoevaart's uncle Jan's flat during the first deportations in 1942, before moving in above the photography shop.

Other Ajax Jews like Schelvis and Johnny Roeg also hid and survived the Holocaust. In a city that lost about 80 percent of its Jews,
those at Ajax seem to have fared unusually well.

In part this was because Ajax members were richer than the orange
sellers and rag-and-bone merchants of the Jewish Quarter. The wealthy
had the best chance of finding cover: Anne Frank's family, for instance,
was able to hide above the offices of her father's own company.

However, the Jews at Ajax also benefited from belonging to a
predominantly gentile club. They knew gentiles, and a few of those
gentiles were very brave. Jews who lived in the Jewish Quarter and
played for Jewish soccer clubs practically knew only Jews. In the war,
that mattered.

It seems that Ajax—not as a club, but as an informal network—
saved people, and Jews were not the only beneficiaries. When food
became scarce, the first-team players would eat together at the club
after training, and in the *Hongerwinter* of 1944–1945, while thousands were dying in Amsterdam, the club sent twenty young members to rural Friesland to fatten up. The solidarity among Ajax
members—most of them drawn from Amsterdam's upper middle
class, many of them friends since childhood—was exceptional. But
among its chief beneficiaries was an Englishman.

The bowler-hatted Jack Reynolds had had a brief career as a professional soccer player at the start of the twentieth century. Later he
coached St. Gallen in Switzerland, and then went to Germany to
manage the national team, but the Great War got in the way. And
so in 1915 he moved to Holland to coach Ajax.

He was still there when the Germans invaded in 1940, teaching
his players to skip rope, running a local cigar shop, and speaking
his very own version of Dutch. The invaders interned every Briton
they could lay their hands on. Reynolds was taken to an Upper
Silesian camp called Tost, where he must have met the author
P. G. Wodehouse, whom the Germans had chanced upon in the
French seaside resort of Le Touquet.

I shan't describe Tost, because Wodehouse has already done so—in rather loving tones, in fact, in his famous broadcasts on Berlin Radio. "I was not at my most dapper," he informed listeners on August 6, 1941, "when we arrived at Tost Lunatic Asylum, which had been converted into a camp for our reception." However, perhaps because of having been at boarding school, Wodehouse felt he had little cause for complaint:

"An Associated Press man, who came down to interview me later, wrote in his piece that Tost Lunatic Asylum was no Blandings Castle. Well, it wasn't, of course, but still it was roomy. If you had had a cat, and had wished to swing it, you could have done so quite easily in our new surroundings." Admittedly,

> Nothing can take away the unpleasant feeling of being a prisoner, but you can make an effort and prevent it getting you down. . . . We at Tost were greatly helped by the fact that we had with us the sailors from the *Orama*, who would have cheered anyone up, and the internees from Holland.
>
> Many of these were language teachers and musicians. . . .

And one was Reynolds. He seems to have spent the entire war at Tost, which invalidates the story Wodehouse later told about his early release. After the war, accused of having promised to broadcast on Berlin Radio in exchange for being freed from Tost, the author would claim,

> What happened was this. I was released on June 21, 1941, a few months before I was sixty. I should have been released automatically on reaching the age of sixty, and I imagine that I was given my freedom a little earlier because of the agitation, which had been going on in America for my release. . . .
>
> I see now, of course, that I was tricked into making these talks, and I naturally feel a damned fool, but I hope I have made it clear

that there was never anything in the nature of a bargain with the Germans. I was released before there was any suggestion of a broadcast, and there was never any idea that my freedom was dependent on my broadcasting.

But Wodehouse was the same age as Reynolds! The author was born in October 1881, and the Ajax manager one month earlier. Yet Reynolds spent the whole war locked up. Wodehouse may not have done a deal with the Germans, but his treatment was thoroughly exceptional, and for him to pretend otherwise was disingenuous.

Ajax did not forget Reynolds: his "Technical Tips" on soccer continued to appear in the *Ajax-Nieuws* after his departure, and for two years the journal published regular news of him. On October 25, 1940, it reported that "good old Jack" had been moved to a German camp, could receive letters in Dutch, and would be sent a fortnightly "*Ajax-pakket.*" In May 1941 the journal joked that he had had to hire a secretary to open all his mail from Ajax members. In August 1942, the journal said Reynolds had written to say he was fine.

The journal's next mention of him, in October 1945, quoted an English newspaper report that "ex-Gillingham player Jack Reynolds had died in a concentration camp." However, the *Ajax-Nieuws* assured readers that the news was premature. Reynolds was alive and in England.

He returned to Amsterdam that month, and in November the journal published his note of thanks "to all who stood by me and my wife so marvelously during my imprisonment." This note appeared above Jaap van Praag's, a conjunction that speaks for Ajax's wartime network. No Spartans returning from camps appear to have published thank-yous in their club journal.

Reynolds had returned to Amsterdam full of anecdotes of Tost. He talked about having laid a cricket pitch, about playing soccer under German guard and, the journal proudly reported, "Don't be startled—about one hundred cigarettes and an ounce of tobacco a week." The Ajax parcels had done the job.

"The most miserable hours of his imprisonment," continued the journal, "were . . . Sunday afternoons between two and four p. m., when his yearning for his wife and for Ajax sometimes grew too strong for him." Now Reynolds had pledged "to build a team as never before, you can count on that." As a tribute, the journal published a special "*Ajax-Limmerick*" in English:

> *We are able to win and we shall, Jack,*
> *Please point out again what our teams lack . . .*

Reynolds would remain in Amsterdam until his death in 1962. On the way to his grave in Amsterdam-East, his funeral parade stopped to pay its respects at the Ajax Stadium, where in later years Johan Cruijff, Marco van Basten, and Dennis Bergkamp would practice their art in front of the *Reynolds-tribune*.

III.

Reading of this proud wartime network, I wondered why Ajax kept so quiet about the occupation. When I finished writing the Dutch version of this book, I still did not understand. Since the mid-1960s almost the entire Netherlands has been engaged in an endless debate about the German occupation, so why not Ajax too? As Susan Smit said, "Ajax's attitude is strange, a bit dark. I find it difficult to explain."

I finally understood Ajax's reticence when I read the investigative reports published in March 2000 at the time of the club's centenary by Robert Misset in the *NRC Handelsblad* newspaper and by Arthur de Boer in *Het Parool*. (De Boer's articles are among the best historical journalism I know.) I also began to understand a lot more about the Dutch war and the limitations of those two great labels, *goed* and *fout*.

After the Canadians liberated Amsterdam on May 5, 1945, Ajax changed a phrase in its club anthem from "*Heil, Ajax, heil*" to "*Hup, Ajax, hup*" and created a "Purge Committee." This was chaired by a former Dutch international named Jan Schubert, who had spent eighteen months in hiding during the war and was determined to punish the collaborators who had tarnished Ajax's name. Schubert was assisted by a rather twisted lawyer named Emile Catz: an NSB (Dutch Nazi Party) member until the party discovered he was Jewish, and *persona non grata* in Britain after he had visited the country in a failed attempt to kidnap his mother.

Catz also sat on the Dutch state's postwar purge tribunal. This, coupled with Schubert's ardor, meant that Ajax's Purge Committee was tougher than most. Since Catz knew exactly whom the state was punishing, it was hard for the club to be more lenient.

Ajax's Purge Committee's decisions had been forgotten until Arthur de Boer excavated them. Finding the lists of expelled members, he then searched the files of postwar purge tribunals to discover what these people had done. It turned out that the committee had expelled seventeen members and donors, and suspended one member, for their behavior in the war. Eighteen was a large number: in all of Dutch soccer, only a few hundred players received any sanction from their clubs after the war. Ajax's Purge Committee dealt with some terrible cases.

The Holocaust in the Netherlands had been a fairly bloodless affair, free of the spontaneous slaughter of Jews by local people seen in places like Ukraine or Lithuania. In Holland, it was a mechanical sorting operation: ringing doorbells, escorting people to trains, impounding their belongings afterwards. All this went smoothly. As Adolf Eichmann fondly recalled at his Jerusalem trial in 1961, "The trains from Holland—it was a delight." Among the people he had to thank for that were several Ajax men.

The captain of Ajax's "Golden Team," winners of the Dutch championship in 1918 and 1919, was a gaunt and quiet center-half named Joop Pelser. A bookkeeper turned soldier turned cigar-shop owner, Pelser also won the Dutch baseball title with Ajax and sat for decades on the club's board. He was well liked. Four of his brothers played soccer for the Ajax first team, and so would his eldest son Harry. Until 1945, Ajax without the Pelsers would not have been Ajax.

In the late 1930s Pelser, his wife, Maria, and their son, Harry, had joined the NSB. After the German invasion, their younger son, Jan, joined the Waffen-SS without telling his parents. Maria, though a fanatical Nazi, tried to get him back, but the boy was sent to the Eastern Front. In July 1942, as the deportations of Dutch Jews began, Joop Pelser started work at the Lippmann Rosenthal Bank. Harry also had a job at the LiRo—found, or so he later claimed, through a Jewish girlfriend whom he knew from cricket.

The LiRo, previously a Jewish company, had been swallowed by the Germans and turned into an accessory to the Holocaust. Joop Pelser would tell agents from the Dutch Security Service after the war, "It was my task to go with a policeman and someone from the Lippman Rosenthal company (who estimated the value of the objects) and to make an inventory of the houses from which Jews had been taken." He was paid 200 guilders a month. The Pelsers moved into a better house, where they stuck NSB posters in the windows. Maria boasted to neighbors that her husband guarded the Jews assembled at the Hollandsche Schouwburg theater. At other times, when the neighbors refused to return her son's soccer ball, she threatened them with deportation.

Jan Pelser deserted from the SS in 1943. On an Amsterdam tram he shot dead a German officer who had demanded to see his leave pass. The boy and his parents went into hiding (the most characteristic Dutch response to World War II) but were caught within two weeks. Joop Pelser was jailed for two months for failing to report a sexual assault by a German officer on a Jewish woman. He then resigned from the NSB and abjured the party before a Catholic priest. (It had long pained him that his party membership barred him from communion and confession.)

After the Liberation Pelser went into hiding again, this time from the Dutch authorities. However, when they sent him a letter inviting him to collect his savings, he showed up and was promptly arrested. "Reputation: very bad," said his dossier. Ajax's Purge Committee expelled the former member of honor.

Maria Pelser and their two eldest sons were captured, too, and interned by the Dutch authorities for fourteen months. In March 2000 Harry Pelser, by then in his eighties, told the *NRC Handelsblad*:

> I spent a year digging potatoes. I was led away from the Tribunal in a brown sweater and brown trousers. I was still wearing them fourteen months later, only my right shoe was broken . . . I was allowed to keep the picture of my girl, my future wife. I had it under my pillow for fourteen months. I understand that nobody will accept whinging from a former NSBer. But that time made wounds that never healed again.

His father would deny before a postwar tribunal ever having guarded Jews at the Hollandsche Schouwburg. He did admit to having made wrong choices, but had "seen no other way out financially." In March 1947 the tribunal sentenced him to three years and three months in jail, minus the time he had already served. He was never seen again at Ajax, where he remains a non-person to this day.

So do many others. Foeke Kermer, a half-back in the fifth team and a youth coach who brought his boys cake and soup, never returned to Ajax because he was serving a life sentence in prison. During the war, according to the legal dossier found by De Boer, Kermer had "behaved like a beast." In the town of Haarlem alone he had captured fifty people hiding from the Germans, and as a camp guard was said to have beaten prisoners to death with his bull-pizzle.

The former first-team player Piet van Deijck was jailed for six months for having plundered the homes of deported Jews in the employ of the notorious Abraham Puls, a soccer fan whom he had met at Ajax. Van Deijck was also suspected of reporting Dutch citizens to the Germans, but this was never proved.

Another who briefly disappeared at the end of the war was Jaap Hordijk, the man who today is always quoted as saying there "wasn't much going on" with Jews at Ajax. Hordijk was purged by the club for having played in the Third Reich: he had been a regular during the war with the German side Potsdam '03, and had represented "Holland" in Nazi-sanctioned "internationals" against "Flanders" and "France." All these matches began with Hitler salutes. You might ask what choice Hordijk had, given that he had been sent to work in Germany, at a film company in Babelsberg ("We didn't make propaganda films, just feature films, operas," he assured *Vrij Nederland* in 1979). But he did not have to play soccer. Nobody did. As one Amsterdam soccer player wrote home from Germany, "I played here a couple of times for a German club, but now foreigners are also obliged to perform the salute before the match, and so I have quit." Challenged on the matter in *Vrij Nederland*, Hordijk explained, "Again, it's not that I had such a bad time there. . . . " His ban at Ajax was soon lifted, and now he is often cited as an expert on Ajax's Jews.

However many players Ajax's Purge Committee punished, it solved nothing. Schubert was blamed by fellow members for the rest of his life for having been nasty to Ajax men ("How could you do that to your own people?"), but in fact he never came close to cleaning up the club. He just scoured the edges. The "possible ongoing cases" mentioned by the committee were later forgotten. A few people were punished, but many more let off. Harry Pelser and the reserve goalkeeper Piet Weppner, another LiRo Old Boy, were allowed to leave the club quietly, without the stigma of expulsion. Silence was best for Ajax. Harry Pelser soon returned to the club, and in 1998 received a gold pin in honor of fifty years' membership from Ajax's chairman

Michael van Praag, who is indeed the son of Jaap, the man who hid above the photography shop.

Other criminals had never left Ajax in the first place. "There were so many I would rather not have seen again after the war," Joop Stoffelen, the club's postwar captain, told *Het Parool*. Yet they were tolerated. The plunderer Piet van Deijck was merely suspended, and welcomed back the day he got out of jail. In 1950 the *Jubilee Book* celebrating Ajax's fiftieth birthday said, "Ajax has had a very great deal of pleasure from him, both inside and outside the lines." Later Van Deijck would join the club's board. Perhaps even more than other Dutch institutions, Ajax—though mostly anti-German in the war—was stuffed with erstwhile collaborators afterward.

IV.

My initial reaction to all this was outrage. Ajax let monsters off the hook just because they bought their round in the canteen or were nippy down the flank. As the ninety-three-year-old former club chairman Jan Melchers told *Het Parool* in 2000, "Regarding the war, the view at Ajax was always: see no evil, hear no evil, speak no evil. . . . Hide it away, don't talk about it."

Wim Schoevaart—whose cousin was killed in the war, whose uncle had hid Jaap van Praag, who almost alone at Ajax now remembers the war—still protects the culprits. But I can see why he does it.

Of course men like the former LiRo employee Harry Pelser (who said, "I don't believe my department directly had to do with the Nazi thefts") should have been expelled from Ajax. Of course Piet van Deijck should never have been allowed back. But the problem, as Ajax knew, was that collaborators could not be punished in moderation. In Holland after the war it was all or nothing.

Being labeled (however wildly) a collaborator (however minor) often meant the end of a person's social existence. The Netherlands might have been gray and cowardly in the war, but it was unforgiving afterward. The Dutch celebrated the Liberation by shearing the heads of women who were said (by someone) to have slept with Germans. Few asked what the shearers themselves had done.

The mood never mellowed much afterward. Former Resistance newspapers like *Het Parool*, *Vrij Nederland*, and the Communist *De Waarheid* remained dominant after the war, often run for decades by the people who had founded them in the first months of the occupation. They were not about to let anyone off lightly. The wartime government-in-exile and its hangers-on, newly returned from London, were also on a mission to punish.

The average Dutchman was in a tricky position after 1945. He had been gray and cowardly in the war, and afterward was not about to risk a public defense of anyone tagged a collaborator. On the other hand, he might have some sympathy for a man who had worked for the LiRo in order to feed his family. (I don't, by the way.) Furthermore, even if the average Dutchman felt that collaborators should be punished, he might not think they deserved to be punished into the twenty-first century, and their children with them. Many NSBers had done no more harm than sell Fascist newspapers on street corners, but any wartime peccadillo could mean tar and feathers forever. Once branded *fout*, you were *fout* for the rest of your life, and so were your children (and in some cases your grandchildren) for the rest of theirs. A sports club, too, could easily become known as *fout* just because a couple of prominent members had been *fout*, or were said to have been *fout*.

The Pelsers' postwar fate is typical. Rejected by their relatives, they never again discussed the war at home. Harry Pelser seems never to have mentioned it to anyone until the *NRC Handelsblad* got hold of him fifty-five years after Liberation, at which time his three daughters still knew nothing about his family's war. "I have wanted to confess everything, because I could no longer bear the weight of the war," the tearful old man told the newspaper. "The shame and the sorrow have broken me." This may well have been true.

There are other complicating questions: Who *was* actually *goed*? And who was *fout* in the war? I am not advocating an undergraduate moral relativism that says no one can judge people who lived in different times and circumstances. In *Eichmann in Jerusalem*, Hannah Arendt points out that to deny the possibility of such judgment would be to render any system of justice unfeasible. Arendt says the judge who sentences a murderer can reflect, There but for the grace of God go I, without allowing the thought to stay his sentence.

A few Dutch people were undeniably *goed* in the war, and a few were definitely *fout*. A torturer like Ajax's Foeke Kermer was *fout* and deserved everything he got. But most people were neither distinctly *goed* nor completely *fout*; and, confusingly, some were both. Joop Pelser, for instance, guard at the Hollandsche Schouwburg, was undeniably *fout* for the year of his life that would mark him forever. But in the same period he was also *goed*: Pelser warned a Jewish friend of one of his sons of an impending raid, and hid him in his house for four months. Nonetheless, Joop Pelser will always be remembered as *fout*.

His son Harry was also *fout*, but was he more *fout* than the Dutch railway men who always made sure the doors on the trains to Westerbork were shut, or more *fout* than the policemen who collected Jews, even though they could have refused? Only one man in the Amsterdam police force ever did say no, and he was ostracized by his colleagues after the war for his disloyalty. Yet in Holland, at least until the 1990s, little was said about the policemen, while the eighteen-year-old who had joined the NSB in a bout of romantic feeling was *fout* forever. Many at Ajax were unwilling to condemn nice guys like the Pelsers to eternal misery.

But there was another reason why Ajax was so gentle. Those who had aided the Germans in the war were known as *landverraders*, "traitors

to their country." Everyone agreed that betraying one's country was a
bad thing. However, to paraphrase E. M. Forster, many people thought
it better than betraying one's soccer club. There must have been vast
numbers of Dutchmen who felt more loyal to club than country. So
fully did a club like Ajax occupy the lives of many of its members that
it became a sort of extended family. The Pelsers or the Schoevaarts were
only extreme cases: it was the norm for fathers, brothers, and sons to
spend the whole weekend playing at the club, while the women poured
the beer.

Millions of Dutch people grow up in a club culture of this kind;
I did. I know it exists in some form in most countries, but I have
never seen it as strong anywhere else. At various times in recent decades Holland has had the highest proportion of registered soccer
players in the world. That is partly because of the peculiar nature
of the country. For most of the twentieth century the Netherlands
was divided into different groups by a sort of friendly agreement.
There were Protestants of various varieties, Catholics, socialists,
Communists, and the generally more bourgeois liberals. Each "pillar"
of society, as it was known, had its own political parties, radio broad-
casters, modes of speech, and sports clubs. Protestant clubs never
played on the Lord's Day. Ajax was a bourgeois club, and Ajax men
would have considered themselves members of a particular caste.
Belonging to Ajax was probably a clearer identity, a more tangible
tie, than being Dutch. The *Ajax-Nieuws* had said as much in August
1941: "What the members of the club do outside the sports field
in political or religious regard, we as sports folk must not judge. As
club fellows we have to feel as one, that is the overriding demand."

This solidarity, which in wartime had aided men like Jaap van
Praag and Jack Reynolds, would afterwards protect the collaborators.
If a member of the Ajax family betrayed his country, the instinct was
to cover up—for fifty years, if need be. When this was impossible, as
with the Pelsers, people would make excuses. They were good men,
they hadn't really done anything to help the Germans, they had had

no choice. Ajax's Joop Stoffelen told the *NRC*, "Harry Pelser didn't betray any people, that's impossible." But Stoffelen had no way of knowing that.

The phrase "little bread NSBers" became a Dutch postwar commonplace, used to explain away the treachery of an acquaintance who had "only done it because he needed the money." The Pelsers were often defended at Ajax as "bread NSBers," as if plundering deported Jews for money was better than doing so from conviction. Joop Pelser's legal file contains a letter from a Resistance hero stating that Pelser had not even had the money to visit his sick son in a hospital in Haarlem, and had "joined the NSB from necessity." It may even have been largely true. Schoevaart's silence on World War II may be immoral, but it is understandable.

9

CAPTAIN OF FRANCE, COLLABORATOR IN GORCUM
Soccer and the Annals of Resistance

A twenty-five-year-old Frenchman stared across the deserted ground of Racing Strasbourg. Oscar Heisserer, captain of France, half-back of Racing and until recently a soldier on the Maginot Line, had come to see what remained of his club after the French capitulation.

Neat, thin, pale, and blond, Heisserer looked more German than French. In Strasbourg, capital of the Alsace, most people had something of both nations. At times all eleven players in Heisserer's Racing team had Germanic surnames, like Hummenberger, Roessler, and Keller. The Alsace was forever passing from France to Germany and back, like a ball in a closely contested semi-final, and this summer of 1940 the Germans had recaptured it for the umpteenth time.

Heisserer was just turning to leave the Racing ground when three cars pulled up, disgorging SS men. One of them, a local pharmacist, pointed at the soccer player and shouted in German, "That's him!"

Heisserer was taken to Strasbourg's SS headquarters, where the local chief told him that, since the Alsace would be German for the next hundred thousand years, he would be well advised to join the SS. "Yesterday I was a French international and captain of the national team," Heisserer claims to have replied, "So how can I join the SS today?" After three hours he was allowed to go home, but the SS chief told him, "You will regret this."

GORCUM, AUTUMN 1941

The train to Gorcum passes through a classic Dutch landscape of mist, green fields, and canals. The town should only be about half an hour from Rotterdam, but it's off the main Dutch railway lines, in a cul-de-sac, hard to reach. Nobody goes to Gorcum.

Even World War II was threatening to pass the town by. There had been a brief flurry of excitement on May 14, 1940, the day before the Dutch capitulation, when Mayor Van Rappard decided that, with the Germans waiting on the far side of a local river and British airplanes circling overhead, Gorcum had to be evacuated. At five in the morning the church bells rang, and as the Germans marched into town the local population cycled out of it with their belongings in bags around their necks. In the event, the RAF decided not to do anything. By the end of that day most *Gorcummers* had returned home disgruntled, particularly the people who had drowned their dogs, thinking they would be gone for years.

The town resumed its usual calm until, on the evening of September 5, 1941, a man named Arie de Jong was voted out as treasurer of the local soccer club Unitas (another classical name from the late nineteenth century). It had been quite a humiliation: De Jong, a former player and a nice man, received just nine votes from the general meeting. There were various reasons for this, but one of them was that after the German invasion he had joined the NSB, the Dutch Nazi party.

Initially De Jong seemed resigned to his defeat. "He will now have a lot of free time that he can use for other things," state the minutes of the general meeting. However, a few weeks later Unitas received a letter from District Inspector Henke saying he was opening "a closer inquiry" into the affair.

The Netherlands today is still suffused with resistance stories of the *Soldier of Orange* variety. Yet Dutch soccer in the war barely featured an anti-German act. This is strange, because if the Dutch were going to commit public resistance, you would expect it to be at soccer matches. In an unfree country the sports stadium is often the only place where tens of thousands of people can gather to shout more or less what they like. The climactic scene of John Huston's film *Escape to Victory*, set in Paris in wartime, has the French fans breaking into the "Marseillaise" when the German team is given a last-minute penalty; after Sylvester Stallone saves, the fans storm the field. Resistance through soccer happens, after a fashion, in real life too: I have written elsewhere of how the revolutions that helped bury the Soviet Union began at sports grounds. The Egyptian revolution of 2011 was made in large part by organized soccer fans fighting the security forces in Tahrir Square. The game is not always just a game.

In the occupied Netherlands (where soccer grounds were virtually the only noisy places) it was occasionally something more. Willem II Tilburg, a club named after a Dutch king, which played in the red, white, and blue of the Dutch flag, became so popular a national symbol that even opposing fans would cheer it on. Fans of the Amsterdam club De Volewijckers (associated with the Communist Resistance) traveled to The Hague in 1943 to beat up fans of ADO (associated, somewhat unfairly, with the NSB).

However, wearing national colors or hitting NSB-ers (an absurd species despised even by the Germans) were fairly safe forms of resistance. Dutch soccer clubs virtually never broke the bounds set by the occupiers. What happened in Gorcum is almost unique. The French story is different: resistance heroes like Oscar Heisserer were more common over there.

STRASBOURG, SUMMER 2001

On a beautiful June morning Heisserer and I are sitting in his living room on the quiet rue de Dorlisheim—or, if you prefer German, the Dorlisheimerstrasse—surrounded by soccer photographs. On one of them Heisserer crouches beside the legendary Ben Barek, as the French team of 1946 pose before their meeting with the England of Lawton and Matthews.

Now that his once-blond hair has mostly disappeared and his features have grown soft and round, Heisserer, with his brown skin, ironed blue shirt, and elegant sandals, has come to look French. His voice, too, has the rises and dips and the changes of tone that go with French, but we are speaking German. Heisserer makes grammatical errors and throws in the odd French word, but for an eighty-six-year-old who has barely spoken the language since Liberation, he doesn't do at all badly.

"Of course I had a very good career in French soccer," he says. At the World Cup of 1938 on home turf he captained France, and with Racing Strasbourg he always finished high in the league and once reached the Cup final.

Then in 1940 the Germans crossed the Maginot Line and brought the Alsace "home into the Reich." The region had been swallowed just as Austria had. It was now officially Germany.

Some time after Heisserer's interview at SS headquarters, the German *Reichstrainer* Sepp Herberger visited Strasbourg and invited him to play for Germany. Heisserer would have been a great trophy for the Nazis: a hero of the Alsace opting for the Reich.

Germany's invasions had already proved an effective method of acquiring players. In the part of Poland annexed at the start of the war, the Germans had found Ernst Willimowski, who remains to this day quite probably the best Polish soccer player ever. He scored twenty-four goals in twenty-two internationals for Poland before the war, including four in a 6–5 defeat by Brazil in the Racing Strasbourg Stadium at the 1938 World Cup.

After Poland was invaded, Willimowski declared himself German. He was of partly German ancestry and spoke the language. He joined a police club in the German town of Chemnitz, scored thirty-seven goals in five games, and was picked for the national team. There "Wili" underwent the customary initiation into the side: his trousers were pulled down and he was thumped on the bottom by the whole team, a ritual the German players called the "Holy Ghost."

Heisserer was meant to join Willimowski in the German team as a pin-up for the expansion of the Reich. But he politely turned down Herberger's offer. "I can't be a French international *and* a German international. That's not possible, is it?" The coach returned home to Mannheim and never bothered him again.

However, Heisserer's problems were only just beginning. Strasbourg had been turned on its head, everything French made German. In local soccer, Racing was rechristened Rasensportverein Strassburg, while little Red Star Strasbourg had been adopted by the SS and renamed SS Strassburg.

The SS imported players for its new club from as far away as Austria, but it was also determined to procure the best soccer player of the Alsace. Heisserer says, "They didn't leave me alone. They offered me money—wow! Constantly, every day they came to me, for two or three years, and said, 'Have you reconsidered?'"

"It has already been considered," Heisserer would reply.

He and his brother stayed with Racing. They never lost a derby against SS Strassburg. "We always wore *bleu-blanc-rouge*, the French colors, and at every match many spectators were arrested for demonstrating. It was like France against Germany, you know. We always had a lot of spectators, fifteen thousand or twenty thousand during the occupation." These must have been the largest demonstrations against the Germans in occupied Strasbourg.

From a drawer Heisserer produces a team photograph, which to my surprise is not of his own team but of their hated rivals SS Strassburg. He points out dead faces. "That's Keller, Fritz, a French international." Fritz Keller, scorer of seventy-four goals for Racing (ten more than Heisserer), remains a French legend. Strasbourg's university stadium is on the rue Fritz-Keller, and there was once even talk of naming Racing's ground after him.

Heisserer points to another face: "That's a German, Willi Heiss, a very good soccer player. He ran away from Germany when Hitler took command, was in the French Legion for five years, then became a professional soccer player in Marseille. Was captured, and crossed into the German Afrikakorps. Wasn't SS at all. But he had his family here, he couldn't go away, you see? I said to him, 'Willi, if you go to Africa you won't come home again, you know?' And unfortunately he didn't come home, he was shot by an English plane in Tunisia, was *der Willi Heiss*, a very good friend of mine."

Isn't Heisserer angry with the SS players? They had made the opposite choice to his.

"To be honest, not many of them were really SS. They were more or less forced to join. It was a crazy time. You know, it took a lot of *courage* —how do you say that in German?—to say no."

I asked Heisserer where on earth he had found the courage. In the war he was at the peak of his soccer powers, with a family to protect. The Germans were not asking him to lie or hurt or kill somebody, just to play in a good team with many of his friends. All around him people agreed to much worse.

Heisserer listened to me politely. Then he shrugged. "I still had illusions. I was a famous man here in Strasbourg. All the people knew Oscar, and I was in the national team. I thought, the Germans will accept this of me. And I think that's why they didn't do anything. They always thought, well, at the end of the song he'll change his mind."

The Germans killed many big fish, but they let Heisserer live fairly happily in Strasbourg until 1943, when they called him up to serve in the Wehrmacht.

GORCUM, AUTUMN 1941

One Saturday morning in November 1941, two months after the NSB-er De Jong had been voted out at Unitas, District Inspector Henke took the train to Gorcum. There he visited the club's chairman, Lammers, to ask what the members had against De Jong.

The Unitas chairman was a local worthy, a sort of accountant at a steel-wire factory, an older man in a three-piece suit with his hair plastered back. He was also a shrewd character. Of course he did not talk politics with the district inspector. Instead, he told him that De Jong had been voted out as treasurer because he had been incompetent, and because he had quarreled before the war with the popular Unitas member Baltus Meijer. There was undoubtedly some truth in this, though Baltus Meijer had later forgiven De Jong after suddenly perceiving the relativity of all things during the evacuation of Gorcum.

The district inspector had also wanted to speak to De Jong but decided against this in order to catch his train back out of town, a decision with which anyone who has ever visited Gorcum will sympathize. Lammers did remark brightly that De Jong could always be found on the high street, selling the NSB newspaper *Volk en Vaderland*.

Soon afterwards Unitas received an official letter ordering that De Jong be reinstated as treasurer. In addition, Huub Sterkenberg, the Unitas member who had proposed a new treasurer, had to be suspended from the club for a year. The mildness of the authorities' demands is striking. There was no hint of physical threat.

Yet Unitas politely refused. The members had voted, and it was against club rules to change anything. In April 1942 the authorities wrote back to say they would jolly well have to anyway. The matter was becoming more serious.

On Tuesday, June 23, 1942, De Jong walked into an Unitas board meeting and handed Lammers a letter. It stated in a single sentence that De Jong was henceforth plenipotentiary of the club. "What is the meaning of this?" asked Lammers. De Jong explained that he now had the final say over everything. One by one the other club directors walked out of the room, leaving De Jong sitting there alone.

Two evenings later the directors all returned to the Unitas ground to hand De Jong their letters of resignation. Because there was training that evening, and because club members had heard something was afoot, the ground was packed. When Lammers told the members what had happened, many of them resigned on the spot. More followed in the next few days, until there was barely a man left to don the famous red shorts.

Now the mayor of Gorcum intervened. In the 1960s L. R. J. van Rappard would become famous as a sort of Dutch Colonel Blimp, a hater of hippies, branded a "Fascist" by the Anne Frank Society. In his 1979 memoirs Van Rappard would argue that the real heroes of World War II were not the Resistance fighters but the mayors and civil servants who had stayed at their posts. He himself had served as mayor of Gorcum from 1939 to 1971. Not that he was all bad: he had annoyed the Germans sufficiently to be imprisoned by the German *Sicherheitsdienst*, the SS's intelligence service, and would eventually spend eight months of the war in hiding. A collection of busts of Van Rappard, ordered by his wife, is apparently still gathering dust in the attic of a Gorcum hospital.

The Mayor, who had become an Unitas donor since moving to town, was determined to save the club. He summoned the old board to tell them it was ridiculous that Unitas was about to provoke its own closure, particularly since De Jong had never once tried to discuss politics. He assured the former directors, "I have found as chairman of the Dutch bee-keeping society that a plenipotentiary can't actually do much." However, the directors maintained that it was disgraceful that the occupiers had interfered with a soccer club. It was an offense against the Unitas constitution!

In the best Dutch political tradition, it was decided to negotiate. The club's former directors, Van Rappard, De Jong, and the local NSB chief Bakker (who employed De Jong as a bookkeeper at his factory) sat around a table and found a compromise. The old directors would resume their posts, De Jong would join the board, and after a while he would quietly resign. Everyone's face would be saved. All that remained was for the Unitas members to approve the compromise.

On Friday evening, July 17, 1942, 157 members and donors met in the local Roxy cinema. It was the most exciting thing to happen in Gorcum since the evacuation (and the second most exciting thing in a very long time indeed). Chairman Lammers told the audience what had happened, speaking so calmly and legalistically that you might almost forget that the Germans were just then killing millions of people in the Soviet Union. A typical sentence: "Mr. Sterkenberg has also acted entirely in accordance with the rules, and no measure contravening our regulations can be taken against him either."

When De Jong got his turn to speak, he said he was certain this was "a matter of a political nature." (This was probably easier for him to accept than the thought that the members just didn't like him, or that he was a useless treasurer.) He said that on the street you could hear "butchers, grocers etc. proclaiming that the NSB-er had been kicked out of the board." Baltus Meijer had asked him "to place the interests of Unitas above the interests of the NSB" (apparently the great ideological struggle of the 1940s), but De Jong could not. However, he appealed to the members "to set aside the hatred they feel for me," because he would be sad if Unitas folded.

Then Sterkenberg, who liked to hear himself speak, rose from the audience. A solid citizen in little spectacles, proprietor of a ladies' underwear store, he had been a goalkeeper once but was now too fat. He said it was strange to reflect that fifteen years ago it had been he who had proposed De Jong as a board member. But he had been mistaken; he had long ceased to admire De Jong; the man must be kept off the board whatever the cost: "Thy youths will not be able to practice your sport and will have to miss your matches. Thy shalt have to make that sacrifice. Think of your club anthem, in which we sing, 'We will not make way for anyone' . . . "

Van Rappard again begged for moderation, but the Unitas members were now resolved to boldness: only forty-six voted for the mayor's compromise motion, and sixty-two against. The NSB-er De Jong had to go. The Second World War had reached Gorcum. Unitas was going to disappear.

STRASBOURG, 1943

Heisserer had been expecting the army call-up papers. For months he had been telling his pregnant wife, "Oscar will never be a German soldier."

"That's fine," his wife would reply.

While he tells me this, Heisserer starts to cough. He apologizes. Then he is weeping, although he keeps talking. "My wife died two years ago, you see? We did it together, and she was a hundred percent *d'accord*. She was expecting a child. And that didn't change anything.

Scenes from Ajax's De Meer stadium in the 1930s. (Above) The opening ceremony of 1934; (left) a league match from 1936; and (below) Ajax crowned Dutch champions in 1939. (SPAARNESTAD FOTOARCHIEF/ ANP FOTO)

(Above) A packed Sunday market in Amsterdam's Jewish Quarter, summer 1940. Within three years most of the city's Jews had been killed; (left) a vendor of smoked fish at the Sunday market, summer 1940; (below) another vendor, summer 1940. The original Nazi caption to this photograph read, "With real Jewish gestures, this Jew recommends his merchandise." (ALL THREE PHOTOGRAPHS COURTESY OF THE NEDERLANDS INSTITUUT VOOR OORLOGSDOCUMENTATIE, OR NIOD)

(Left) German troops singing in Amsterdam, 1940. Dutch bicycles had not yet been confiscated; (below) a German "*Propagandarnarsch*" through the streets of Amsterdam in 1943, celebrating the tenth anniversary of Hitler's seizure of power. (BOTH PHOTOGRAPHS COURTESY OF NIOD)

(Far left) Meijer Stad (middle), product of Rotterdam's Jewish Quarter, with two members of his Dutch Army Unit in The Hague, March 1940. Two months later, the army would crumble in the face of the German invasion; Eddy Hamel (left), Ajax's outside-right of the 1920s, "A terrifically nice, popular soccer player."

(This page and opposite, top) England plays Germany at White Hart Lane, December 4, 1935; at the Spurs ground, the Swastika flies at half mast in mourning for Britain's Princess Victoria. The German team was generally welcomed throughout Europe in Hitler's first years in power. The arrest of fourteen anti-Fascist demonstrators outside the ground was the only incident on an otherwise peaceful afternoon. England thrashed the Germans 3–0. (ALL PHOTOGRAPHS HULTON GETTY)

Soccer featured at Napola, Nazi Germany's National Political Teaching Institute—
a sports lesson in Potsdam, 1941. (AKG LONDON)

That infamous photograph: the England team gives the Nazi salute before the kick-off of the friendly game in Berlin, May 15, 1938. (EMPICS)

Disabled veterans of World War I watch Allied Servicemen play British Army Team at Stamford Bridge, March 29, 1941. (HULTON GETTY)

The opening fixture of a regional wartime league: Millwall host Norwich City before a healthy crowd at the Den, October 21, 1939. (HULTON GETTY)

(Right) Dignitaries discover soccer: A. V. Alexander, First Lord of the Admiralty, meets the West Ham players before the Football League Wartime Cup Final, June 8, 1940. West Ham went on to beat Blackburn Rovers. Meanwhile, France was falling to the Germans. (Below) September 1945, West Ham plays Aston Villa in the Football League (South) at Upton Park that is being restored after wartime bomb damage. (BOTH PHOTOGRAPHS FROM EMPICS)

The annual ceremony to commemorate the "February Strike" of 1941: flowers are laid at the Dockworker statue in front of Amsterdam's Portuguese Synagogue. (PHOTOGRAPH COURTESY OF NIOD)

(Below) Ajax is champion of Holland in 1973. Flowers for the chairman, Jaap van Praag. (SPAARNESTAD FOTOARCHIEF)

(Bottom) The golden—or "diamond"—Ajax enjoys a romp against Bayern Munich in the European Cup quarter-final in 1973. In the middle, wearing the captain's armband, is Johan Cruijff. Months later, his teammates would vote to strip the obstinate and domineering Cruijff of his captaincy, and he left for Barcelona, signaling the end of a great team. (SPAARNESTAD FOTOARCHIEF/NATIONAL FOTOPERSBUREAU)

"I was called up on a Wednesday, and on Thursday I was gone. From here I went to the Lorraine, I had false papers made—well, a whole novel."

The SS immediately arrested his wife. The Heisserers had expected this, and so had spread a story that he had run off with another woman. "Even a German friend of mine swore that I had left with another woman. Everything so that nothing would happen to my wife, you understand? I didn't just run away, it wasn't easy. I had made my decision, and couldn't do anything against my own conscience, could I?"

The SS men screamed at the pregnant Mrs. Heisserer, "*Ach*, your husband, we'll definitely catch him, and then we'll carry him around the Kleberplatz in a cage!" But they didn't catch him. Heisserer reached Switzerland, where he was interned for two years and made to perform hard labor. It has been reported that he helped some Jews escape from France to Switzerland—something he didn't tell me. After he disappeared from Strasbourg, the Germans caught his brother instead. Heisserer told me, "He also played for Rasensportverein, for Racing, and when I disappeared they put him in the German Army. He ended up in Danzig, in a U-boat. But he came home in 1945, you know. He was a very good soccer player too."

Heisserer returned home in the spring of 1945 as a soldier in the French Army that liberated Strasbourg. "And then I saw a daughter I hadn't seen before, and that daughter is now the wife of the French Minister for French–German Relations."

GORCUM, 1942

De Jong was now plenipotentiary of an empty husk. Unitas had almost no members any more. But Mayor Van Rappard was still determined to save the club. He did so with surprising ease. He got

Unitas and the NSB to agree that a new board would be chosen, including neither the old directors nor De Jong, and that a "neutral person" would be appointed to ensure there were no "politics" at the club. On December 4, 1942, Unitas was revived. Two days later the first team beat Overmaas 3–0.

But Huub Sterkenberg, the man who had opposed De Jong, was to die in a concentration camp. Van Rappard would claim in his memoirs that the shopkeeper's deportation "stood in no relation to the Unitas affair, even if this was asserted in a malicious attempt to show me in a bad light." Unitas members believe otherwise.

WHY?

The thought of resisting the Germans (as distinct from merely reading underground newspapers) probably never even occurred to most people in the occupied Netherlands. They obeyed the law, as they had before the war and as they would afterwards. Only in the 1960s, when the next generation asked why they hadn't resisted, did it seem that in the war everyone had made conscious moral choices.

It was not just that people were frightened of joining the Resistance. They simply weren't that interested. After all, life was continuing more or less as before: the family, the job, the soccer club. The Resistance was for Communists, fanatics, and criminals, and it put ordinary people in danger. The name "Putten," in particular, still conjures dreadful images in the Netherlands: over five hundred men from this village were deported and killed in 1944 in reprisal for a Resistance ambush on a car carrying four German soldiers.

It has been estimated that a mere twenty-five thousand Dutch people were active in the Resistance, about 0.25 percent of the population, and the annals of Resistance in the nation's soccer clubs stretch little further than Unitas. What distinguished this club from thousands of others?

Initially Unitas felt it was doing nothing illegal. In fact, the board was forever insisting on its legality. In a 1947 pamphlet on the affair, Lammers expressed his surprise that "a political party thought itself so powerful it could act at will, putting aside all law and fairness."

The club assumed the Nazis would be reasonable and law-abiding. And the strange thing is that in Holland they were. As long as you weren't a Jew or a gypsy or a Resistance fighter, in the occupied Netherlands until 1944 you could write letters, appeal against decisions, and make compromises. There was no need to mount the barricades. That knowledge gave Unitas courage.

But when the club's general meeting rejected De Jong for the second time, Unitas did genuinely endanger itself. Running such risks was rare in the Netherlands. The reason the members dared do it was probably because their leaders had. Unitas's directors were the first to oppose De Jong's return as treasurer, and the first to resign from the club. After that it was easy—indeed, almost obligatory—for the other members to resign too. You could hardly be the only one to say, "Wait a minute, I could get into trouble. Anyway, I've already paid my membership fees." You would look silly. Brave leaders set Unitas apart.

The courage of these individuals remains mysterious, but Heisserer's is less so. In France many more people said no than in the Netherlands: an estimated four hundred thousand French people were active in the Resistance, or 1 percent of the population. Particularly in the Alsace, fighting back came with the territory. At one point, when Heisserer was trying to explain to me how he had dared turn down the Germans, he said, "I want to show you a photograph of my father," and shuffled off. He had already told me his father had been a butcher and weightlifter nicknamed "Hercules," so famous in the Alsace that when Heisserer entered the *lycée* at Haguenau he became known as "the son of Hercules."

Heisserer returned carrying the picture of a giant man with a huge waxed moustache and a bare, bemedaled chest. I could hardly believe that this character from a nineteenth-century funfair was the father of a living person. "He was the strongest man in France, you could say," Heisserer told me.

He was trying to explain where he came from. The Alsace, unlike the Netherlands, had a history of toughness. Heisserer pointed to the year of his own birth: "1914, can you imagine, we're now in 2001! In three weeks I'll be eighty-seven. With the war, before the war, during the war, after the war, *ja, jajaja*! Well, that's the fate here, you see? In history there is always only war, and we are a borderland. The war, the great one of '14–'18, and long ago too—we know our history well!"

In France, and particularly in the Alsace, there was a culture of war: 1940 was just a rerun of 1914 and 1870. The son of Hercules was prepared. In the Netherlands, where no one had shot at humans since Napoleon, people were more afraid.

STRASBOURG–POSTSCRIPT

Heisserer retired from soccer in 1948. "If I could have just one thing. . . . My best years were taken from me. In 1939 I was twenty-five years old, you see? From my twenty-fifth year to my thirtieth I couldn't play for France. They stole my most beautiful five years."

GORCUM–POSTSCRIPT

Arie de Jong was expelled from Unitas after the war and banned from the club's ground for life. But quite soon he was allowed back, as the Unitas board chose to regard not him but his employer Bakker as the evil genius in the affair. However, De Jong would only ever come to the club to watch the occasional game, I was told by Frans Roussa and Arie Roza, the last two survivors of the Unitas first eleven of World War II. "I did speak to him once or twice later, and he was a very pleasant man socially," said Roussa. "He became an outcast," added Roza. "He'd stand there all by himself," said Roussa.

Eventually De Jong moved to another town. When Unitas celebrated its seventy-fifth anniversary in 1973, it was awarded the Royal Dutch Medal of Honor for its resistance in the war.

10

THE NETHERLANDS
WAS BETTER THAN THE REST

As a child in Leiden I learned that the Dutch had been good in the war. I learned that nobody bought in the shops of people who had been *fout* in the war, and that the formerly collaborationist *De Telegraaf* (which I thought of as the only Dutch newspaper not to have been in the Resistance) was still universally loathed (though it also, mysteriously, contrived to be the country's best-selling daily). The average Dutchman had spent the war delivering his illegal newspapers after feeding his hidden Jews. I was proud of the Dutch.

I suspect that children in Leiden today no longer have to swallow this myth. Their parents and teachers are relatively relaxed about the war. Not only did they themselves not experience it, but in most cases their own parents didn't either: they can accept without trauma that most Dutch people were grey or cowardly in the war.

What survives of the Dutch myth is the notion that Holland was better than the rest. All right, the Dutch did not prevent the Holocaust, and like the rest of Europe they stole Jewish property, but, they often claim, they still did more than most. Amsterdam's February

Strike of 1941 was the only mass action in Europe by gentiles for Jews. "Not in Moscow, not in Warsaw, but in Amsterdam, and that is the undying glory of Amsterdam," wrote Mari Andriessen, sculptor of the Dockworker statue that stands beside the city's Portuguese synagogue commemorating the strike. Anne Frank, too, is part of Amsterdam's "undying glory."

That the Netherlands nonetheless lost three-quarters of its Jews was inevitable, runs the new Dutch argument. In a little country bordering on Germany, without mountains or forests, there was nowhere for Jews to hide. The tragedy of the Dutch was that they (unlike other peoples) were honest, competent, and law-abiding. The Nazis exploited these virtues to trick them into deporting the Jews. Like Adolf Eichmann at his trial in Jerusalem in 1961, the Dutch would come to accuse "those in power" of having abused their "obedience."

The Dutch had no chance against the Germans, and if they had resisted *en masse* they would have been slaughtered with the Jews. In the field of sport, playing on was the only sensible option. That is the usual line of defense, anyway. It is worth testing these theories against the experience of other countries.

––––––

In late 1940, a few months after invading Norway, the Germans decided to Nazify Norwegian sport. They appointed a "sports *Führer*," and tried to place a Norwegian Nazi (or "quisling") in charge of every club.

The result was a nationwide sports strike that remained largely unbroken until the Liberation. Norwegian skiers, skaters, and soccer players refused to play under quisling leaders. Almost all eight hundred members of Lyn Athletic Club resigned after the sports *Führer* tried to impose a Nazi director. With many thousands of other Norwegians, they were banned from sport "for life."

The Nazis strove to make Norway's official sports championships run as usual. Nobody came. In Oslo's Ullevål Stadium, which could accommodate forty thousand people, soccer matches in wartime were regularly played in front of just ten. A semi-final of the national soccer championship in Bergen in 1942 apparently drew a crowd of only twenty-seven. Eventually local quislings were deputed to watch sports matches.

However, games were hard to organize for want of participants. The sport of bandy (similar to ice hockey) virtually ceased in Norway during the war. At the national speed-skating championships of 1942 there was only one competitor in the senior class. A soccer club in a coastal town could find no opponents other than at the local mental asylum.

Sportsmen organized "illegal" events in remote country districts to keep fit. Dozens of participants were arrested, among them the three Ruud brothers, international skiing champions. One brother, Birger, told by a Nazi sports leader that it was his duty to take part in a certain tournament, is said to have replied, "When the day comes that it is my *duty* to participate in a skiing contest, on that day I will burn my skis."

So worried were the Germans by the sports strike that Himmler apparently visited Norway to investigate. Many Norwegian sportsmen were deported to German concentration camps. This failed to break the sports strike, which continued to inspire the country, spreading resistance even to tiny hamlets that until then had been only dimly aware that the German invasion had happened. "Local athletic leaders came to play a big role in various aspects of the Home Front," wrote Tore Gjelsvik in his *Norwegian Resistance 1940–1945*, "athletes being particularly important in building up the secret fighting groups which were then under formation."

"Do you know what I should like to do?" Professor O. K. Hallesby, a fundamentalist divine, is supposed to have asked at a wartime meeting of Norway's Joint Christian Council. "Go up the Palace Hill, wave my hat, and shout, 'Hurrah for your young sportsmen!'"

A sports strike was one of the paths not taken in the Netherlands.

———

In the courtroom at Eichmann's trial in Jerusalem was Hannah Arendt, who was reporting it for the *New Yorker*. Later she would extend her articles into *Eichmann in Jerusalem: A Report on the Banality of Evil*, the most intelligent work of journalism I know. What concerns me here are her three chapters, as shocking as they are inspiring, which compare the fate of the Jews in the various European countries outside the Third Reich.

The Holocaust in the Netherlands, wrote Arendt, "was a catastrophe unparalleled in any Western country; it can be compared only with the extinction, under vastly different and, from the beginning, completely desperate conditions, of Polish Jewry." She blamed, in large part, the strong Dutch Nazi movement, second in Europe only to Germany's. It was true that a relatively large number of Dutch Jews had found hiding places, but it was also true that a relatively large number of the hidden Jews were betrayed. Of the approximately 28,000 Jews hiding in Holland, more than 11,000 did not survive.

Belgium (which I had always thought of as *fout*) turned out to have saved half its Jews. The Belgian police had dragged their feet, railway workers left doors of the deportation trains open or arranged ambushes, and many Jews found hiding places. Paul Spiegel, later chairman of the German Jewish community, spent the war hiding with his mother at a Belgian farm—an Anne Frank story with no diary and no betrayal.

In Norway in 1940 there were only 1,700 Jews, most of them refugees from Germany, a group that in most countries was treated as the lowest of the low. Yet when the Germans ordered their deportation, several quislings resigned from the Norwegian government. Whereas the Dutch queen Wilhelmina, in her wartime speeches on the BBC, granted the Jews five brief mentions in five years, Norway's queen was always urging her people to help the Jews. Nine hundred Norwegian Jews were smuggled across the border to safety in Sweden.

Italy kept promising the Germans it would round up its Jews, but it never did. The Italians seemed unable to take anti-Semitism seriously, wrote Arendt. Even Roberto Farinacci, leader of the Italian anti-Semitic movement, had a Jewish secretary. When the Italians did pass a law against Jews, they all but sabotaged it by making countless exceptions. For instance, if just one member of a Jewish family had joined the Fascist Party, the whole family was exempted from all measures. Only when the Germans themselves occupied Italy in 1943 did they manage to deport 7,500 Italian Jews to Auschwitz—less than 10 percent of the number living in the country.

All over Eastern Europe, people used the opportunity presented by war to slaughter the local Jews. The exception was Bulgaria. This Nazi ally allowed Hitler to deport the fifteen thousand Jews from the bits of Romania, Yugoslavia, and Greece that he had given the country, but the measures taken against Jews in Bulgaria itself were "simply ridiculous," wrote Arendt. All baptized Jews were exempted from the measures, whatever their date of baptism. A baptism epidemic ensued. The Germans, after a lot of trouble, eventually managed to get a law passed making non-baptized Jews wear a very small star. The few Jews who actually wore it received, according to a German official, "so many manifestations of sympathy from the misled population that they are actually proud of their sign." The Bulgarian government promptly abolished the star.

In other countries the Germans tried to herd the Jews into a ghetto in the capital, the better to deport them. The Bulgarians reversed the process, sending the Jews out of Sofia into the countryside so as to disperse them. Many Bulgarians tried to stop the banished Jews on their way to the station, and when that failed they demonstrated in front of the king's palace. Not in Amsterdam, not in Rotterdam, but in Sofia. The Germans wanted to talk to Bulgaria's Chief Rabbi, but he was being sheltered by Metropolitan Stephan of Sofia, who had said that "men had no right to torture Jews and to persecute them." Not one Bulgarian Jew died in the camps.

But the country that fared best in Arendt's pan-European comparison was Denmark. "The story of the Danish Jews is *sui generis*, and the behavior of the Danish people and their government was unique among all the countries of Europe," she wrote. In a little country bordering on Germany, without mountains or forests, something unheard-of occurred. The Danes not only protected their Jews, but unlike the Italians and Bulgarians they also told the Germans that killing Jews was wrong.

"The Danes," wrote Leo Goldberger, one of the Danish Jews saved from the death camps, "point out that the special set of circumstances that prevailed in their country during the war makes comparisons with other countries inappropriate." It is true that what happened in Denmark was probably unfeasible in the Netherlands. Even so, the comparison is illuminating; so much so that in 2004 I visited Denmark to explore it further.

Denmark, conquered as easily as Holland in the spring of 1940, was allowed more or less to rule itself for the first three years of the war. This was a crucial difference with the Netherlands, which was run by a coterie of mostly Austrian Nazis. The Dutch royal family and cabinet had fled to London in May 1940, leaving instructions to the country's top civil servants, the secretaries general, to keep things functioning without anarchy. The secretaries general aimed not to upset the occupiers. When the Germans asked them to sack a Jewish concert master, they considered objecting, before passing the order on to the orchestra anyway. "Perhaps a middle way can still be found," they noted in their minutes.

In Denmark by contrast, the Danish king Christian X and his government stayed in office and very largely kept running things during the war. The occupied Danes even held elections. Every day King Christian rode his horse through Copenhagen, greeting his subjects as he went, living proof that the Danish establishment remained in the saddle. The German occupying troops only handled military matters, leaving everything else to the Danes. In the first few years of war, Germans and Danes got along fairly smoothly. The Danish historian Therkel Straede writes that the German occupation here "passed off more mildly than in any other country." Hitler praised Denmark as a "model protectorate."

Indeed, Danish relations with the Germans verged on collaboration. Very few Danes ever lifted arms against the occupiers. Jorgen Kieler, a Dane who didn't merely help rescue about 1,500 Jews but also committed armed sabotage (one of his wartime explosions made the front page of the *New York Times*), told me in 2004, "I felt very often that I was living in another world from other Danes. The feeling of isolation plays a major role. I did not get rid of it until I sat down and wrote my autobiography five years ago."

The wartime Danes may have been collaborationist, but they were not anti-Semitic. The 7,800 Jews in Denmark in 1940 had integrated to the point of becoming invisible. As it happened, they were practically the only ethnic minority in the country. Almost all other Danes belonged to the Danish Lutheran Church—a church that would play a crucial role in the Jewish rescue.

Danish Lutheranism was a peculiar variant of the German creed. The Danish church's founding father, Nikolai Grundtvig, born the son of a country pastor in 1783, had taken as his key text the Book of Genesis. Grundtvig read the Creation story to mean that human life had value in itself, even before Christianity arrived. His slogan was, "Man first, then a Christian." This implied that religious differences were secondary, contradicting Luther's own anti-Semitism, and the usual Protestant obsession with schisms.

In the autumn of 1940, after the Germans had arrived, the pipe-smoking theologian Hal Koch gave a series of lectures on Grundtvig to packed halls around Denmark. Koch's audiences understood that he was not simply talking about theology. He urged Danes to act as a group. He said there was "the need for the entire nation to combine politicization, individual and collective responsibility, knowledge of all facts, and negotiations with the Nazi, as long as that was possible."

A year later, he moderated a public debate on the "Jewish question"—
itself an astonishing fact—in which he called on Danes to reject the
merest hint of discrimination.

Other churchmen took a similar line. Their influence was vast.
Admittedly Denmark in 1940 had perhaps the lowest percentage of
churchgoers in Europe, but most Danes still used the church for bap-
tisms, weddings, and funerals. Lutheran pastors remained respected
authorities. Because they were virtually state functionaries, and King
Christian was head of the church, the church was in effect the moral
arm of government. Whenever the Germans hinted that it was time
for measures against the Danish Jews, the Danes would reply that
there was no "Jewish question" in Denmark.

That Christian wore a yellow star around Copenhagen is a myth,
because the star was never imposed in Denmark. But it *is* true that
the Germans were told that if the star were imposed the king would
be the first to wear it. When someone tried to burn down the Copenhagen synagogue in December 1941, Christian sent a message of
support to the Chief Rabbi. The arsonist was caught and given a stiff
sentence, which was later stiffened further by the Danish Supreme
Court. The Germans had never seen anything like it.

In 1942 Christian received a birthday telegram from Hitler. He
replied with a brusque, "My utmost thanks. Christian Rex." The lack
of deference drove Hitler wild. General Hermann von Hanneken
and the SS man Werner Best were sent to Copenhagen to sort Denmark out.

But by the summer of 1943 it had become clear that Germany
was going to lose the war. Inevitably, the willingness to resist grew
all around Western Europe. There were riots in Danish shipyards,
strikes in several cities, and after Von Hanneken proclaimed martial
law there were executions. On September 8, Best sent a cable to Berlin
saying it was time to deal with the "Jewish Question." Ships arrived
in Copenhagen harbor to carry off Denmark's Jews.

But, wrote Arendt, "The German officials who had been living in the country for years were no longer the same." Von Hanneken refused to supply troops to deport the Jews, and even refused to issue a decree making the Jews report for "work." The special SS units used in Denmark often objected to "the measures they were asked to carry out by the central agencies," according to Best's testimony at the Nuremberg trials. He himself got Berlin to promise that the Danish deportees would be sent to Theresienstadt, the Nazi show camp for protected Jews, and not to the death camps.

The deportations of the Danish Jews were scheduled to begin on the night of October 1, 1943. As neither the Danes nor the local Germans were willing to carry them out, special police units had been sent from Germany. However, Best would not let the units force their way into Jewish homes, so they could only arrest people who opened the front door voluntarily. Just 477 Jews—many of them old and confused—opened the front door that night. The rest had been tipped off.

The German naval attaché Georg Ferdinand Duckwitz (who after the war would be made West German Ambassador to Copenhagen) had warned Danish politicians about the planned deportations. The politicians told the Chief Rabbi Marcus Melchior, and in the synagogue on the morning of September 29, the day before the Jewish New Year, he had alerted his congregation. "You must leave immediately, warn all your friends and relatives and go into hiding," he urged.

Finding hiding places in Denmark was "very easy," wrote Arendt. Gentiles had been pressing their house keys on any Jew they could find. "At one point I had four keys in my pocket for houses entirely unknown to me," one Jewish woman would later recall.

By one estimate, 90 percent of Lutheran ministers joined Denmark's rescue and resistance efforts. Copenhagen's cantor was lent 25,000 Danish crowns (more than his annual salary) by a Lutheran priest named Rasmussen to pay for his family's escape to Sweden. After the war, Rasmussen refused repayment. The Sunday after the attempted deportations, Denmark's pastors read a letter from their pulpits: "Whenever Jews are persecuted . . . it is the duty of the Christian church to protest against such persecution, because it is in conflict with the sense of justice inherent in the Danish people and inseparable from our Danish Christian culture through the centuries." Five Danish Lutheran priests were killed in the Resistance, others went to prison and concentration camps, and about one hundred had to go underground until the liberation.

Among Denmark's many heroes, the hospital workers of Copenhagen also stand out. One Danish ambulance driver telephoned all the people with Jewish names he could find in the phone book and offered to drive them to safety. Jews were installed in hospital beds under gentile names like "Hansen" or "Petersen," or disguised as visitors, staff, even funeral mourners.

At Copenhagen's Kommunehospitalet all one thousand staff were involved in the rescue. Half the town must have known what was going on. Yet there were barely any betrayals.

Quite the contrary: the Danes were aided by German sabotage. As Leni Yahil wrote in *The Rescue of Danish Jewry*, it seemed that "there hardly was one German left in Denmark who was prepared to execute the action against the Jews along the lines followed in other places." There is a story of a German Army patrol stopping a garbage truck in which Jews were hiding, and lifting the lid to reveal them. Then one soldier exclaimed, "Abraham, Isaac, and Jacob," dropped the lid, and waved the driver on.

The Danish Jewish journalist Valdemar Koppel recalled being caught fleeing one night by two Gestapo men, who asked him if he was Jewish. "Certainly," Koppel replied, "and you?" They drove him to the Elsinore police station, explaining on the way that he had been stupid to flee given that he was married to a non-Jewish woman, and debating with the student who had been trying to help him escape whether the German invasion of Denmark in April 1940 had been illegal. The student spent four or five days in solitary confinement with nothing for company except a copy of the weekly newspaper *B. T.*, which he succeeded in memorizing word for word. He was then handed over to the Danish police—akin to being released, except that he was given coffee and cigarettes too. Koppel was also eventually freed.

If you sit on the pier in Helsingborg at the southern tip of Sweden, and look across the sea, Denmark is so near that you can make out individual Danish trees, church steeples, the sun reflecting off roofs. The Sound is only a couple of miles wide here. On the Danish side is Hamlet's Elsinore, or "Helsingør" as the Danes call it. That is where most of the Danish Jews embarked in 1943. Over several nights, Danish fishing boats ferried them across to Sweden. Some made the journey in just an hour. A Swedish journalist who had stood on the beach watching one of the Danish boats arrive recounted in his newspaper,

> Someone on board starts singing "Du Gamla, du Fria" [the Swedish national anthem]. And everybody joins, as best they know. They remember a word here or there of the text, but nevertheless, bright, happy voices join in a mighty chorus.
>
> It is almost more than you can bear. Tears run down the cheeks of tall, hefty men standing on the beach, watching. Here they come, hunted from house and home, driven from their jobs and sometimes torn away from relatives, and there they come, singing . . .

Within days 7,200 of Denmark's 7,800 Jews were safe in Sweden. At this point any other country would have declared the operation a triumph. The Danes did not forget the four-hundred-odd Jews who had been caught. An eighty-four-year-old schoolteacher named Hanna Adler was released thanks to a petition signed by hundreds of her former pupils, by civil servants from the Ministry of Education, and by the Mayor of Copenhagen.

The Danes then ensured that none of the Jews sent to the Czech ghetto at Theresienstadt would be transferred to the death camps. "In the ghetto," wrote Arendt, "they enjoyed greater privileges than any other group because of the never-ending 'fuss' made about them by Danish institutions and private persons." They received food parcels, and a visit from a Danish delegation (which passed on King Christian's regards in a whisper), and were released on April 13, 1945, before the end of the war. About fifty of them had died in Theresienstadt. "Only" 116 Danish Jews, or 1.5 percent of the total, were killed in the Holocaust.

Arendt concluded, "Politically and psychologically, the most interesting aspect of this incident is perhaps the role played by the German authorities in Denmark, their obvious sabotage of orders from Berlin. It is the only case we know of in which the Nazis met with open native resistance, and the result seems to have been that those exposed to it changed their minds." In other words, the Nazis in Denmark, being told every day that killing Jews was wrong, came to believe that killing Jews was wrong.

This is probably only part of the explanation. The Germans in Denmark, in letting the Jews go, were also taking the path of least resistance: to have killed them regardless of Danish anger would have made their occupation of Denmark difficult. But whatever their motives, the Germans did yield to a civilians' revolt. Nor did they punish the Danes with mass executions. The Germans in Western Europe ruled with a degree of consent. They could suppress the two-day February Strike in Amsterdam by killing eleven people, but they could not quell a nationwide revolt, because they needed their troops in the east.

Once again, as at Unitas in Gorcum, it seems the Danes were brave because their leaders were. The king made a public commitment to the Jews, Danish political leaders refused to take even the mildest measures against them, pastors read a letter in church opposing their persecution, and so an atmosphere was created in which ambulance drivers and fishermen saved their lives. It was similar in Norway, where king and government had called on their citizens to resist the Germans for as long as possible.

The story of the Danish Jews is a fairy tale—so much so, in fact, that it makes Danes uncomfortable. When I went around Copenhagen speaking to rescuers, Jews, historians, and other experts, I was struck by how little postwar Danes had made of the story. Behind the Museum of Danish Resistance, where you'd hardly notice it, a stone sculpture stands in the grass: a Medusa-like tangle of women, an Israeli gift symbolizing the rescue. But in its neglect (the arm of one of the figures is broken) the piece epitomizes not so much the rescue as Danish silence about the rescue.

This is curious. The Dutch for decades propagated a false myth of having saved the Jews. The Danes, who really did save their Jews, rarely talk about it. In part, this is precisely because the Holocaust didn't hit Denmark. Here there is no trauma to relive as there is in the Netherlands. This struck me when I visited Bent Melchior, son of the wartime chief rabbi, in his comfortable bourgeois living room. On his walls were photographs of children and grandchildren, Jewish art, and a copy of a letter of support from Christian X to his father. It looked like a life without tragedy. To postwar Danes, there just didn't seem to be that much to say about the Jews and the war.

It was an Israeli historian, Yahil, who wrote the first major book about the rescue, in 1969. Like most subsequent foreign accounts, it is a paean to the "special character and moral stature of the Danish people." This kind of talk makes most Danes uncomfortable. It makes some of them want to throw up.

In the 1990s, when Danish historians finally turned to the rescue of the Jews, they tended to debunk the conventional story of heroism. For instance, they emphasized the large sums charged by some fishermen to ferry Jews, even though most of the rescuers demanded nothing, and others contributed their own money.

Jorgen Kieler, the rescuer I met, was also anxious not to sound like a hero. He told me that saving Jews had been less risky in Denmark than elsewhere, as the Germans in Denmark did not punish it with death. However, one reason the Germans didn't is that the Danes united for the Jews. The Nazis would have had to punish the entire establishment. By contrast, in Holland it was a matter of picking off a few isolated resisters. In any case, the Danes could not have known in advance that the German punishments would be soft.

I asked Straede, the historian, why every Dane I spoke to added some caveat intended to diminish the rescue. He said, "There is a consensus to feel unease about it, because whenever you are confronted with it, it is always because some American Jews bring it forward to you with ridiculous ideas of heroism, a simplified view of history that the good guys are fighting the bad guys, and so on. We know that our motives are more tainted."

The Danes had a haven a few miles across the sound; the Dutch did not. Yet the Dutch might have achieved something had they not just debated the size of the "Forbidden for Jews" signs.

11

SOLDIER HEROES
British and German Soccer in the War
(and Long After)

I.

My taxi turned into the Preston North End ground off Sir Tom Finney Way, and I walked through the rain past the Sir Tom Finney Stand to find Sir Tom Finney in the office he shares with two other people. He led me upstairs to an executive box where we could talk in peace.

The warmth of the executive box pleased Sir Tom. He pointed to the exposed stand opposite, where he and his wife usually sat. I looked at the empty stand (it was a Friday afternoon) and a giant portrait of a younger Finney, painted on the seats, looked back at me.

Preston North End's eighty-year-old honorary president has spent almost his whole life at this ground, in a small town twenty miles from Manchester, in northwestern England. He turned professional here at age seventeen, in 1939, and played in the team that won the War Cup final of 1941. Preston held the mighty Arsenal at Wembley, and beat it in the replay at Blackburn Rovers. When I said it must have been strange playing a Cup final in a bombed-out London in the middle of war, the famously amiable Sir Tom agreed that it had been. But then he said, "I mean, I wasn't all that interested in the war when I was playing. I was only eighteen. And the main concern was to go down and beat them, you know. And to hold them to a draw in London was really quite an achievement. . . . I wasn't really all that interested in the—I mean, other than the fact that we wanted England to win the war."

Most histories of British soccer hardly mention the war. Phil Soar's 261-page *Encyclopaedia of British Football* deals with it in a paragraph. Nicholas Mason's *Football!* passes seamlessly from the Italy–England match of May 1939 to the Dynamo Moscow tour of Britain of late 1945. Byron Butler's *Official Illustrated History of the FA Cup* covers the epoch in a sentence, "And the Cup stayed with Portsmouth for six dark years."

When the war does feature, the same few anecdotes are generally trotted out. The guest-player rule allowed little Aldershot to field an eleven of internationals from their local army camps; bombs and other wartime exigencies forced Spurs to share White Hart Lane with Arsenal, and Manchester United to move in with Manchester City; and England's Stan Mortensen once appeared as a substitute for Wales. No one takes anything that happened in soccer in these years very seriously. It remains patriotic to emphasize the provisional, cheery insignificance of the wartime game, as if everyone had been too busy fighting Hitler to bother. British soccer in the Second World War remains an almost untapped social phenomenon.

In Germany, league soccer continued as if nothing were happening, even as the Allied bombs flattened the country, and as the one essential commodity for top-class soccer—young men—was being dispatched to its destruction on the Eastern Front. The German national team thrived until Goebbels pulled the plug late in 1942. For most of the war in Europe's two main combatant nations, the ball rolled on.

II.

Peter Croker, who would be transformed by the war into a professional soccer player with Charlton, remembers exactly where he was when it began. At eleven in the morning of September 3, 1939, he recalls, "I was at the cricket. Both teams were there. The game was due to start at eleven-thirty. There was some umming and awing about whether we should play or not. Then it was decided, on a majority of the married players, that it would be better if we went home."

An air-raid siren went off while they talked, but the cricketers assumed it was a practice alarm and ignored it. They had other worries. "Then a chap came running across the ground in a full gas kit," Croker reminisces. "It was a warm day, and he got to us, and he pulled up the pipe of his gas mask, and he said, 'Take cover! Enemy aircraft approaching!'" Croker's imitation gives the man a computer-like voice. "He must have been sweating like a pig. He gave most of us the best laugh we had in the war."

Soccer, too, had closed down immediately on the outbreak. The FA still remembered its dismal First World War. In August 1914, the association had offered to abandon soccer and put all its grounds at the disposal of the country, but the War Office had said that was not necessary, and so the clubs had blithely played on.

That young men were having fun when they should have been dying in France outraged the puritan tendency. Britain's middle and upper classes used soccer to chastise the working classes for their lack of patriotism. Some newspapers refused to publish match results, and on September 8, 1914, *The Times* published a letter from the temperance leader N. F. Charrington to the king, saying the game's continuance during the fighting was a disgrace. Later that season, when Charrington rose to make a speech on military recruitment at half-time at a game at Craven Cottage, he was dragged away by two Fulham officials, even though he had permission to speak. The puritans

hassled soccer until 1916, when the FA curtailed the game and conscription was introduced.

The FA had resolved that in future wars it would put out more
flags. When Chamberlain croaked over the wireless that sunny Sunday morning that "consequently this country is at war with Germany,"
the association suspended all soccer, just three matches into the season.
A Bolton fan named J. H. Dilworth took his club to court demanding
the refund of his season ticket, but was told to forget it. The judge
pointed out that no one had got their money back when King Edward
VII's coronation was postponed because of illness. Southend did re-
imburse its season-ticket holders, though.

But the Home Office said it wanted recreation to continue as
much as possible. So, within days of banning soccer, the FA unbanned
it again. Now regional leagues and friendly matches were permitted,
though crowds could at first be no larger than eight thousand. The
restriction seemed unnecessary: almost no one came to watch these
pointless early wartime games. "The passion of the players had
dropped to almost zero, and the public would rather go to the cinema
or walking," grumbled an Ajax Amsterdam member living in London,
in a report he wrote for the *Ajax-Nieuws* in September. He said
Chelsea had recently played Southampton before fewer than two
thousand spectators in a ground that could fit seventy thousand.
"Imagine the desolate sight. . . . Some time ago the Ajax veterans'
team drew a larger crowd on Saturday afternoon. . . . So you see, on
the soccer front, too, nothing is stirring and people feel that 'something' has to happen."

The social researchers of Mass Observation agreed. "Only 9 percent [of pre-war soccer fans] continue to attend *regularly!*" they noted
in a report on sport on December 13, 1939. Mass Observation, es-
tablished by the anthropologist Tom Harrisson in 1937, was one of
the first bodies to try to find out what the man in the street thought
by asking him. This revolutionary method produced surprising results.
George Orwell, for instance, was fascinated by the finding that many

people could not understand official propaganda: most thought "immorality" must always refer to sex, while one man thought "movement" had to do with constipation.

Working-class sport was exactly the sort of pursuit that official Britain ignored but Mass Observation did not. "Sport is the biggest English industry," its report began. "The amount spent in betting alone each year is more than the amount of money spent in the largest staple industry, building, and much larger than the nation's milk bill."

Now the war was destroying sport. Mass Observation found that most soccer fans no longer went to matches, either because they were working on Saturday afternoons, or because of travel difficulties, blackouts, evacuations, or cancellations of matches. Others scorned the meaningless regional games. Nearly half of all supporters said the war had lessened their interest in sport (though 9 percent said the war had increased it).

Yet interest in sport, however diminished, remained strong. Forty-nine percent of those polled by Mass Observation read the sports news more closely than the war news; only 30 percent read the war news more closely. As Mass Observation concluded, "People find the war at present completely unsatisfactory as a compensation for sport." Yet newspapers had slashed their sports coverage since the start of war, and most sports publications had closed. (One of the rare survivors, the *Sporting Record*, ran the fantastic headline seventeen days after war began: "If Only Hitler Had Played Cricket He Wouldn't Have Had Such An Un-Sporting Record.")

In short, an unofficial Britain was yearning for its pre-war sport. The report said, "Sports like soccer have an absolute major effect on the morale of the people, and one Saturday afternoon of League matches could probably do more to affect people's spirits than the recent £50, 000 government poster campaign urging cheerfulness, even if it were repeated six times over and six times better, as it easily could be."

But soccer picked up as the war took time to get started. Most British professional soccer players spent the first few months of "phony war" in barracks, or working as policemen or air-raid wardens, with almost nothing to do. The Germans had yet to start bombing, and until Hitler invaded France in May 1940 no British troops went to the Continent. There was ample time for soccer.

The regional soccer of wartime soon acquired a jokey character. Players hitch-hiking to a match from distant barracks would some-times arrive only after kick-off or not at all, and chancers in the crowd would volunteer to take their place, so that they could say for ever af-terwards that they had played for Manchester United. No one trained much. But a lighter, more entertaining soccer ensued. Players showed off tricks, knowing that results hardly mattered in the various contrived regional cups and leagues and constant friendlies. The average number of goals per game doubled, from three in the last pre-war season to six in the first months of war. On New Year's Day 1940, the *Manchester Guardian* said goalkeepers "must be questioning the wisdom of Dr. Johnson's preference for being attacked rather than ignored." The game also grew friendlier: the traditional post-match handshake between opposing players is said to date from World War II.

By the time the war arrived in Britain, soccer had reemerged. Late in May 1940, as the German Army reached the French coast at Boulogne and the British Expeditionary Force appeared trapped near Dunkirk; as Harold Nicholson, Parliamentary Secretary at the Ministry of Information, said that shortly "the Germans may land thousands of men in Britain" and the War Cabinet debated making peace with Hitler—at this time Huddersfield made a nine-hour motor trip to London for the War Cup. Then, while British soldiers were being rescued from Dunkirk by the armada of little boats, Chelsea–West Ham drew a crowd of 32,797 in London. The racing correspondent of the *Daily Mail* reported after the fall of France, "The people were stunned by the news just after the first race at Wolverhampton yesterday but, of course, carried on and presumably

the meeting today will go through, if only as a gesture of stoutness."
(The crucial phrase in this sentence is "of course.")

There were angry letters to the *Radio Times* about the immorality
of reporting sports results at such a time, but others thought the
steadfast devotion to sport demonstrated British fortitude. No mere
war could stop soccer. The president of the Football League said in
July 1940 that while the coming season would be very difficult, what
with possible invasion attempts, evacuations, and so on, there was
no reason not to continue.

One difficulty he had not foreseen was the Blitz. On August 24,
1940, the Luftwaffe, which had previously mostly been bombing
Kent airfields, dropped its first bombs on London. It may have been
an accident—the pilots did not know where they were—but the RAF
retaliated over Berlin. From September 1940 through the following
May, London was bombed almost nightly. The docks were a particular
target, and the nearest clubs, Charlton and Millwall, suffered terribly.
So many locals were evacuated, and so great was the fear of bombs,
that at times Charlton drew crowds of three hundred or so in a stadium that could accommodate seventy thousand. "It looked a bit
desolate really," said Croker, who by then had got into the Charlton
team as other players disappeared into the services. "And if it was
wet, the chances are that when you came out of the tunnel there
wouldn't be anybody on the terrace opposite you." He thought Millwall was more dangerous, though: "The visitors' changing room had
a glass roof."

People in many cities grew afraid of coming to matches, as stadia
were obvious targets. Yet though the Germans conducted "Baedeker
raids" on cultural landmarks, it never seems to have occurred to them
to bomb a soccer match. Many British and German grounds were
bombed (Selhurst Park and Birmingham's St. Andrews several times),
but never during a game. This makes sense, since the raids were almost
always at night. However, Helmut Schön, a wartime German international and manager of West Germany when they won the 1974

World Cup, would claim long after the war "that the English were too tied to the game of soccer to bombard a full stadium." It wouldn't have been fair play.

III.

The British authorities did nothing to discourage soccer during the war. There was no need to worry about shirkers in this war, as conscription had long since been introduced, and in any case almost all the troops were just hanging around their barracks in Britain. The war was going to last for years, and if working men could be given a treat on Saturday afternoons at little expense, why stop it? Most people agreed. Mass Observation could not find a single peacetime fan who opposed the game continuing in wartime. "Even more amazing, only two percent of those who professed no interest in sport at all during peacetime were against sport in wartime." (These people might have opposed sport in peacetime, too.)

But the authorities did not merely tolerate soccer; they did their utmost to keep it going. Most accounts of the British wartime game emphasize the constraints: the small crowds, the regional leagues, the incomplete kits. Wartime soccer, like wartime jam, is always depicted as ersatz. Yet the truly remarkable fact is how *little* the game was disrupted. Many of the prohibitions that characterized the British war barely touched soccer. Crowds numbering tens of thousands were allowed to gather in stadiums in the midst of the Blitz; teams traveled long distances to matches while official posters urged "DON'T TRAVEL unless it is absolutely necessary" and while petrol was being imported from the United States by convoys that were often sunk by U-boats; new kits were provided, if less often than before, even as Britons were urged "to be seen in clothes that are not so smart." Orwell and others grumbled about horse racing continuing unhindered (it was considered the sport of the rich), but no one seems to have attacked soccer.

Wartime soccer was a gift the upper classes gave to the working classes. This was the "people's war." Victory depended on the working classes remaining willing to fight. That rendered the traditional class divide an embarrassment. The ruling classes, brought up on cricket, rugby, and shooting, felt obliged to reach out to the masses. They planned a postwar National Health Service and universal secondary education, and they began showing an interest in the people's game. Soccer entered the communal British soul during the war as it never had before. If ever national unity was embodied in wartime, it was in the packed crowd at a charity soccer international with hordes of dignitaries in dutiful attendance. "The Royal Box was nearly always crowded when we played a charity international at Wembley during the war," wrote Hapgood in *Football Ambassador*. "At one match there were seven Cabinet Ministers present." It is a tally that may never have been equaled since.

The king and queen, Winston Churchill and his wife, the Norwegian king, and the New Zealand prime minister all showed themselves at soccer grounds, and General Bernard Montgomery, while plotting the invasion of Europe, often went to watch his local club Portsmouth. (In 1944, when he probably had other things on his mind, he was made club president. He would keep the post for decades, one of many British servicemen to take from the war a lasting affection for Pompey.)

Montgomery seems genuinely to have liked soccer, but some of the other dignitaries forced to attend games must have suffered dreadfully. Hapgood tells a story of a wartime match against Wales that even today makes you wince with embarrassment:

> Usually, when distinguished persons inspect us, they just shake hands and pass on. But this afternoon, when Mr. Brook Hirst, chairman of the Football Association, presented me to His

Majesty, the King paused and said, "How many times have you played for England?" I replied, "Forty-three, Sir." The King then asked, "How old are you?" "Thirty-four, Sir." The King gave me a friendly smile, "The same numbers reversed," he said. Odd that, until that moment, I hadn't noticed the coincidence.

In similar vein is the letter West Ham received later in the war from Major Frank Hopkinson, commanding officer of the Hammers' player Dicky Walker in North Africa. Hopkinson wrote to say what an excellent, brave sergeant Walker was, and to ask "how the old club is doing." He then admitted, "I am afraid that I didn't play soccer as you know it! I went in for those games called Rugger and Hockey! They did me very well—I had the honor of playing for the Midlanders at Rugger and Cambridge University and England at Hockey. However, I always enjoy a good soccer match!!!" It was brave of him to write (he wrote again later to say that Walker had been mentioned in dispatches) and West Ham reprinted his letters in its match programs.

The war changed in the summer of 1941, when Hitler invaded Russia, and the air raids on Britain declined. Some of the sandbags clogging London streets disappeared, theaters reopened, life became easier, and soccer began to recover. All kinds of games were played, by army, navy, and RAF teams as well as by clubs. Charity internationals between England, Wales, Scotland, and the gaggles of foreigners exiled in Britain became so frequent that an FA committee reported in May 1943, "It is a fact of no little interest that war-time has seen an increase rather than, as might have been expected, a decrease in the number of matches on an international basis."

From 1942 onward, the plainer it became that Britain would win the war, the more people went to soccer. On Boxing Day 1942, 323,000 saw the opening matches of the War Cup, and the four quarter-finals in April 1943 drew more than one hundred thousand spectators between them. By January 1945 attendances were 40 percent up on the previous year. Soccer was as good as back.

IV.

The FA library on Soho Square contains two tomes of an unpublished 1972 Ph.D. thesis by an Ohio State University student. John
Ross Schleppi's *History of Professional Association Football in England
During the Second World War*, from which I have borrowed liberally
in this chapter, is the sort of book that could never be written again.
Schleppi traveled around Britain at about the turn of the 1970s in-
terviewing aging soccer luminaries such as Bill Shankly, Joe Mercer,
and Stan Mortensen, who seemed delighted to reminisce at length
about the war with a young American. The clear impression from
their interviews is that they seldom let the Second World War in-
terfere with their soccer. Arsenal's Denis Compton confided that
he thought the war "was the best time of my life as far as soccer
was concerned," and Mercer told Schleppi, "For seven years I probably played twice, sometimes three times a week. . . . It was a funny
kind of thing in the war. . . . Sometimes I didn't know who I was
playing for: the army, the command, the unit, England, or the club.
I know once the C. O. said when I wanted a pass to play, 'Mercer,
I don't know whether you want a pass to come into the camp, or
to stay out!'"

Many of the best players seem to have experienced the war as an
endless soccer match. Stanley Matthews, for instance, played so many
games for so many different sides that in August 1943 his club Stoke
City publicly proclaimed itself extremely dissatisfied with his conduct.
He had not played a game for Stoke since war broke out.

Even being sent to serve abroad was seldom an obstacle. Sir Tom
Finney told me, "When I was called up I thought, well, I'm not going
to see much soccer. I knew we were going to a hot climate, but I
didn't know where until we arrived. And of course it was Suez, Egypt.
I was stationed at a base depot there and playing an awful lot of
soccer really. And athletics, and generally, you know, it was a real

surprise to me. Because they had a very good side there, called the Wanderers, which was pretty well a semi-professional team really."

I asked Sir Tom if he had returned from abroad a better player.

"Oh, absolutely, yes," he said. "I was more or less a seasoned player when I came back."

V.

Millions of Britons seem to have spent much of World War II thinking about soccer. This jars with the way we now recall Britain's war—Dunkirk, the Blitz, Burma, D-Day—but it makes sense. The first few months of the British war are often referred to as the "phony war," but in fact the same phrase could be applied to much of the rest of the conflict too. About thirty thousand Londoners were killed by bombs, and other cities suffered terribly too. It would be mad to minimize any of this, but on the whole, outside the capital, danger was the exception. For most of the war, most Britons, even most young men, were stuck on the island with little to do. It has since become customary to remember the heroism rather than the tedium. Jack Rollins's *Soccer at War*, for instance, concludes with a roll of honor of nearly eighty professional soccer players who fell in the war. But analyzing his list yields surprising results.

Establishing how all the players on Rollins's roll died is impossible. Many were definitely killed by the enemy. (To name but a few: Carr of Sheffield United and Roberts of Nottingham Forest were both reported killed in action in June 1940, presumably in France; Lieutenant Harry Goslin, captain of the Bolton Wanderers team that had joined up together at the outbreak of war, died in action with the Central Mediterranean Forces in 1943; Arsenal's full-back Cyril Tooze fell in Italy in February 1944, a month after his sometime teammate Flight Sergeant Bobby Daniel was reported missing after flying operations.) But a startling proportion of the men on Rollins's list were killed in traffic accidents (this at a time when cars and even motorbikes were scarce). After car headlights were banned in September 1939 there had been a doubling in the number of road accidents. Headlights were quickly restored and now equipped with masks that threw a narrow beam straight downward, which did not help much. The Home Guard—a nationwide volunteer force— added to the challenge of driving by occasionally firing at cars at night, or erecting tripwires made of clothesline across the road. Drunken soldiers returning to camp late at night were particularly vulnerable.

The accident toll among soccer players was remarkable. In June 1940 Tom Cooper of Liverpool, Derby and England died in a motorcycle accident. Six months later the former Arsenal center-forward Jack Lambert, who ran the club's nursery at Margate, was killed in a motor accident. In 1941 the Luton keeper Coen died in a flying accident, and J. R. Smith, the Millwall and England winger, was hit by a crane in an accident in the docks but survived. Chivers of Blackburn died in April 1942 in a pit accident. Preston's Tom Taylor was killed in the same month in a motorcycle accident near his army camp, six days after scoring a hat trick in a guest appearance for Middlesbrough. Jack Wilkinson of Sheffield Wednesday died on his motorbike on February 13, 1943, the same day Stan Mortensen was almost killed in a practice parachute jump. Four months later the Barnsley outside-right George Frederick Bullock died in a road accident. The former Arsenal and England player Herbie Roberts succumbed to the skin infection erysipelas in Middlesex Hospital on June 19, 1944. (Arsenal players seem to have been particularly unlucky.)

In the month Roberts died, the Allies landed in Normandy. This was one of the most dangerous passages of war for British soldiers, yet I cannot find a single record of a professional soccer player dying in the campaign. At least two were wounded, though: Robinson of Barnsley lost a leg in Normandy (the FA would refuse his club permission to stage a benefit match in his aid), while Bob Thyne of Darlington was blown up by a mine. But he had recovered sufficiently by October to play for Scotland against England in front of a crowd of ninety thousand at Wembley.

All these deaths and wounds were horrendous. However, for British professional soccer players serving in World War II, danger seems to have been rarer and more banal than one might imagine.

VI.

When I was a student in Berlin in 1990, one of my professors once described to me how his secretary bullied him. She decided whom he could meet and where he had to be all the time. This sort of strictness was considered fairly standard in Prussia, and my professor did not seem to mind. He said, "You know, I have a lot of respect for women. I was raised by women. All the men had stayed in the war."

The year I lived in Berlin, which was the year after the Wall fell, I was constantly struck by how much Germans had suffered in the war. Not nearly as much as the Jews and Slavs and others they had slaughtered, but suffered nonetheless. Waiting at a bus stop in West Berlin once, I fell into casual conversation with an old woman who told me she was going to visit her ailing sister-in-law in the East. They hadn't seen each other in the twenty-eight years the Wall had stood, but had remained close, largely because they were both mourning the same man. "My husband disappeared in the last few days of the war," said the woman chattily. "I think the Gestapo came for him. Afterwards I went looking for him everywhere, but neither hide nor hair. His sister misses him terribly too." Then the bus arrived, and we got on.

Germany in 1945 has been described as a "moon landscape," with millions of its own people dead. Stalingrad alone had claimed eight hundred thousand German soldiers, while Allied bombs killed six hundred thousand civilians, ten times as many as died in the UK. More houses were destroyed in Hamburg alone than in all of Britain. Yet even in those last days of war, on April 22, 1945, with the Allies virtually at the gates of Munich, the city's two big clubs Bayern and 1860 Munich met in a friendly. (In case you are interested: Bayern won 3–2.) German soccer had continued for most of the war almost as if nothing had changed.

I once saw a German match of 1943 between Hamburg SV and First Vienna, preserved on a Belgian newsreel. It seems to have been the semi-final of the championship, but there was some pretty poor soccer on display: one player accidentally punches a ball into his own net, and later a goalkeeper stands motionless as a soft, bouncing shot finds his far corner, though he does raise an arm in contrition afterward. Another goal prompts a pitch invasion, in which the most notable participant is a man with a briefcase, waving his hat in abandon, a beam of light falling on his face. You would never have guessed there was a world war on.

Watching footage of the various German war finals, you get the impression that spectators were always smiling, that female fans outnumbered men, and that no one in the Reich wore Nazi or SS uniforms. That was how the cameramen chose to depict it. The Nazis never sought to turn wartime soccer into a Leni Riefenstahl–style extravaganza. The point of the game was distraction, not propaganda: soccer was a space where Germans could escape from the war, where life continued as it always had. The great forward Fritz Walter, mobbed by German sailors on a boat in Italy in the middle of the war, would later reflect, "For them I am the embodiment of concepts that seem to be lost forever: peace, home, sport . . ."

The German game soldiered on throughout the terrible years. It had paused briefly for two months on the outbreak of war, but then resumed and survived almost unbroken until the autumn of 1944. Air raids were so frequent by then that kick-off times were often kept secret until shortly before the game, yet seventy thousand people attended the 1944 league final a few days after the D-Day landings. Guest players were permitted, many smaller clubs folded, and teams sometimes started games with fewer than eleven men, but, unlike in Britain, fully competitive soccer continued.

Both Germans and Britons remarked during the war on the surprising resources the Reich devoted to soccer. The official match program for the German War final of 1940, after boasting about the number of games being played, smirked, "And that while at the same hour the men and women of the British Isles fearfully await the German general attack, where the pitches of English soccer clubs have been ploughed and torn up, in the hope that this panic measure might be of some use at the decisive hour." (Trenches had indeed been dug in some British school and amateur pitches.) A crowd of eighty thousand would watch that day's German final, the writer added.

The reason the Nazi authorities were even more encouraging toward soccer than the British was that they were less sure of their people. It was relatively easy for Churchill to make the case for fighting the war: the Germans had started it, and if unchecked they would subjugate Britain as they had the rest of Europe. Britons accepted, with only a few grumbles, that their living standards had to fall.

To most Germans, the need for war was much less obvious. Most of them were cheered by the largely pain-free conquests of Poland, Denmark, Norway, the Low Countries, and France. German soldiers had arrived in Holland with orders from their families to send home some Dutch bacon. However, people were less enthusiastic about a war of conquest if it was going to make them poorer, and in 1941 many Germans had grave doubts about the wisdom of invading the Soviet Union.

In Britain, the rhetoric was of sacrifice. But few Germans saw why they should make sacrifices for a war that was supposed to make them richer. The regime was therefore always trying to persuade them how much of their pre-war existence remained intact. Hitler was angry when food coupons were introduced in 1939, and indeed a wave of passive resistance immediately swept industry, notes the social historian Tim Mason. Rations remained higher in Germany than in Britain throughout the war, as the Nazis tried to provide Germans with both guns and butter. But providing soccer was cheaper.

From the day the Nazis seized power they had begun swallowing all of German society. Every institution from primary school to dentists' association was Nazified, given an approved leader, and had tabs kept on it. The giant Nazi Kraft durch Freude ("Strength through Joy") association grew until it had become everything from theater company to travel agency to nationwide sports club. The KDF spurred companies to build sports fields, hire coaches, and establish teams with such vim that by 1940 it could claim about eight million people playing games under its aegis. The regular sports clubs had about three times fewer. Their numbers shrank further as the war went on, while a profusion of services teams emerged. Some of these, sponsored by soccer-mad officers, were soon thrashing famous clubs.

The Nazis never quite trusted the game, though. The thousands of German soccer clubs, fervently supported, mostly pre-dating the regime, were an alternative focus for the loyalty of millions. A sports club is a mighty thing: a group of people in one town with a shared passion and communication channels. Soccer always had the potential to jump up and bite Nazism on the nose. No totalitarian regime could tolerate that. The Nazis seemed destined to abolish soccer clubs. The KDF, in particular, was keen to displace the clubs altogether. (So, at different times, were the SA and the Hitler Youth. The internal struggle between Nazi bodies has been described as "institutional Darwinism.") Late in the 1930s there was talk of merging clubs with KDF works teams to create one sports association for each town, run, of course, by the regime. A few mergers did occur: one, in 1938, produced the future professional soccer club Vfl Bochum.

But the regime knew how attached fans and members were to their clubs, "most valuable property of the German *Volk*," in the words of the *Reichssportführer* himself. In 1942 Hitler decided to let the clubs be. There would be time to deal with them after the war, when things were quieter. (In fact, after the war it would be the Allies who briefly banned German clubs.)

For the while the Nazis let most clubs continue much as before. Each one was assigned a *"Dietwart,"* a sort of political commissar, and sometimes players were tested on important facts like the date of Hitler's birthday, but the clubs were allowed to continue choosing their own chairmen, a gross breach of Nazi custom. And every now and then they would do something irritating. In 1940, Bayern Munich's players took the opportunity of a friendly match in Switzerland to visit the club's former Jewish chairman Kurt Landauer in his Geneva exile. The Nazis were furious. The bonds within a club were just too strong for them.

When the Germans invaded Holland, they caught up with Landauer's brother Franz, who had sought refuge there before the outbreak of war. He was sent back to the Reich to stand trial on some charge or other, and his escort on the journey, a Gestapo man, happened to ask whether he was related to the Landauer of Bayern Munich.

"That's my brother," said Franz Landauer.

"Oh, that's fine. I'm a Bayern fan," said the Gestapo man. And they had a relatively pleasant journey. Franz Landauer was acquitted at trial, but later died in Westerbork.

Soccer could be a dangerous alternative passion to Nazism, and the most dangerous and passionate fans in the Third Reich were probably the Austrians. They had begun turning against Germans as the war grew grimmer, and the only place where they could express these feelings safely was the soccer stadium. You would never know this from reading the Austrian FA's official 1964 history of the Austrian game. It says only, "Sport too, was crushed under bombs in the years of the tragic interlude, and Austrian soccer awoke from the ruins to new life in the April days of 1945." However, that is nonsense. Austrian clubs played in German soccer during the war, and when they met German teams riots were common. The Security Service of the SS reported after a match in Vienna in 1940 between Rapid and the German side Fürth: "The trouble went off when the referee entered the field and it became known that he was a Berliner. He was greeted with whistles and jeers. . . . There were enough opposition elements in the crowd who, with the slogan 'Against the Germans of the Old Reich,' managed to carry with them those of good will and party members."

When the German club Schalke visited Vienna later that year, the SD reported anti-German chants, fights, stone-throwing, and fanatical support for the home team among the tens of thousands of spectators, writes the historian Michael John. The Schalke team bus was demolished, and the tires slashed on the limousine of the Gauleiter of Vienna, Baldur von Schirach. It could only have happened at a soccer match.

VII.

"Many are dead, and many don't trust themselves to speak," Albert Sing told me on the phone.

Alone among Germany's wartime internationals, Sing in 2001 was both very much alive and positively eager to speak. When I arrived at the station of the beautiful Swiss lake town of Lugano he was waiting for me, a sturdy little man in his early eighties with spiky white hair and a dog. First things first: Sing gave me a tour of the town, while talking unceasingly in the Swiss-German accent he had acquired over the last half century. He had come a long way from the Eastern Front.

When Germany had played their last pre-war international just four days before the invasion of Poland (a 2–0 defeat to Slovakia in Bratislava), Sing had been nowhere near the national team. He was still just a budding young soccer player with the Stuttgarter Kickers. Nor did he seem likely to get a chance soon, as most soccer players were called up on the outbreak of war. Everyone had to be seen to be doing his duty.

But this was just propaganda. In fact, war had made it all the more imperative that the national soccer team continue playing: Germans had to feel their lives had been only mildly disrupted, as in a rail strike or a snowstorm. In those early days of war the Foreign Minister Von Ribbentrop wrote that he "placed the highest value on German teams appearing abroad and foreign teams coming to Germany." The Third Reich would play thirty-five internationals from the outbreak of war until November 1942.

Eventually Sing, the dog, and I arrived at the family villa outside Lugano. It was perfect in a Swiss sort of way: a neat garden, a pendulum clock, paintings of local landscapes, and a photograph of a grandson on the wardrobe. The Sings had lived here ever since he briefly coached the local club decades before. His wife, a German-speaker from the Alsace, brought coffee, and in the hours of our conversation she returned with endless refills until I was virtually bursting. Sing just kept talking. I had expected a man who had played soccer for Nazi Germany and fought on both Western and Eastern Fronts to be reticent in telling a journalist about his life, but he was delighted to be given the chance.

Sing was born in a village near Stuttgart just after the Great War, one of seven children of impoverished parents. In summers he was sent to work on his aunt's farm, where they would all go to bed early to save electricity. He remembers his aunt starting her bedtime prayer, "Our Father, who art in heaven," and falling asleep before she finished. "Since I was a boy, I had to fight," Sing concludes. It is his favorite theme.

Then came war. "I was on the Western Front from the first day, May the eighth, nineteen"—he pauses briefly, trying to work it out— "forty. We went through Luxembourg and Belgium into northern France and stayed at the front until the French campaign was over. I was in communications. Thank God I never got into a situation where I had to shoot someone. It would probably still be on my soul today."

After conquering France, he returned on leave to Stuttgart and played three matches for the Kickers. This was his first soccer in months or perhaps years, he says. Still, he must have played well, and someone must have put in a good word for him, because Sepp Herberger, who had to pick his eleven largely on hearsay, suddenly called him up for the national team. Sing made his debut for Nazi Germany at left-half against Bulgaria on October 20, 1940. Germany won 7–3, but Sing confesses, "I didn't play particularly well, and Herberger didn't pick me again. I was physically unfit because the war was demanding for a soldier." He disappeared from the national team for eighteen months, spending a lot of time playing for the Paris Soldiers eleven. This was fun, except for the day when they were running on the athletics track and French partisans threw hand-grenades at them. A couple of players were killed and another lost a leg, but Sing was unhurt.

In that terrible year of 1941, Germany played nine internationals without him, losing twice. The defeats infuriated Goebbels, who never quite came to terms with the unplanned element of soccer. "Definitely no sporting exchanges when the result is the least bit unpredictable," he noted after the 2–1 defeat to Switzerland on Hitler's birthday. Germany always had to win. To make sure that happened, in 1942 Herberger was allowed to choose a squad that would go into training camp for three weeks before every international. Sing was in it. He would play in the Third Reich's last eight soccer internationals from April through November 1942.

I had come to see him in the hope he would have something to say about the political dimensions of these matches. "It was pure propaganda, that we played in the war," he had once told another journalist.

I quoted this line back to him.

Sing said, "What really offended me is that before the match, when the anthems were played, we had to give the salute until our arms were practically falling off!" Sitting at his table, he demonstrates the Nazi salute for about thirty seconds. I feel uncomfortable, but he apparently does not. "And then afterward, when the anthems were finished, the 'Horst Wessel Song' was played as well." Horst Wessel was an early Nazi who had been killed in a political brawl; the song was the party anthem.

I asked Sing how he felt about such things in the light of history. Obviously playing for one's country was a glorious thing, but . . .

"No!" he shouted. "I am still proud today that I was in the national team, and also incredibly annoyed, because I am sure I would have played a record number of internationals if I had had a normal career."

He was also annoyed by the popular notion that as an international soccer player he had had an easy ride in the war. "Advantages," he mumbled. "I was stationed in Paris. Before the match against Romania, for instance, I first had to go to the three-week training camp in Upper Silesia. . . ." And he described all-night train journeys standing in packed trains from Paris to Stuttgart to Hof to Dresden to Breslau to Gleiwitz. "And I arrived at Gleiwitz at four o'clock, and at six we had a practice match. I went to the groundsman and got a piece of bread, otherwise I'd have fallen over on the pitch. And it was always like that, you understand?" Often he would report back in Paris after an international and then leave immediately for another.

We were sitting happily around his living-room table, quaffing coffee and listening to the birds sing in the garden and were getting on well, but a tension was emerging in our conversation. I wanted to talk about soccer and Nazi Germany; Sing wanted to talk soccer: his best matches, Herberger's brilliant training methods, prizes he had won as a coach with Young Boys Bern in the 1950s. It was not that he seemed embarrassed to talk about Nazism. He just thought other things were more interesting.

I tried again. Germany's away matches in wartime had been particularly complicated diplomatic affairs. Herberger would tell his players before the game to behave impeccably so as to win friends for their country (the old "fair play" message) but foreign spectators sometimes used the matches to stage mini riots. I asked Sing whether he had experienced hostility playing in Nazi satellite states like Slovakia, Bulgaria, or Hungary.

Not at all, he said. They always got friendly welcomes everywhere—sporting friends, you know. And he told me a story about a match against Switzerland in Bern on October 18, 1942. "It's very peculiar," he began. "I have lived in Switzerland since '50, but to this day I can't properly understand what happened. The Swiss—as far as I can see, from what I can gauge with hindsight—they weren't Nazis. But they always lived in fear, that just as he [Hitler] had marched into Norway, into Belgium and Holland, that Switzerland was a little thing he could snap up without trouble."

He told me about the game: it seems to have been a thriller, with four goals from the converted Pole Willimowski, and a 5–3 victory for Germany. (I checked these facts later, and Sing's memory was right in every particular.) Then, as the German players walked off the field towards the exit to the changing rooms, Swiss spectators queued up beside the exit.

"I came off the pitch, and the spectators were lined up giving us five-franc pieces. When I got to the changing room my hands were full of them. I still can't understand why they did it. Either they had so much fear of us that they wanted to offer us something, or maybe they felt sorry for us. Perhaps they really wished us well, I don't know. Anyway, I was very surprised and pleased. I had maybe two hundred francs. In those days we didn't get a match bonus or anything. And you couldn't buy anything in Germany, and in Switzerland you could

still buy everything. So we went shopping, got the wife a present."
Willimowski reports that they went to the casino.

We ate lunch in a restaurant a hundred yards from Sing's house,
at a table in the shade beneath the trees. He told me he came here
all the time, and always ate the same dish, which I had to have, too.
But when the waiter came, and Sing tried to explain in German that
we would both have the risotto with liver, the man could not understand him. Like most people in Lugano, he was an Italian speaker.
Although Sing had lived there for decades, he barely spoke a word
of the language. I took advantage of the confusion to order myself
some risotto without liver. We also had wine: it had been quite a
liquid day, yet Sing had not been to the toilet once.

Over lunch, liberated from my questions about Nazi Germany,
he told me about his brilliant coaching career in Switzerland after
the war. It was Sing who had introduced at Young Boys Bern the
Holy Ghost, the custom from the old German national team of beating a new player on his bare bottom; Sing who had chosen the West
German hotel for the World Cup of 1954 in Switzerland, which the
Germans won; and it was his successor as manager of some Swiss
club or other who had lost fourteen matches in a row, some season
forty-odd years ago. As Sing told me all this, he leaned halfway across
the table in his excitement.

I told Sing that I liked him, that he seemed a nice man, that he
was clearly not a Nazi, and that I understood he had just wanted to
play soccer. But he had ended up representing the most murderous
state in history. How did he feel about that?

Sing answered very calmly, "I didn't experience it like that. I was
happy that I could play my sport. The ultimate consequence would
have been if I'd said, 'I won't play.' But then I would have been sent
to the front."

I left it at that. Neither of us wanted to ruin our pleasant rapport
by discussing embarrassing subjects. At no point did I mention being
Jewish. I would have been discomfited, and he would probably have

found it boring. "*Bene*," he said to the waiter, and we wandered back to his villa.

I asked Sing about the pressure from the Nazi regime to win matches. Modern players sometimes complain about the pressure in contemporary soccer, where a single slip can cost a club millions of dollars. Sing said it was not so much that the party told you to win as that you knew what would happen if you played badly and were dropped from the squad. "You'd go to the front," he laughed. "That was very simple, nobody said that, we realized it ourselves." And if you were sent to the Eastern Front in 1942, you would very probably die.

But the regime was gradually losing patience with the national team. After Germany lost 3–2 to Sweden in Berlin on September 20, 1942, the Foreign Affairs Secretary Martin Luther wrote, "100,000 have left the stadium depressed; and because victory in this soccer match is closer to these people's hearts than the capture of some city in the East, such an event must be prohibited for the sake of the domestic mood." (He was apparently reporting Goebbels's comments.)

The last international soccer match of both Albert Sing and Nazi Germany was a 5–2 victory over Slovakia in Bratislava on November 22, 1942. Fritz Walter, who was playing for Germany, recalled in 1959,

> It was still 1–0 when the referee's whistle shrilled during one of our attacks. The usual minute of silence for the fallen was observed. Whereas there was usually deathly silence for these 60 seconds, there was seething and murmuring on the terraces of the Pressburg stadium. [Pressburg is the German name for Bratislava.] Slovakian soldiers were still fighting on the side of their German allies, but the masses felt no sympathy for this alliance.

After the match the German players were sent to the front, partly to pacify the mothers who had lost their sons and kept asking why others were swanning about playing soccer. "A month after the dissolution of the national team two players were dead," Sing told me.

"Urban and Klingler. They went to the front and fell straight away." Klingler had scored a hat trick against Slovakia.

Sing spent fourteen days trundling through the winter in a goods van toward the Caucasus, where the German Sixth Army had been encircled in Stalingrad. It was his great good fortune that the national team had kept playing just long enough for him to miss the battle, but he still saw enough to become fast disillusioned with the war. The war on the Eastern Front was indescribably awful for everyone involved: little food, fatal temperatures, and acre upon acre of enemy land that the simplest German soldier could see was too big to occupy. "We didn't have the people for it, and we didn't have the resources. We couldn't fight a war against the whole world and think we could win it. I said, 'I hope we'll lose the war, because otherwise I'll be a soldier forever to carry the thing on.'"

In our six hours of conversation Sing never once mentioned Germany's victims. He never denied that Germans had done terrible things, and he never offered a defense of Nazism ("It's nonsense, just as Communism is nonsense," he said), but the main victims of Hitler he was aware of were the German soldiers.

Sing survived the Eastern Front by a series of miracles. He was also stripped of his rank and locked up, by his own account because he refused to donate his monthly pay to the Reich on Hitler's birthday. Eventually he managed to get out of the Ukraine and return home to Stuttgart on leave. While there he decided he did not want to go back to the front. "At the end of my leave I reported to Stuttgart train station, and every five minutes the loudspeaker announced," and here Sing puts on a deep, mournful voice, "'Soldiers on leave to Chemisel! Platform five!'

"They were building a new front at Chemisel from the soldiers arriving there. I said to myself, 'You'll end up in a company with total strangers, and no one will ever come home.' I thought for a while, and just then, on another platform there was a train to Vienna. I knew that Karl Decker who had played in the national team with me was in Vienna. I'd been through there before. And I decided that somehow from Vienna I'd go to Bucharest and find my regiment. I rode blindly to Vienna.

"When I found Decker, he immediately sent me to a hospital, supposedly with a stomach ache. Then it was obvious how I could disappear. In Vienna they hid people: it was a game down there. That first Sunday I played a game for a Vienna eleven against Budapest, and afterwards I played every Sunday. Of course there were match reports in the press. It was completely clear to me that I was in danger of my life. If it had come out, I'd have been shot as a deserter. And for the people in Vienna it was enough if I just trained the junior team. They didn't need me to play. They didn't want me to take the risk. They said, 'Albert, leave it at that.'

"I said, 'No, I want to play, it doesn't matter to me any more, I've had enough. Let them shoot me for it.' I didn't give a shit any more. So I played. We reckoned, rightly, that my regiment wouldn't be able to find out where I was. And nobody else was looking for me."

Deserting during the death-throes of the Third Reich to play soccer in Vienna was less of a risk than it might seem. Returning to the Eastern Front would have meant a greater chance of death. Eventually Sing reported to a reserve regiment in Germany and was sent to the Western Front.

His war ended at dawn one day in late March 1945. He was driving a Volkswagen crammed with German soldiers fleeing the American advance when suddenly he found himself face to face with an American tank. From twenty yards it fired into the car. His passengers fled, but bullets pierced the engine at the front of the Volkswagen and hit Sing.

The Americans drove up and said, "Get out!"

"I can't," said Sing.

He almost died. He spent six months in a tent hospital for German POWs near Brest and was operated on several times. "And that last operation, they took out the bit that had been shot through and made an emergency exit here," he gestures down his front. "I eat and drink, and it comes out through there." I finally understood why he hadn't gone to the toilet all day. The solution was not perfect: Sing said he often dirtied his trousers. "It's not easy, I'll say that, in certain situations."

Yet he played soccer in Switzerland until the age of thirty-nine. He told me of his cracking shot from twenty-five meters ("a giant bomb," he said, in German soccer slang) that won Young Boys the Swiss Cup final against Grasshoppers in 1953. "And the Grasshoppers goalkeeper became a doctor. And in 1956, when I had an operation to have the bullets and the car splinters taken out of me, he was senior doctor in the hospital in Zurich. While I was being prepared for the operation—I'd already had the injection and was half gone—he came in wearing a surgical mask, and he said, 'Well, Albert, this is the revenge for that Cup final goal!'" When the car splinters were removed from Sing's stomach, they still bore the khaki camouflage paint of the Volkswagen.

Then I had to go to Strasbourg to meet Oscar Heisserer. Sing dropped me off at the station and said he hoped to see me again.

VIII.

At last it was all over. On May 6, 1945, two days before Germany officially surrendered, the English Football League's Management Committee met in Manchester to consider various postwar issues, among them television and its relationship with soccer. The committee resolved that the secretary would ask for details from the Association of Protection of Copyright of Sport.

On May 26, Manchester United and Bolton met in the League North Cup final. "The entertainment began fully an hour before kick-off," reported the Manchester *Guardian*, "the most arresting item being a display of energy by a one-legged man in a red singlet and white shorts who insisted on hopping around the field as a mark that United 'could do it on one leg,' so to speak."

And at six in the evening of August 6, the day the first atomic bomb fell on Hiroshima, the BBC Home Service reported,

> President Truman has announced a tremendous achievement by the Allied scientists. They have produced an atomic bomb. One has already been dropped on a Japanese army base. It alone contains as much explosive power as two thousand of our great ten-tonners. The President has also foreshadowed the enormous peacetime value of harnessing atomic energy.
>
> At home, it's been a Bank Holiday of thunderstorms as well as sunshine; a record crowd at Lord's [for the England–Australia cricket match] has seen Australia make 265 for five wickets.[1]

World wars were over for the century, but they had marked German and British soccer forever. The last era of European warfare, which stretched back into the nineteenth century, had imbued both countries with the cult of the soldier: the brave, hardy, willing man who gives his body for the good of all.

In Britain, where most of the nation's wars are still regarded fondly, this cult remains explicit. It infests the conservative male realm of soccer. The most despised figures in the English game are cowards and whingers: players who shy from a tackle, who won't run until they drop, who dive. As Liverpool's German full-back Markus Babbel said, English fans expect you to get up even if you've broken your leg. Soccer matches have become Britain's weekly enactment of military valor by proxy.

I wrote in *Soccer Against the Enemy* that British managers often praise their players by comparing them with soldiers. Eulogizing his

---

[1] I have taken this sequence of events from Schleppi.

England captain Bryan Robson, the team's then manager Bobby Robson told the author Pete Davies, "You could put him in any trench and know he'd be the first over the top . . . he wouldn't think, well, Christ, if I put my head up there it might get shot off. He'd say, c'mon, over the top." Few foreign managers would have understood what any of this meant, let alone said it.

Robson was delighted when another of his England captains, Terry Butcher, played out a match against Sweden in 1989 with blood streaming from a head wound. "Have a look at your skipper. Let none of you let him down," the manager told the rest of the team while the doctor stitched Butcher together at half-time. The tabloids took the same view: "You're a Bloody Hero Skipper," said one headline. It was as if Butcher's valor and suffering were in some way comparable to those of the troops in Passchendaele or Normandy.

Bobby Robson may have been an extreme case (the writer Brian Glanville has noted that he seemed obsessed with the Second World War) but he was by no means alone. Butcher's head wound remains an iconic image of English soccer. And the later England manager Kevin Keegan, though from a younger generation, frequently described his defender Stuart Pearce in soldierly terms (probably copied from the tabloid press). Ireland's manager Mick McCarthy, raised in England, said in November 2001, after his team had held out against Iran in Tehran to qualify for the next year's World Cup, "For me heroes are people who fight and die for their country in wars, but in a soccer sense these lads are true heroes."

British fans express the same ethos when they call themselves "So-and-so's blue-and-white army," while British hooligans used to think of themselves as re-enacting the Allied liberation of Europe in World War II.

In other words, in the general British male imagination, to be a soldier remains the ideal. The other great soccer nations have lost this warrior cult, or never had it in the first place. The French last won a glorious war under Napoleon, and the Dutch, the Brazilians, the

Italians, and the Argentinians have even fewer military triumphs to crow about. Few of their males aspire to being soldiers, and largely for that reason they play a less valiant sort of soccer.

Germany is a trickier case. I was sitting on a bus in Berlin one day during the first Gulf War in 1991 (buses were interesting places in Berlin in those days), chatting to the woman next to me, and when she heard I was English she said, "Tell me, why do the English like war so much?" The Germans just could not understand the popular support the Gulf War enjoyed in Britain. They hated war. The German experience is that you fight for an evil regime, lose millions of men, and are then defeated. They have not supported any war since Hitler. The Germans barely have an army, and the cult of the soldier disappeared decades ago.

And yet that cult has shaped German soccer just as surely as it did the British game. A country's style of play is often said to reflect enduring national characteristics, but in fact it can suddenly be created. In the late 1960s, Cruijff and his manager Rinus Michels created a flowing, attacking, highly disciplined style at Ajax—call it "total soccer" if you like—and it became a style to which Dutch teams have aspired ever since.

In that first match of the Nazi era in 1933, the Germans seem to have played softer, slower, and more skillful soccer than the French. According to the press of both countries, it was usually like that in those days. Then Germans were subjected to twelve years of rhetoric about war, valor, strength, and above all *Kampf*, a word so central to the Nazi mind that Hitler used it in the title of his autobiography. *Kampf* literally means "struggle," but even before Nazism the German word was used with much greater frequency than the English one. A battle was a *Kampf*, any attempt to do anything difficult was a *Kampf*, and the Nazis often described life itself as a *Kampf* (often a *Kampf* for existence). Everything became an aggressive confrontation. The word was also obsessively overused in German soccer of the Nazi era. A match was a *Kampf*, a battling soccer player a *Kämpfer*, and to play in a battling manner was *kämpferisch*. After Germany lost to Sweden in 1941, Herberger noted, "The forwards are too soft! No *Kämpfer*!! Against Sweden one can only win with strength and *Kampf*, speed and hardness!!"

His words echo the Hitler Youth motto, "A German boy must be lean and mean, quick as a greyhound, tough as leather, and hard as Krupp steel." This was the sort of language that the men in German soccer imbibed every day for twelve years. Nor was it entirely new to them. Just as the German cult of the soldier pre-dated Nazism, so did the use of military language in soccer. The Nazi influence simply made it even more common. Here is Fritz Walter writing about a wartime game between his air force team, the "Red Hunters," and a Cologne side: "Both goalkeepers are under constant fire. . . . The Hunters' defenders . . . defuse the dangerous projectiles. Leine's bomb [a hard shot] whizzes narrowly past the post. . . . The men of Cologne carried their hopes of victory to the grave."

Many German match reports of the Nazi era read like this. After that first international in the Third Reich, the 3–3 draw against France in 1933, a headline in the Nazi Party newspaper *Völkischer Beobachter* had chastised the German manager: "Neither theory nor tactics will decide, Herr Nerz, but only the spirit of *Kampf*." Soon the entire German press was writing in this vein.

Any aspiring German player could understand that soldierly virtues were valued most. When the young bank clerk Fritz Walter joined the army he received a letter from Herberger saying, "A good soccer player is also a good soldier!" (The overuse of exclamation marks may also have been inspired by Nazi rhetoric.)

The Nazi atmosphere pervaded everything, and inevitably it changed the style of the national soccer team. By 1938, when the German and Austrian teams had to be melded together, the soft, skillful German game of 1933 had vanished. Now the problem was that the Germans played a more aggressive, more *kämpferisch* sort of soccer than the stylish Austrians.

The world war only intensified the German cult of the soldier. The nation's press was filled each day with the brave, manly sacrifices of the *Kämpfer* at the fronts. No doubt many of the soldiers, suddenly acquainted with the horror of war, rejected this ethos. Others probably found it appealing: after all, it turned them into heroes. And a few saw the connection with soccer. Sing told me of a period he spent under siege in the Ukraine: "It was a bitter time, I tell you. Thirty degrees below zero. Once we didn't get food for fourteen days. There was a dead horse lying on the ground with its legs in the air. We ate from it for fourteen days. . . .

"And yet I learned an incredible amount from that. Not to give up, you understand. You are only lost when you give up. In Bern they still talk about the 'fifteen minutes of Young Boys,' when we would suddenly roar back into the game. You mustn't give up!"

When it was all over, Germany's postwar authorities tried to eradicate the cult of the soldier. The army was all but abolished, references to the dead *Kämpfer* frowned upon, and the word *Kampf* itself began fading from the communal vocabulary. Yet cults that have lasted for decades do not disappear just like that. More to the point, Herberger was still in charge of the national team, and he largely perpetuated the German game of the Nazi era. In 1954 Herberger won the World Cup with a team of *Kämpfer* who defeated a more skillful Hungarian side in the mud of Bern (the image of the trenches of World War I escaped few observers). The West German captain that afternoon was another survivor of war, Fritz Walter.

Herberger would remain manager until 1964. He then gave way to his anointed successor Helmut Schön, who had played under him in the national team in the Nazi years. Schön remained manager until 1978, when he gave way to his anointed successor, Jupp Derwall. In other words, there was a long continuity in the era that had begun with Herberger in 1937. Generations of German soccer players were raised in a style of play set under Hitler.

Until about 2000, German soccer was characterized by *Kampf,* strength, and never giving up. The military antecedents of this style are now forgotten, and would be considered an embarrassment if remembered, but they do matter.

Berti Vogts, German manager from 1990 to 1998 and known as *"der Terrier,"* once referred to the "German virtues" in soccer. If he was trying to suggest that these were enduring national characteristics, he was wrong. The traditional German game derives not from the "German character," whatever that may be, but from a particular historical epoch: the decades of war that began in the 1860s. This soldierly tradition faded from German life but perpetuated itself in soccer for decades after the war, simply because in soccer no one ever felt the need to eradicate it. West Germany's 1949 constitution never had a clause about playing like Brazil.

12

OF BUNKERS AND CIGARS
The Holocaust and the Making of the Great Ajax

I.

Ajax after the war was stuffed with collaborators. In the 1950s a host of Jewish Holocaust survivors entered this middle-class Amsterdam family, and over time helped turn it into the world's best soccer club.

Getting the survivors' stories is difficult. When I first walked into Bennie Muller's cigar shop and asked to speak to him about Ajax and the Jews, he grabbed his head and rubbed his eyes. Muller was captain of both Ajax and Holland in the 1960s. He doesn't look even half Jewish with his straight, light-brown hair, but when he was four years old German soldiers and Dutch policemen came to his house to take away his Jewish mother. She survived the war, saved by her marriage to a gentile, but eight of her ten siblings did not. Muller, who like many Amsterdam Jews trained as a diamond cutter, asked me, "Must we do this? Everything will be dredged up again." Then he led me into the back room of the shop, gave me a seat "for two minutes," and talked for an hour and a half.

When I arranged an interview with Muller's old teammate Sjaak Swart, I did not even dare mention my book. The outside-right, who won three European Cups with Ajax in the 1970s, has always been secretive about his half-Jewish origins. On the phone I told him I wanted to interview him about the club's centenary. When I turned up one morning at the restaurant of the ice rink he runs, Swart had forgotten our appointment. At first he tried to send me away, but then he relented, and after we had talked for two hours I was the one saying, "No, really, I have to go now."

"Coffee?" he appealed desperately. During the conversation we had both dropped hints about being Jewish, but never quite confronted the subject. I hope Swart (known as "Mr. Ajax") will forgive me this book.

Maup Caransa, the multimillionaire Jewish businessman in whose honor Ajax in the 1960s were sometimes known as "Caransajax," sent me a friendly letter saying he wouldn't meet me. Other witnesses were dead.

Salo Muller, masseur of the great Ajax, was the only one of the club's Jews who spoke to me easily about the war. When I met him, I could see why Johan Cruijff used to knock on his door every time he distrusted the Ajax club doctor's diagnosis. The skinny physio who brought me coffee, water, and lukewarm water has the perfect treatment-table manner. For years Salo was Cruijff's personal healer. The best picture in Ajax's centennial jubilee book shows the masseur in a pair of white Y-fronts standing over a prone Cruijff, who is staring into the distance like Jesus on the Cross.

The last time Salo Muller saw his parents, he was six years old, and they were standing among hundreds of other captured Jews on the stage of the Hollandsche Schouwburg theater (quite possibly guarded by the former Ajax captain Joop Pelser). "I wanted to go to them and I was taken away by a German," the masseur recalled. "I sat screaming in the crèche for a week."

The silence of Ajax's other Jews was natural. Being a Jew born in Holland before the war is still not easy. Of the 140,000 Jews who lived in the Netherlands when the Germans invaded, more than 100,000 were dead by 1945. The survivors emerged to find their world erased. The Jewish Quarter was deserted at the Liberation, Bennie Muller told me, "It was all ruins. Torn-down houses. They had been pulled apart from inside, all the wood taken out to make fires."

Amsterdam's Jewish soccer clubs of before the war never recovered. Jewish boys of the late 1940s who wanted to play soccer had to find somewhere new. One day in 1947 Sjaak Swart and Bennie Muller played the first match of their lives together for a tiny club named TDW that no longer exists. A couple of years later they both arrived at Ajax. "I looked up to it as a little boy, because I came from a small club for working people," recalled Bennie Muller.

In fact, had it not been for the war he and Swart would never have ended up at a relatively posh club like Ajax. Both came from poor families: Muller was a classic product of the Jewish Quarter, grandson of a fruit seller named Levi Sluiter, while Swart's father sold herring at the market. Proletarian Jews like them had always played for proletarian Jewish clubs. But the Holocaust had destroyed the old clubs and changed everything.

Swart made his first-team debut for Ajax in 1956, and Muller followed two years later. In 1959 Salo Muller arrived and soon became a legend in his Buddy Holly glasses and woolly hat, sprinting to the rescue of felled players faster than any other physio in the league. From then on Dutch Jews loved Ajax. To those who had survived the war, Holland's landscape was like an empty room: the great synagogues almost devoid of worshippers, the half a table of relatives at a wedding. But that empty room felt a little less empty when you all visited the stadium together on Sundays to watch Swart and Bennie Muller, sturdy soccer players who proved that Jews weren't weaklings whom the big, strong Dutch had to save from the big, bad Germans.

When Swart and the two Mullers arrived in the first team, Ajax was a measly semi-professional outfit, unknown outside the Netherlands. But momentous changes were on the way. In the early 1950s, a child from down the road in Betondorp ("Cement Village") had begun hanging around the Ajax Stadium. Little Johan Cruijff helped the groundsman raise the flags on match days, brought the players studs in the changing room, and kept goal in their training sessions whenever they let him. He joined Ajax at the age of ten, and two years later, when his grocer father died, his mother was given work cleaning the changing rooms. Cruijff was adopted by the Ajax family.

On February 2, 1964, the seventeen-year-old with a rigid side-parting made his debut alongside Swart in an away match at GVAV (Cruijff's mother had only recently given him permission to travel to away games). Though still too skinny to lift a corner into the goal-mouth, he scored Ajax's only goal in a 3–1 defeat. Ajax was not very good then.

II.

Ajax's transformation into the best team in the world began that February afternoon, but would probably never have happened without the ill-assorted bunch of war-forged individuals surrounding Cruijff.

Not all of them were Jews. In fact two of the main men behind Ajax's rise, the brothers Freek and Wim van der Meijden, are known to this day as the "bunker builders." During the war, Freek, the elder brother, had turned the little family firm into a giant contracting company working for the Germans. The brothers built barracks and gun positions, and the bunkers along the coast that would give the Van der Meijdens their undying nickname. A postwar court dismissed

Freek's extremely lengthy defense variously as "nonsense," "fallacy," and "just too childish," and sentenced him to three years in jail.

Soon afterward the "bunker builders" resumed their usual seats in the main stand at Ajax. The club would not allow them to become members, but they threw parties and bought drinks in the boardroom after matches, and soon began to strengthen the team. In 1954 a cautious form of semi-professionalism had entered the hitherto amateur Dutch game. By the 1960s Ajax was probably the best-paying club in the country.

The Van der Meijdens financed transfer fees, gave the players cars (Volkswagens, of course), supplemented their salaries and match bonuses, and took care of any fines imposed by Ajax. They found houses for players and directors in the new Amsterdam suburb of Buitenveldert, which, curiously, was just then replacing the desolate old Jewish Quarter as the home of many of Amsterdam's Jews.

In his restaurant, Swart told me, "I had a cigar shop, Wim and Freek helped me with that."

"The bunker builders," I replied (the Pavlovian reaction to any mention of their names).

"I don't know that," said Swart. "People say that. No, we mustn't talk about that. We mustn't talk about *that*."

(In case you were wondering, Amsterdammers do not live off cigars. "Cigar shop" is a generic Dutch tag for anything resembling a newsagent.)

The Van der Meijdens eventually found a crucial ally in their long quest to become Ajax members. Jaap van Praag was the Ajax man who had spent much of the war hiding motionless above a photography shop. He had emerged in 1945 to hear that his parents and little sister had been killed in the camps, and that his wife had run off with another man. He plunged himself into his work and his club, and eventually decided he wanted to be Ajax chairman.

On July 16, 1964, Van Praag, backed by the bunker builders, took the post from his former best friend Jan Melchers. One member of his first board was Jaap Hordijk, the man banned by Ajax at the end of the war for having played "internationals" in the Third Reich.

A year later the bunker builders were declared Ajax members. About the same time, in 1965, the club suddenly began buying a string of players for sums unprecedented in Dutch sporting history. "The club's capital should be on the pitch," Van Praag liked to say. Suddenly Ajax began to resemble a professional soccer club. Cruijff told me in his mansion in Barcelona in 2000,

> It was at some point halfway through the '60s. I was the second full pro in Holland, that was in 1964, if I'm right. Just think, it hasn't been going that long. Piet Keizer was the first, I was the second.

The bunker builders had provided the momentum. But if much of Ajax's new money was *fout*, a lot of it was Jewish. The main source of that was Maup Caransa, one of five children of a coal merchant from the old Jewish Quarter.

Caransa's surname indicates descent from the Portuguese Jews who came to Amsterdam at the end of the sixteenth century, the small community that produced (and later expelled from its synagogue) the philosopher Baruch Spinoza. Caransa was a tall, reddish-blond boy with blue eyes who did not look at all Jewish. He wrote to me that he "could not remember ever following Ajax before the Second World War, as there was just no time and no money." As a child he sang at the services of the Portuguese synagogue, and by the age of twelve he was selling oil and coal from a cart. Decades later, Caransa would tell an Arab sheikh who asked where he had made his money, "Like you, I began in oil." The owner of large swathes of Amsterdam was often referred to by old friends as "the oil man" or "the Portuguese."

In 1936, Caransa's father Salomon did what most inhabitants of the Jewish Quarter spent much of their time fantasizing about: he won 100,000 guilders in the state lottery, an unimaginably large sum.

Caransa and his three brothers lay behind the front door with an axe until the money was brought to the bank. Then the family's future seemed assured. Caransa went to Paris for six weeks and blew 850 guilders, more than he had with him.

When he got home his father gave him a beating and his mother, Rachel, said, "You're too lazy to work." Caransa packed a little suitcase with a towel and a bar of soap, mumbled, "I don't need you," went to sort the washing in a Jewish hospital, and ate in a soup kitchen. In 1941, at the last minute, he married a Catholic woman: his mixed marriage and gentile appearance would save his life.

He sat out the war in the Jewish Quarter, so that if his parents returned they would know where to find him. They never returned, and nor did his brothers. Caransa was left with only his sister, Femma.

After the war he began wheeling and dealing in car tires, jeans, army supplies, and, most of all, Amsterdam real estate. He built the Maupoleum—voted the ugliest and most hated building in the Netherlands before it was torn down—and eventually he owned most of the remnants of the Jewish Quarter. "I threw myself into my work," he said.

So did an entire class of Jewish men of his generation. They never gave themselves time to think about the Holocaust. Coming to terms with it was impossible anyway. They never laid their heads on the table and said, "God, what have they done to me?" Instead, straight after the war they made children (a striking number of Dutch Jews were born in 1946 and 1947), named them after murdered relatives, and then devoted themselves to building up their own businesses because they never wanted to depend on anyone else again. The gentiles had shown they could not be relied on. If the Nazis came back, these men intended to be rich enough to save their families.

This group of Jewish entrepreneurs bestrode Amsterdam. It was a different time, a poorer city, with few large companies. The local papers were full of the doings of a handful of local wheeler-dealers, many of them Jews. In newspaper cuttings from the 1960s you read breathless accounts of Caransa buying up the city, boasting about the Rembrandt self-portrait on his wall, driving a Rolls Royce.

Many of these Jewish magnates fantasized about retiring early from business and, by implication, from society. They never did. They were probably terrified of the void. Meijer Stad only sold his company when he was eighty; Jaap van Praag, who at the end of the war had sworn to retire at forty-five, was still working when he drove his car into a canal at the age of seventy-seven; and Caransa was still doing the occasional deal in his eighties. In 2000 the Dutch business magazine *Quote* valued him at about £65 million.

Jewish businessmen like Caransa did not want to be posh, didn't aspire to chair a hockey club or a museum. "I'm not a cultured man," Caransa liked to say. The ultimate reward most of them sought was a top-of-the-range German car (Stad had a Mercedes calendar in the bathroom). Large banks and companies quoted on the stock market were too chic to go into soccer in the 1960s, but Caransa and his ilk were happy to put their money into Ajax.

Their rewards were intangible. A soccer club is a sort of family, and that is particularly true for people who don't have families of their own. Fans of other clubs began calling Ajax a "Jew club" in the 1960s, but really it was more like a postwar Dutch-Jewish family. It wasn't made up of blood relatives, but then nor were many Jewish families after the Holocaust. A survivor who was about the same age as your murdered grandfather became your "grandpa," other people were "uncles," you invented cousins and tried to resume life. For men like Caransa and Salo Muller, Ajax must have been that sort of family. Meeting at the club, they would hug and ask, "Hey, you earning any money?"

These men clustered at Ajax. There was the Jewish textile baron Leo Horn, a hero of the Amsterdam Resistance, who under the name "Dr. Van Dongen" had hidden other Jews and ambushed German munitions wagons. After the war Horn had become a famous referee, overseeing Hungary's 6–3 hammering of England at Wembley in

1953, and prompting England's Billy Wright to rate his refereeing qualities "second to none throughout the whole world." From 1945 until his death in 1995 Leo Horn took the sleeping pill Mogadon.

There was Japie Kroonenberg, who came from an even poorer Jewish family than Caransa and became his rival as a property baron. There was Cohen, a butcher from the Rembrandt Square who used to give the Ajax team a banquet if it won the league, and whose granddaughter Sharon married Ajax's midfielder Ronald de Boer.

Sometimes these magnates gave Ajax money and sometimes just services. Caransa advised Van Praag to take out a debenture loan to finance the roof of the main stand. Horn played host (often in the sex club Yab Yum) to the foreign referees starting to arrive in Amsterdam for European ties, and would sometimes even accompany Ajax to away matches. On the rare occasions when he himself was assigned an Ajax match, people at the club would smirk: victory was guaranteed. Famously, Horn once just smacked Sjaak Swart on the bottom during a game for kicking a Feyenoord player.

The "textile Jews" would often employ players for afternoon work. Cruijff himself briefly worked for a man named Blitz, making extra money by selling bargain items at a mark-up to his mother, friends, and neighbors. Ajax's great outside-left Piet Keizer ("Cruijff is better, but Keizer is the best," wrote Holland's best sports journalist Nico Scheepmaker) schlepped bales of material around Leo Horn's storeroom. The young defender Ruud Krol, who would play for Holland in two World Cup finals, learned to sew in the employ of Horn's brother George.

The Horns and the Krols had a special bond: Ruud Krol's father, Kuki, had been in the same ten-man Resistance group as Leo Horn, and had hidden George Horn and many other Jews in his flat above a café. (Kuki Krol talked to me at length about this, but after nearly sixty years was still too emotional to speak on the record. He had never managed to shake off the war. He was still paying dearly for having chosen to be *goed*.)

Even the Van der Meijdens seem to have become honorary members of this extended Jewish family—godfathers, if you like. They had no problems with Jews. Salo Muller remembers one of them (people seldom distinguish between Wim and Freek) showing him pictures of an Amsterdam synagogue he was helping to restore.

The "golden Ajax" was built on *fout* money and Jewish, but all of it was the product of the war.

III.

The non-Jewish players of the great Ajax (and there were a few) inhabited a Jewish environment that was almost unique in the postwar Netherlands: the chairman, the sugar-daddies, the masseur, a couple of teammates, journalists, Arie Haan's agent, the players' favorite baker—why, you'd almost think there were a lot of Jews in Holland.

Salo Muller says the changing room "was a wonderful environment for an Amsterdam Jew." Jews and gentiles alike would tell Jewish jokes and use Amsterdam-Jewish expressions. When the other players teased Salo Muller, the big goalkeeper Heinz Stuy would shout, "Don't let those *goyim* get to you!" and the masseur would correct his pronunciation of *goyim*.

Not that there was any tolerance for religion in the great Ajax. When Stuy and the Mühren brothers tried to pray before meals, the other players would time them: "Hey, Heinz, eighteen seconds!" Salo Muller was once forbidden from observing Yom Kippur because Ajax had a match against FC Nuremberg, but the day that mattered most to him was May 4, when the Netherlands mourns its war dead with two minutes' silence. At 8 p.m., the designated time, it is common for cars to pull over on to the hard shoulder of the motorway and pause.

Salo Muller told me, "The other boys didn't feel that involved with May 4. I do, of course, because my whole family was killed in

Auschwitz and Sobibor. Well, if we were sitting in the changing room on May 4, I observed two minutes' silence.

But nobody else did. Rinus Michels, the manager, once said on May 4, "'Boys, quiet for a moment.' But still: then a couple go and piss."

Nonetheless, the Jewishness of the environment rubbed off on virtually the whole team (even the wild-child right-back Wim Suurbier was married to a Jewish girl for a while) and on no one more so than Cruijff. There is a common belief among Jews that Cruijff is Jewish (there was a chorus of *oy vey*'s when he lost his fortune investing in a pig farm in the late 1970s). Cruijff is not Jewish, but, as Salo Muller says, "He was always surrounded by Jews."

Cruijff had a certain amount in common with Amsterdam's Holocaust survivors. Like most of them, he was the son of a tradesman from Amsterdam-East who had died too young. He too always carried his father with him (Cruijff regularly holds conversations with his father's ghost). Probably as a consequence, he too was fanatically driven. He too was a tough businessman. He even had his own Jewish family, because his mother's sister married a Jewish diamond dealer.

Many Dutch Jews I met seemed to regard Cruijff as a sort of Jewish patron saint. They recounted their personal experiences of him, always involving some sort of benevolent laying-on of hands, perhaps in the form of a spoken greeting or the signing of a Hebrew card on the birth of a child. One Jewish journalist—naturally, a close friend of Cruijff's—assured me that Johan was a fan of Isaac Bashevis Singer.

But the most compelling story was told by the late Joop van Tijn in *Vrij Nederland* on Cruijff's fiftieth birthday in 1997. In the early 1970s, Van Tijn had been master of ceremonies at the bar mitzvah of a boy named Guy, who was a keen but mediocre soccer player. As a present, Van Tijn had recorded an interview with Cruijff about the toughest opponents he had ever faced. Cruijff named a couple of professionals who were very good, but then said that the best defender of all was Guy, that little kid at AFC. He'd hardly ever got past him. Van Tijn wrote,

> I at least was master of ceremonies, but what did Cruijff have to do with it—except that he seemed to enjoy doing something like this? It was the highlight of the bar mitzvah. All super-expensive presents from super-rich uncles and aunts across the whole world (the boy's parents were wealthy) paled in insignificance.

IV.

Without Cruijff no great Ajax, but it would never have happened without the entourage either. In 1964, the year Cruijff made his debut, Ajax had competitors even within its own city: the Amsterdam club DWS won the Dutch championship that season, and another local side, Blauw Wit, also played in the premier division.

Then Van Praag became chairman of Ajax and, thanks to the bunker builders and the Jewish boosters, the club gained in allure. A player who signed for Ajax could expect extra cash, a soft job in a textile warehouse, and the chance to play with top-notch signings as well as with excellent local boys like Cruijff, Swart, and Bennie Muller.

Ajax finally achieved greatness on December 7, 1966, on an Amsterdam evening so misty that the crowd at the Olympic Stadium sensed rather than saw the team's destruction of Liverpool. "If anyone talks about the start of Ajax, they talk about the mist-match against Liverpool," Cruijff told me. "Bill Shankly and so on. He was the coach at the time."

The visit of an English side had sparked great excitement in Amsterdam. At a pre-match lunch Caransa threw for both teams in one of his hotels, he ran from table to table shouting, "I'm crazy about Ajax! I am completely confused!" That Ajax should beat the English was considered inconceivable. "It would be like an Amsterdam amateur team beating Barcelona now," Bennie Muller explained to me. "Ajax?" Shankly is supposed to have said before the match, "That's a cleaning fluid."

On the way to the game, Swart's car wouldn't start, so he, Cruijff, and center-back Barry Hulshoff had to take turns pushing it to get it going. They arrived at the stadium late and exhausted. But at the end of the match, as far as anyone could make out through the mist, Ajax had beaten Liverpool 5–1. "It was a super surprise," Bennie Muller told me. Swart said, "Sometimes you had the ball and heard sounds, but you didn't really know where you were."

Shankly told the press that Liverpool would win the home leg 7–0—"and you better believe it." Many in Holland did. Caransa, who accompanied Ajax to Anfield, losing at poker on the plane first to Cruijff and then to Keizer, was again a bag of nerves. He told Cruijff, "If you lot score one in the first fifteen minutes, I've got an extra bonus for you."

"I'll discuss it with the boys," replied Cruijff. "But you know we think in large sums, just like you."

"I never calculate a loss," said Caransa.

Ajax drew 2–2 at Anfield, thanks to two goals by Cruijff. Shankly visited the Dutch changing room afterward to congratulate the visitors on a brilliant performance.

And for the next eight years we had the great Ajax. Its game of one-touch passing, overlapping full-backs, and goalkeepers who knew how to pass a ball became known around the world as "total football." I asked Swart if that was what it was called at Ajax. "We never said that. It was a name that came from outside, from the English."

Did Ajax players have a name for the style?

"No."

The great Ajax was the sort of team that will never exist again. The famous forward line of Keizer, Cruijff, and Swart had all grown up within a mile of the ground, and Keizer's and Cruijff's parents had dated each other before choosing their spouses, suggesting fascinating permutations that never were. Certainly Keizer and Cruijff had a preternatural understanding. With the outsides of their feet they sent each other backspun passes that always bounced just so.

They were almost all local boys, with the *joie de vivre* of a village team. Suurbier would sometimes turn up for morning practice still wearing his clothes from the night before, and then lead the pack in the sprints. Gerrie Mühren, a Catholic boy from the village of Volendam, once juggled the ball for several seconds during a European semi-final against Real Madrid as if he were playing on the street. The Bernabeu stadium gave him an ovation.

Foreigners were stunned by Ajax's simplicity as much as by its brilliance. Swart's book about Ajax's run to its first European Cup final in 1969 (a 4–1 defeat by AC Milan) contains a telling juxtaposition of photographs: the Benfica squad prepares for the quarter-final by performing crouching leaps in unison, while somewhere else at the same time its prospective opponents throw snowballs. The Benfica players may not have believed that the morning after the match Swart and Bennie Muller would be tending their cigar shops.

Then one day it ended. Young Johnny Rep replaced Swart on the wing and scored a brilliant goal that had the entire Ajax crowd on its feet, except a "textile Jew" named Sal van Thijn, who sat and grunted, "I'd rather see Sjaak miss."

Swart retired in 1973 after a record 603 games for the club, missing the World Cup of the following year that would make Rep famous. Salo Muller had left earlier in the 1972–1973 season after a quarrel with the board. "Ajax's only Jewish chairman should never have let his only Jewish physiotherapist go like that," he complained to me. Ajax's only Jewish chairman resigned in 1978 after fourteen years in power. Kuki Krol recited a poem at the farewell party. The new chairman, Ton Harmsen, was considered another protégé of the bunker builders.

The Jewish businessmen left one by one as the big companies moved into soccer. On the night of October 23, 1977, Caransa, who had begun funding smaller clubs, was knocked to the ground on the steps of the Amstel hotel and driven off in a car. The kidnapping made the front page of the *New York Post*. Kurt Waldheim, Secretary General of the United Nations, said, "I condemn such actions." Caransa was released after ten days, for a ransom of 10 million guilders that he had negotiated himself.

It would be nice to say the specter of the war had since ceased to haunt Ajax, but it hangs around to this day.

13

THE MOST POPULAR TEAM
IN ISRAEL

"These Israelis must be crazy," was the general opinion in the Netherlands when Ajax drew Hapoel Haifa in the UEFA Cup in 1999. The
Hapoel chairman spoke of "a Jewish derby" and "our brothers in Amsterdam," while the Israeli journalist Eli Shvidler was quoted in the
Dutch press as saying that Ajax was "probably the most Jewish club
in the world and certainly the most popular team in Israel." In the
same articles, Ajax spokesmen were quoted metaphorically shaking
their heads.

Ajax won 3–0 in Haifa. For the formality of the return leg, the
Amsterdam Arena was decked out as usual with Ajax flags decorated
with stars of David and the names of Dutch provincial towns. (One
Israeli told me that when he first saw an Ajax home match he thought
he was dreaming.)

That night Ajax was awful. In the second half Hapoel scored from
a penalty and missed another, and something happened that I cannot
remember ever having seen in a soccer ground before: the home crowd
began supporting the visiting team. "*Olé!*" the Arena shouted as

Hapoel passed the ball around, and when the hard-core fans in the F-side chanted, "Jews! Jews!" for once they weren't referring to Ajax. At the end they gave the Israelis an ovation.

Three months later, on a day so wet it could be Amsterdam, I am fed hummus and salad in the Hapoel canteen in Haifa. Then I go downstairs to a box-room to meet the manager, Eli Gutman, who with his cropped hair and square face looks like an Israeli Army colonel. Sternly, he says, "We were happy after the match: firstly we had won, secondly we knew that Ajax had reached the second round." I say it must have been the first time Hapoel had received an ovation abroad. "No. It also happened at Besiktas." Only at Valencia had Gutman ever seen a swastika.

Gutman loves Dutch soccer. In 1994 he spent a week as an intern at Barcelona, where he had been allowed to talk to Johan Cruijff, then the club's manager, for fifteen minutes a day. "He asked me things about Israel, about religion, about Jerusalem, and whether there was still a war in Israel. I felt a lot of sympathy."

When I go back upstairs to the canteen, the players are having lunch and I am fed again. Chess is being played at one table, and at another the long-haired Croat Giovanni Rosso sits alone reading the newspaper, probably to find out what he has been up to. The idol of Israeli women speaks fluent Hebrew and, according to the Israelis, never wants to go home again.

I sit at a table with the Israeli internationals Ran Ben-Shimon and Ofer Talker. Ben-Shimon is a vegetarian—no chicken on his plate. He also turns out to be a frequent visitor to Amsterdam. "I go there for the streets of Amsterdam and the things you find as a tourist there." He grins. Like most Israelis, he was delighted when Hapoel drew Ajax.

Talker, an Indian Jew, adds, "It used to be the Jewish club."

"Isn't the chairman a Jew?" asks a bearded teammate.

"Half Jewish," I reply.

"Half Jewish, that's enough."

Ben-Shimon says the match in the Arena was the greatest experience of his career. "I did something for the first time in my life: I took off my shirt and threw it into the Ajax crowd."

Oh yes, they say, funny story about Ajax's visit to Israel: Brian Laudrup, then playing for Ajax, turned out to have a female cousin working on a kibbutz. Amid great media fanfare the two Danes were presented to each other. "She was a very nice young woman," says Ben-Shimon. "Big, big headlines," adds Talker.

Why are they so keen on Ajax? "We know from the history of our people that the people in Holland helped us at the time of the Holocaust," says Ben-Shimon. "At the World Cup final in '78 I cried when they lost. It's the history."

"History shmistory!" shouts the bearded teammate.

In Amsterdam, had they visited the Anne Frank house?

"Was she there, too?" Talker asks.

Ben-Shimon says, "I have been there before as a tourist. But not with the team. If you talk about soccer players, you know that soccer players like shopping."

———

You don't belong in Israel unless you have a bumper sticker on your car. Most cars have stickers with political slogans like "Jerusalem, without you I am half a person," or "UN—Unwanted nobodies—go home." My friend Shaul, an Israeli journalist, has chosen a neutral message: "Ajax" says his sticker.

Shaul drives me out of Tel Aviv to watch Maccabi Petach Tikva against Maccabi Haifa ("Israelis are without doubt the worst drivers in the world," he says proudly). On the way he lectures me about Dutch soccer. Shaul often cheers himself up by watching his video of "that match" of 1988. (He means Holland beating West Germany 2–1 in Hamburg, with the eighty-seventh-minute goal by Marco van

Basten, in the semifinal of the European Championship, but I always want to ask, "*Which* match, Shaul?")

Shaul hates Germans. In fact he only supports them when they play against Maccabi Tel Aviv. A friend of his feels the same way: when he visited Amsterdam he paid a prostitute to wear a Maccabi Tel Aviv scarf while he beat her.

Tonight Petach Tikva are playing at home in their cement stadium, but Maccabi Haifa, a much bigger club, has brought most of the fans. When the stadium announcer reads out Petach Tikva's lineup, the crowd chants the same word after each name.

"*Maniac*," Shaul explains. "It's sexual, it has so many meanings, it's perfect for soccer." Israeli fans are tough, he says. They whistle in disrespect at the anthem of every visiting national team. There is an ongoing debate about the propriety of this custom. Before a recent international against Austria (or "the Nazis," to use the common Hebrew word for Austrians) Shaul had written, "Austria, at last a country whose anthem you can whistle at in good conscience."

One of the Maccabi Haifa forwards playing tonight used to play for Ajax, Shaul tells me proudly. All right, he played for the Ajax youth team. Yossi Benayoun came from a barren little place in the Negev desert called Dimona, and was frightened of moving to Amsterdam, so his whole family and under-age girlfriend moved with him. But the Benayoun loathed Amsterdam. In a legendary Israeli television documentary his tearful mother lamented the ugliness and expense of the tomatoes in the local market. And there was no coriander! After various family rows, several Benayouns returned to the Negev. Before Yossi himself gave up and went home, Shaul interviewed him at the family home outside Amsterdam.

"Do you have dreams?" Shaul asked him.

Benayoun looked at him uncomprehendingly.

"Scoring on your Ajax debut like Cruijff, Van Basten, and Bergkamp?"

"No," said Benayoun.

Now he is an Israeli international, but tonight against Maccabi Petach Tikva he does nothing, except for an instant nutmeg of a defender after a turn through 180 degrees.

———

While in Israel I am told every day that the Dutch were good in the war. The Dutch myth, now faded in the Netherlands, still exists in its pure form here. My friend Oren, a Harvard-educated anthropologist, tells me in Tel Aviv that many Dutchmen wore yellow stars during the war in solidarity with the Jews. Tel Aviv is a young person's city, the Amsterdam of Israel. In a café opposite the square where Yitzhak Rabin was murdered in 1995, I drink Turkish coffee with the television reporter Itai Anghel. Other Israelis had told me I couldn't miss Anghel, because he is unbelievably tall, maybe six foot two. It is the sort of café that could have been in Soho or Greenwich Village, and although it's Friday at about 5 p.m. the beautiful young customers aren't getting ready to do nothing until dusk tomorrow. Anghel is a man of the world too. This thirty-something foreign correspondent with a motorcycle helmet on his lap has even made an item about Ajax's Jewish aspect, though unfortunately the footage illustrating the item was of Ajax's rival PSV Eindhoven.

Maybe Anghel can tell me why the Israelis believe the Dutch were good in the war. Anghel looks at me as if I am a moron. It's because, he says, the Dutch *were* good in the war. Admittedly at the start of the German occupation they neglected the Jews, but later they changed. He learned that at school.

"When did they change?" I ask.

Anghel doesn't know exactly.

"The February Strike?" I prompt him.

He just knows the Dutch were good. Anghel says I must understand that Israelis don't expect much of other countries. Most of Europe energetically assisted the Holocaust. In Kosovo, which he visited recently, an Albanian SS unit had gone from house to house with the

Germans, pointing out Jewish families. I say the Dutch also helped the Germans round up the Jews. It makes no impression.

The Israelis are right in a way: the Dutch *were* good in the war. Not the Second World War, though, but the war of 1973. When the Arabs invaded Israel on Yom Kippur, and the country was fighting for its survival, it received unconditional support only from the United States and the Netherlands. The Arabs took revenge with the oil boycott, inflicting the car-free Sunday on Holland. The Dutch prime minister was filmed cycling to work. This made a big impression on Israelis, who did not know that Dutch prime ministers generally cycle to work anyway.

After 1973 came 1974, the World Cup with the great Dutch team that made a lasting impression on Israel. In 1975 the tournament gave rise to a legendary comic sketch about the referee Pendelovitch (*pendel* is Hebrew for penalty), who takes a hooligan to court for screaming abuse at him during a game. In court, it gradually emerges that the judge is himself a hooligan who had been screaming much the same sort of abuse at the referee. The case descends into a debate about the line-up of the great Dutch team of 1974. "Rep, Rep! No, De Jong, De Jong!" is a line many Israelis can still recite.

In another Tel Aviv café I have arranged to meet Saggie Cohen, but at first I can't find him. Cohen is a soccer analyst on Israeli television, so I look for a groomed and wealthy man, an Israeli Alan Hansen. Then a small, round, bald man scurries up to me, an Israeli Winston Churchill who is at least as articulate as the original.

Cohen, who has a Ph.D. in the history of science, says that in Holland so much came together. Anne Frank (the only thing the Israelis learn about Holland at school), the cycling prime minister, Johan Cruijff—to Israelis, they merged into a single person.

The team of Cruijff was crowned by the defeat in the final against West Germany, says Cohen. "In the Anne Frank case the Dutch also lost to the Germans, and then too they were morally superior. In soccer, the Dutch élite unit does our work against the Germans."

The love of Holland had to do with everything, he says, with the blonde girls who worked in the kibbutzim in the 1970s, and with Amsterdam. "You have water, we don't; you have civil rights, we don't; you have nicer buildings than we do. Holland was the first country in Europe many Israelis visited in the '70s, when we started going abroad in large numbers. The first Dutchman we met in person was Johan Cruijff. Nobody forgets his first love."

Do Israelis believe Cruijff is Jewish?

"Johan Cruijff is regarded as an honorary Israeli. If Cruijff were to found a party here, he'd win at least two or three seats in the Knesset. Cruijff can write in Hebrew. Did you know that? At big tournaments he has a column in one of the two main Israeli newspapers. And sometimes it says at the bottom, 'Written specially for Israel.'"

I tell Cohen about Cruijff's Jewish family. (A couple of weeks after our conversation, Cruijff would be wandering around Jerusalem in a red-and-white yarmulke bearing the number 14, in town for the wedding of his Jewish nephew Pascal.) "Then he is a Jew," says Cohen. "We have the myth that Jews are at the head of every great cultural movement. We had Moses, Jesus, Freud, and Einstein, so if something like that happens in soccer it has to have come from a Jew."

Do Israelis believe the current Ajax players are Jewish? The Africans, the Scandinavians, the Greeks?

"No, no. We don't think they are Jewish. We assign that quality to them. We know exactly who they are, but we categorize people: they're either for us or against us. Ajax is for us, so they are for us in everything. And we follow them. We follow Davids, we hope his eye operation is a success. We follow Kluivert, we hope he doesn't go to jail.

"Everyone who is against the Germans is a good Jew, so the Dutch are considered honorary Jews. Ajax are the good guys, even if they aren't the most popular team in Israel." Cohen knows this because his TV station has carried out surveys. In the late 1990s Manchester United came first, then Liverpool, Arsenal, Barcelona (Cruijff and many other Dutch players, anti-Real Madrid, anti-Franco, therefore anti-Hitler) and only then Ajax. Now Ajax doesn't figure at all, after a run of disastrous seasons. Many Israelis even support Bayern Munich, says Cohen.

Bayern!?

"I experienced it in my own house. The way they lost the Champions League final in 1999, in the last minute, with Kuffour in agony after the goal: they became human. Now my wife hopes they'll win the Champions League. My wife!"

But how can people support Bayern?

"One thing: if nobody likes German soccer, you get people who say, 'Oh, but I like German soccer. It's exciting, it's good!'"

———

"I like German soccer, it's interesting," says the Israeli sports historian Eyal Gertman. Gertman, known to some of his friends as "the Nazi," just can't understand why the Israelis hate Germans so much. He even tries to explain it in academic articles.

Can he really not understand it?

OK, he understands, but he still thinks it's ridiculous. Surely it's absurd that (according to opinion polls) Israelis hate Germans more than Iranians or Russians? The strange thing is that they hate Germany more as time passes: since 1990 the polls have shown a "regression" of about 10 percent. At Euro '96 one Israeli newspaper ran the headline "Auschwitz, Wembley and Treblinka: We Won't Forget You." Unbelievable, Gertman thinks. And why does everyone support Holland? At least he would guess that the list of favorite national teams in Israel is as follows:

1. Brazil.
2. Holland.
Last: Germany. Second-last: Germany.

Gertman can see that Holland is attractive ("Nice girls, tasty cheese, good soccer"), but surely you can't support a country just because it *liked* the Jews? (Confusingly, Gertman, like many Israelis, often says "Germans" or "Deutschland" when he means the Dutch or Holland.) Gertman says, "If you look at which countries helped the Jews, then it's Denmark and Bulgaria. That's it."

Saggie Cohen more or less agrees. "With a correct historical understanding we would always support Denmark and Norway, and of course England."

Yet when the first notes of the Danish national anthem rang out before a game at the Ramat Gan Stadium in November 1999, the Israeli public launched into its traditional symphony of whistles. Here and there throughout the stadium spectators stood up and said, "Sshhhh! Not for the Danes!" and the whistling quickly died down. But still, the Israelis don't feel for Denmark what they do for the Netherlands.

Cohen points out that, for most Israelis, history consists of a very few periods: the biblical era (no Netherlands), the Holocaust (Anne Frank), the creation of the state of Israel (the Netherlands voted in favor), the wars of 1967 and 1973 (prime minister's bicycle), and, in foreign social history, the soccer World Cup (Cruijff).

But the most important story is the Holocaust. Almost everybody was against the Jews then, but it would be unbearable to believe that the Jews had no friends at all. OK, Denmark and to a lesser degree Bulgaria were their friends, but what are Denmark and Bulgaria? Countries you never hear about. Holland is more famous (Anne Frank, Johan Cruijff, Rembrandt, etc.) and yet in its smallness resembles Israel.

In the last few years Israelis have begun judging other countries based on where they stand in the Israeli–Palestinian conflict (in Cohen's words, "America and Micronesia on the one hand, all the rest on the other"). However, the traditional Israeli way is to judge other countries based solely on where they stood from 1939 to 1945. The only thing that counts is their relationship with the Jews. Austria and Germany were bad in the war, so they must have always been bad. Holland saved Anne Frank, or nearly, so it must have always been good. Just as Israel is the land of the Jews, five thousand years ago and a hundred years ago and this year, so Holland has always been the friend of Israel. Like a lonely adolescent inventing an imaginary friend, the country has made a friend of Holland. The former Prime Minister Yitzhak Shamir has said that the "unique" relationship between the Dutch and the Jews dates back to the sixteenth or seventeenth century. Shimon Peres called the Netherlands "as always, a true friend."

The Dutch Embassy in Tel Aviv is uncomfortably aware that the Israelis have swallowed a myth. But the embassy is in a bind, because it can hardly go around proclaiming that Holland was grey and cowardly in the war. The Dutch Queen Beatrix did venture cautiously in that direction on March 28, 1995, when she told the Knesset, "We know that many of our fellow countrymen put up courageous—and sometimes successful—resistance, and often, exposing themselves to mortal danger, stood by their threatened fellow men. During our visit to Yad Vashem yesterday we saw their names too among those remembered forever under the trees planted there." Then she said, "But we also know that they were the exceptional ones and that the people of the Netherlands could not prevent the destruction of their Jewish fellow citizens."

This could be read as an attempt to refute the myth. Those Dutch! And modest with it! the Knesset members must have thought. Responding to the speech, Prime Minister Yitzhak Rabin said, "Holland, we embrace you. Thousands of Dutch tulips bloom in Jerusalem. If we could we would give them all to you." But in fact even Beatrix's admission of Dutch failure was euphemistic. Very few Dutch people had even tried to "prevent the destruction of their Jewish fellow citizens."

While I was in Israel in January 2000, the country's quality press was starting to debate the Dutch role in the war. Recent official Dutch reports on the confiscation of Jewish property during and after the war had suggested the country hadn't been so good for the Jews after all. "The Netherlands still seems to be trying to avoid a full moral grappling with a past that is at odds with its reputation of resistance to Nazi barbarism," said an editorial in the Jerusalem Post. But the average Israeli knows that cannot be true. A German SS veteran who addresses a hundred skinheads in a barn in Braunschweig becomes proof to many Israelis of the irredeemable evil of Germans, and in the same way there is always proof of Dutch goodness. In the first Gulf War the Netherlands gave Israel Patriot missiles, which were installed by Dutch soldiers. The missiles weren't used, but still. When Frank Rijkaard played for Ajax, he used to vacation on the beach of Eilat. And a quote from Ronald de Boer once ran across a whole page of the daily newspaper Yediot Achronot, "My father-in-law is called Cohen and his father-in-law is called Polak, so how could I not have something with Jews and Israel?" The Israelis like to hear it.

On my rainy day in Haifa I meet Shmu'el Hacohen, an Amsterdam Jew who survived Bergen-Belsen while his family "was slaughtered one by one." Hacohen now runs what is effectively a campaign to persuade the Israelis the Dutch weren't so goed in the war. "Ach," Hacohen shrugs, in Dutch that has remained fluent over fifty-four years in Israel, "what do people know of another country? A couple of facts."

He once asked an Israeli taxi driver, "Sir, what do you know of Holland, of the Dutch Jews?"

The driver replied, "To be honest, all I know of Holland is the black soccer players."

———

When I phone Abraham Klein, he tells me I'm lucky to find him at home. He is only there because the tennis is on, Pete Sampras. Since the death of his wife a couple of years ago, Klein is almost never home.

On the evening of my day in Haifa, he opens the door to rescue me from the downpour. Klein has gone gray but looks trim in his Fifa tracksuit. In his entrance hall dozens of souvenirs are jumbled together: the match ball of England–Brazil 1970, a Vitesse Arnhem pennant, the ball from the Italy–Brazil game in 1982. Straight-backed and silent, Klein leads me up the stairs as if I were a soccer team emerging from the tunnel. He serves me cognac and tea, says Agassi has won the semi-final, and seats me at the kitchen table in a room decorated with more soccer souvenirs, among them a fine toiletries bag from the Scottish FA.

Klein hands me a number of business cards, on each of which he is depicted with a different player: Karl-Heinz Rummenigge, Dino Zoff, Carlos Alberto, Bobby Moore. Israelis apparently considered Klein a mediocre referee, not even the best of his generation, just lucky to be fluent in English. Yet at the World Cup of 1978 he became the most respected referee in the world.

But he was denied the World Cup final between Argentina and Holland. The rumor was that the Argentines opposed him on the grounds that the Dutch and Israelis were politically too friendly. Klein was given the match for third place instead, and in the final, the Italian Gonella, a shameless home referee, allowed the Argentines to kick the Dutch even harder and more often than he let the Dutch kick the Argentines. Afterward the Dutch players said Argentina could only ever have won the World Cup in Argentina.

Before I can ask Klein about this, he produces a scrapbook of the competition that someone with access to the entire world's press has put together for him:

"THIS TIME NO HOME REFEREE" (German newspaper headline) "Abraham Klein of Israel, who was unwaveringly insistent on applying the laws as they are written—with the resultant hail of abuse from the home country, when they lost, and widespread acclaim in Europe. Ironically, his brave, conspicuous performance robbed Klein of his rightful claim to the final." (From a book about the World Cup by David Miller)

THE BEST REFEREE IS KLEIN (Italian headline)

"I hope the brave, little Israeli ref, Abraham Klein, gets the final." (Brian Glanville in the *Sunday Times*)

Over dozens of pages it becomes clear that Spain, Hungary, Israel, the *Kicker* in Germany—that everybody thought Klein deserved the final. Even Jack Taylor of Wolverhampton, who refereed the 1974 final, said so.

It doesn't bother Klein. He refereed so many great matches, and only one man can have the final. "If I look back—and please be careful and write exactly what I say: I don't think that many referees in the world have had such a beautiful career." Furthermore, he was linesman for the '82 final, but if it had finished in a draw he would have led the replay.

It is hard to imagine another referee as thorough. On the way to the 1978 tournament Klein stopped over in Cape Town, where the climate was the same as in Argentina, and so he was already acclimatized by the time he landed in Buenos Aires. He says his first match there was "the most difficult of my career."

Argentina was meeting Italy in its final group match. Klein had prepared by analyzing every detail of the hosts' first two games against Hungary and France. Thanks in part to poor refereeing, Argentina had won each match 2–1 in front of seventy-seven thousand fans in the River Plate Stadium. The Portuguese referee Garrido had sent off two Hungarians in the closing minutes. The Swiss referee Dubach had denied France an obvious penalty, and given a rather less obvious one to Argentina.

"Watching these games I analyzed all the players," says Klein. "Then I could focus my tactics on them in the match. For instance: near the end of the first half against Italy one of the Argentinians fell in the penalty area, and of course eighty thousand people asked for a penalty: whistling, shouting, crying. What I had learned from the previous matches was to stand very close to the Argentine players who made the problems. I will not tell you their names."

Glanville wrote, "There was nothing more impressive in this World Cup than the way he stood between his linesmen at half-time in the Argentina–Italy game, scorning the banshee whistling of the incensed crowd."

Klein explains, "At half-time, when I went into the tunnel, I was whistled by eighty thousand people. And in the second half, when the teams were called out of the dressing rooms, I had the tactic not to enter the field before the players. I knew the crowd would remember what had happened at the end of the first half, and would greet me with whistling and shouting, which is not a good feeling for a referee. I waited until the Argentines came out of the tunnel and then I walked on to the field with them, into the applause."

Argentina lost 1–0 and finished second in the group, which meant that for the next round the team unexpectedly had to decamp from the River Plate Stadium to Rosario. After the match Klein was told to wait in the changing-room. When he was finally allowed to leave, there were still many fans hanging around outside the stadium, but for him they parted like the Red Sea. Nobody said a word.

Did Klein notice that the Argentine Jews were suffering under the military regime? "I was invited by the Jewish community in Argentina, I talked to them. The Jewish people had a bad time in '78. And I know, although they did not tell me this, that they were very frightened when I got this match. You know, sometimes as a referee you look people in the eyes and you see what they are thinking."

"Say you had been given the final," I say. "You knew that Argentina then was bad for the Jews. And you probably had a good impression of Holland."

"Not only for me, but for all Israeli people Holland is a special country. Always they have helped the Jews."

"But then surely you couldn't have refereed the final fairly?" I ask. "Unconsciously you would have been favoring Holland."

"I can tell you that when I am on the field only two things are important for me: to be honest to both teams, and to take all decisions bravely. I believe that referees are all fair, but maybe they are not all brave. At the World Cup 1978 I also refereed Germany–Austria. Well, for a Jewish person Germans and Austrians are the same. But for me they were like Dutch and Brazilians."

"I will tell you something," says Klein, after we have been drinking cognac in a fairly pleasant atmosphere for an hour. "I have spent a year in Holland, when I was thirteen years old. I was coming from Romania and Hungary on my way to Israel, in a train full of children, and on the way I spent a year at school in Apeldoorn. In 1947."

Klein didn't tell me the background, and I didn't feel I could ask. However, years later he explained to the *Guardian* journalist Rob Smyth that he had spent the war in his hometown of Timisoara in Rumania, living with his mother, her parents, and her six sisters in a two-room apartment. His father had left Rumania in 1937. Many of Klein's relatives were killed in the camps, but the boy and his mother survived. After the war he was one of 500 starving children put on a train to Holland to fatten up. The train journey took three weeks. Parents—insofar as they had survived—were not allowed to come.

Klein told me, "If you live in a country for a year, just after the war, and they treat you in the best way, then you have special feelings for that country. I don't think people knew this story when I was in Argentina for the World Cup. Nobody knows it. Not even the people of Holland."

"Why not?"

"Nobody asked me."

Klein has a lump in his throat. "Every time when I am in Holland, I visit Apeldoorn. Apeldoorn was a place for me—and not only for me, for five hundred children—if you are starving, and you come into a free country, with no Germans, where the people are nice to you. . . . I can remember our first meal, we arrived in Apeldoorn around lunchtime, I don't know when we had last eaten soup and meat. They gave us bread, we ate all the bread, and they said, 'Don't eat it all, because you are getting potatoes and meat.' I learned Dutch, of course, a little." After Apeldoorn he joined his parents in Israel. On later trips to Rumania for soccer games, he always refused to visit Timisoara. What he remembered of his hometown, he used to say, he didn't want to remember.

Holland's captain at the World Cup '78 was Ruud Krol. Does Klein know that Krol's father had hidden Jews in the war?

"Leo Horn was a great friend of mine. A year before he died he was here in my house with his wife. Thanks to Leo I knew everything about Krol, everything. But on the field Krol was the same for me as all other players."

You could have refereed Argentina–Holland without problems?

"Like all the other games. No problems. *Nussing*."

14

SOCCER SONGS
OF THE NETHERLANDS

When I began living in the Netherlands again to research this book, there were many things I recognized from childhood. These included always cycling into the west wind, living among giants (the Dutch are the tallest nation on earth), and the rudeness that dominates large swathes of national life. The Dutch are much more polite to white foreigners than to each other.

Of course not everything had remained the same in my thirteen years away. The country I had known in childhood was a socialist paradise, where students could attend university well into middle age at the state's expense, and hundreds of thousands of people never worked because the doctor had said it was bad for them. That was mostly over. In Amsterdam, the hippies and bicycle thieves of the 1980s had become yuppies, some of them stock-market millionaires. The old squats in the city center—once practically the standard form of Amsterdam living—had become penthouses.

But the main change I noticed in 1999 was a national lurch away from liberalism. The usual foreign rule of thumb is that since the Dutch are liberal on drugs and liberal on prostitutes and positively missionary about euthanasia, they are liberal indeed. This rule turned out not to be foolproof. A northern village had launched a nationwide witch-hunt against asylum seekers; there was another witch-hunt against pedophiles; and, as Euro 2000 approached, a third was starting against soccer fans. The leader of the Christian Democrats had even suggested sending in the army to control them, though given the laid-back pacifism of the Dutch Army this would probably have been pointless. The big new political idea was "administrative detention." It meant that if a group of people *looked* dangerous (say, hundreds of overweight, sunburned, drunken, topless males standing in city squares shouting in English, "Get your tits out for the lads"), a mayor could detain them for twelve hours, even if they had committed no crimes. Various African military regimes were said to be studying the same idea.

The new mood surprised me. During my years away I had grasped that the Netherlands was not the paradise of universal brotherhood I had imagined as a schoolboy, but it was still strange to find that it sometimes seemed the opposite.

Speaking to Dutch people as I researched this book, three things in particular surprised me. The first was the frequency of anti-Semitic jokes (as well as digs at Moroccan immigrants) in Dutch conversation. The second was that few Dutch people I met seemed bothered by these comments; indeed, they seemed surprised that I was. The third thing was that many Dutch Jews were distraught about Ajax fans calling themselves "Jews," but we will come to that.

Anti-Semitism in Dutch soccer has a venerable history. Ajax players have been "Jewed" by opposing fans for more than sixty years, but the practice only really took off in the 1960s, the era of Van Praag, Caransa, Swart, and the two Mullers. The most famous incident, in January 1965, involved Bennie Muller and the DWS goalkeeper Jan Jongbloed, who would later defend Holland's goal (albeit rather shakily) in the World Cup finals of 1974 and 1978.

After a clash in the penalty area, Jongbloed apparently called Muller a "pleurisy Jew." (Traditional Dutch swearing usually revolves around diseases. People urge each other to get cancer, or cholera or typhoid or pleurisy. Alternatively, the diseases can function as adjectives.) Jongbloed claimed he had merely told Muller to "get pleurisy," but was nonetheless suspended for two matches. On his return, for a European tie against a Hungarian team, he received a telegram saying, "Good luck to you and your mates. Ben Muller."

When I asked Muller about the affair thirty-four years later, he was still irritated. "If I see Jongbloed now, he tries to greet me, but for me that man is dead. But is there anything strange about it? Isn't it like that everywhere? It's something of all centuries."

Muller told me that both he and his son Danny, who had played professionally in Holland in the 1990s, had suffered racist abuse throughout their careers. "They did it to distract you from your game, and it worked, because you were very sensitive to it. It happens to Moroccan players now." But Muller said that in his day the comments had never referred to the Holocaust: no hissing sounds and the like. "It was the 1960s, so it was still a bit fresh," he explains.

That would later change. In Muller's playing days the Holocaust was only just starting to penetrate the Dutch public imagination. Virtually the first treatment of the subject in the press came during the Eichmann trial of 1961. Also in the 1960s, an almost universally watched TV series about the German occupation by a Jewish historian, Lou de Jong, and a seminal yet personal account of the Dutch Holocaust by another Jewish historian, Jacques Presser, alerted the Dutch to what had happened rather recently under their noses. De Jong had been appointed the Dutch state's official historian of the war, and from 1969 through 1988 he published his *Kingdom of the Netherlands in the Second World War* in twenty-seven volumes. Millions of copies were sold, making it one of the best-selling academic histories in history.

Soccer hooliganism also reached the Netherlands late, confirming Heine's theory about the country. Only in the 1970s did the first Dutch "*sides*," or gangs of young fans, emerge. Dutch policemen, struggling to cope with the novelty, traveled to Britain for advice. They were told to use decrepit old trains to transport hooligans to matches, which was not much help, as the Dutch had no decrepit old trains.

Ajax's "F-Side" began daubing swastikas on walls, and briefly called themselves the "SS." But the other "*sides*" labeled Ajax fans "Jews," on the grounds that Amsterdam was the "Jew city," and soon the F-Siders adopted "Jews" as their own nickname of choice. Around the turn of the 1980s they began waving Israeli flags, perhaps inspired by the Spurs fans who had visited Amsterdam for a UEFA Cup tie on September 16, 1981.

By then the "Jewing" at Dutch matches had changed character: for the first time, it was accompanied by Nazi symbols. In December 1980 the Stiba, a Dutch group that fights anti-Semitism, had alerted various clubs to slogans like "Ajax Jew club," "Death to the Jews," and "Ajax to the gas chamber." The clubs said the fans were too stupid to know what they were chanting. The Stiba replied that "the law is broken by both stupid and clever people."

The Stiba's efforts achieved nothing. The hooligan *sides* were irresistibly drawn to Nazi symbols, because the Dutch rediscovery of World War II had made these symbols into exciting taboos. At the start of the 1980s the war had experienced a revival in the Netherlands. Holocaust memorials were unveiled all over the place, May 5 again became an annual holiday commemorating the Liberation, and a Memorial Cross was created as a decoration for former Resistance fighters. Suddenly the Holocaust was everywhere. Schoolteachers, politicians, newspapers, and the Stiba were always banging on about it. The Dutch establishment clearly thought the murder of the Jews had been a very bad thing. This inspired the hooligans.

On May 7, 1982, Ajax met FC Utrecht at the end of a particularly big week for World War II. On May 4, Holland had mourned its war dead; on May 5, it had celebrated the Liberation, and a monument had been unveiled to the Resistance heroine Hannie Schaft, the "Girl with the Red Hair."

A few Utrecht fans at the Ajax game waved swastika banners and shouted anti-Semitic slogans. Two of them, Peter and Chris (not their real names), were subsequently tried in court. The judge asked Peter what had happened in the camp of Westerbork. Peter replied that perhaps a couple of Jews had been killed. He was sent to visit the camp and seemed to find it interesting. Even when he heard during his visit that FC Utrecht were playing a friendly match in the area that very day, he decided to stay in the camp. Peter had been told to write a report for the judge, and had taken a friend with him to write everything down, because he himself had a hand in plaster.

Chris read Anne Frank's diary in a single afternoon. That was rare for him, he said. A world had opened for both boys, because they had learned almost nothing about the Holocaust at school.

It didn't help. In 1982 Israel invaded Lebanon, and Feyenoord fans adopted anti-Zionist slogans from the banners at anti-Israel demonstrations. The song "Ajax is a Jew Club" soon came to seem too soft. At a match against Ajax, Feyenoord fans obligingly sang, "Ajax Jews, the first soccer deaths!" into the microphones of television crews. The Netherlands was shocked. Feyenoord–Ajax was not a marginal event in Dutch life, but the biggest match in the country's sporting calendar.

Then, in September 1986, about a thousand supporters of the Hague club FC Den Haag marched through the streets of Amsterdam-South (where many Jews lived), singing anti-Semitic songs. One of these, "Jews, We're Coming," was recognized as an echo of the German song of the Nazi era, "*Juden, wir kommen*." Den Haag's chairman Dé Stoop, a wealthy businessman, refused to apologize, saying, "These expressions flow from the fact that Ajax clearly presents itself as a Jewish club." Stoop also blamed Amsterdam's Jewish mayor Ed van Thijn (who as a child in wartime had been smuggled out of the Hollandsche Schouwburg theater) for "acting much too emotionally."

There was national outrage and talk of expelling Den Haag from the league. Stoop addressed the offending fans, saying, "You have no idea what it's like when your friends are taken away in the night and never return. I don't blame you, but singing a song like that is unacceptable." The fans apologized, but then sang the songs again for the benefit of journalists.

In 1988, soon after Den Haag fans had threatened violence at Amsterdam homes where they detected menorahs, the club was relegated. It only returned to the Dutch premier division in 2003.

The problem since has mostly been Feyenoord. If you attend a Feyenoord–Ajax match these days you will be treated to Holocaust songs and imitations of escaping gas, performed not by a gang of teenage hooligans but by thousands of Feyenoord supporters, many of them middle-aged or well dressed or fathers with children. A Dutch banker I knew in London, a Feyenoord fan, told me with a smirk that he had sung "some pretty bad things" at Feyenoord–Ajax recently. Here is a selection of things he might have sung:

> There comes the Ajax train from Auschwitz.
> Sieg, Sieg, Sieg
> > (accompanied by the Hitler salute)

> Sssssssssssssssssssssssssss
> > (the sound of escaping gas)

> What sort of Jew is that?
> That Jew from Amsterdam!
> He screws his own child.
> That is Danny Blind.'
> > (Blind, a gentile, played for Ajax until 1999)

Van Praag is a Jewish plague.
Van Praag under the circular saw.
(Michael van Praag, a half Jew, became
chairman of Ajax in 1989. This song,
like the one about Blind, rhymes in Dutch.)

I asked an elderly Rotterdam Jew named Micha Gelber, a season-ticket holder at Feyenoord, what he thought of the songs. He
replied, "I was in several concentration camps. Of course I experience
the singing as hurtful. More hurtful would hardly be possible. But
after everything I have been through I have an elephant's hide. Anti-
Semitism doesn't interest me. The only thing that would have been
worse than what I experienced was the gas chamber." More worrying
than the songs of uneducated soccer supporters, said Gelber, was that
telling Jewish jokes had become *bon ton* in the middle-class neighborhoods of Rotterdam.

It would be hard to argue that Feyenoord campaigns vigorously
against these terrace songs. On the day in April 1999 that the club
won the Dutch title, the players on the balcony of the town hall and
the fans in the square beneath shared a spot of community singing.
The full-back Ulrich van Gobbel yelled eight times into a microphone,
"Whoever doesn't jump is a Jew!" and later the club captain Jean-
Paul van Gastel admitted to having shouted the same thing. I think
this was the first instance of Dutch professional soccer players chanting anti-Semitic slogans in public.

There is a peculiar debate in Holland about who is to blame for
chants like these: Feyenoord's fans and players, or rather the Ajax
fans? One argument says that the latter, by calling themselves "Jews,"
are guilty of provoking the references to gas chambers. I found this
was a common view among Dutch Jews.

Many of them told me they hated it when Ajax fans chanted,
"Jews!" and waved banners with stars of David (or, as these are now

popularly known, "Ajax stars"). Some Jews said they walked out of the stadium when it happened. This struck me as a characteristically Dutch-Jewish response. Israelis love the chants and symbols of the Ajax supporters, whom they assume to be philosemites, and few London Jews object to Spurs fans calling themselves "Yiddoes." The difference in reaction is probably due to the Holocaust: Dutch Jews (many of whom hardly ever reveal they are Jewish) are more frightened than British Jews or Israelis because their families have generally suffered more.

Nowadays the Jews are almost alone in getting worked up about the sing-alongs at Feyenoord. The Dutch establishment no longer seems particularly bothered. Rotterdam City Council takes no action against the Feyenoord fans singing about gas chambers, even though they are the city's most visible ambassadors. The Dutch press has also ceased to take much notice. The former Resistance fighters and their coterie who ran the Netherlands' newspapers for decades are now retired or dead. The taboo on anti-Semitism has weakened.

The Feyenoord fan who sang, "We're going on a Jew hunt" in 1980 was a rebel who outraged the establishment. But my friend the banker in London is not a rebel. He and his fellow singers don't think they represent a teenage neo-Nazi gang; they represent Feyenoord itself. Don't even the players sing the same songs? And does anyone from the club tell them to stop?

Even members of the Dutch establishment now join in the fun. One evening in 1999 I had dinner in a fashionable Amsterdam restaurant with some well-known Dutch writers and journalists. There was banter between Ajax and Feyenoord fans, and after a couple of pro-Ajax remarks a TV star from Rotterdam shot back, "I smell the stale air of the Secret Annexe." (I think this reference to Anne Frank was a quote from a prominent Rotterdam poet, but I am not very well up in anti-Semitica.)

Another example: before a Holland–Brazil match in October 1999, I was chatting to a leading Dutch journalist in the press room of Ajax's Amsterdam Arena when a colleague came up to us waving a telephone lead. "I had to pay 750 guilders for this," he grumbled.

"Jew club, eh?" joked the leading Dutch journalist.

I am sure I lead a sheltered life, but I cannot recall many such comments in Britain.

The decline in the taboo on the Holocaust in the Netherlands is best demonstrated by the career of Theo van Gogh. A descendant of the painter's brother, Van Gogh made himself a modest name as a film-maker. Then in the early 1980s he began laying into the Jewish writer Leon de Winter, accusing him of milking the Holocaust for his best-selling novels. A representative sample of Van Gogh's argument:

"A touch of Zyklon-B in a country that allowed its Jewish inhabitants to be murdered almost without extending a finger is always interesting. Particularly commercially, of course." And, "Leon, what more do you have to do with '40–5 than I do? I can't glory (even if I wanted to) in deported Uncles and Aunts, Grandpas and Grandmas."

Van Gogh managed to keep this sort of thing going for years. In 1992, after a student magazine published a montage of De Winter lying in a mass grave of murdered Lithuanian Jews, Van Gogh reprinted it in his own magazine column.

Shattering taboos, which is what he thinks he is doing, is a valued pastime in Dutch art. The big taboos used to be sex and blasphemy. From about 1980 they were replaced by the Holocaust. For a minor artist on the make, being cheeky about the gas chambers became a short cut to being considered original, witty, important. It got you into the newspapers. Van Gogh's anti-Semitic provocations made him the subject of court cases for years.

But gradually the outrage began to fade. By about 2000, anti-Semitic tirades had come to be considered rather old hat. To display indignation about them was considered old-fashioned, like getting worked up about someone saying, "Goddamn!" I was often told I shouldn't worry about the Feyenoord songs: they were simply the equivalent of Ajax supporters chanting, "Farmers!" at fans from the provinces. These were just words, I was assured, nothing to do with real gas chambers. Even Herman Menco, the Jewish Feyenoord fan who went to the stadium with peroxided hair during the war, told me, "You don't think those Feyenoorders are 'crashing' because they're anti-Semites, do you? They're just against Ajax."

Of course I know that the Feyenoord fans and the leading Rotterdam journalist are not about to murder the Jews. Obviously the Fourth Reich is not about to break out. I know the average Feyenoord fan is not talking about real Jews, none of whom he has ever met. To him the word "Jew" simply connotes an Ajax fan. (This is why a Dutch rabbi walking through Rotterdam in his skullcap is pursued by shouts of "Hey, Ajax!") In other words, the usual Dutch argument runs, the comments are harmless.

That may be true, but many Dutch Jews still find them hurtful, and a Dutchman who did not lose 75 percent of his family to the gas chambers displays a certain insouciance when he tells them not to be so touchy.

In *Histoire de l'antisémitisme*, Léon Poliakov calls the Dutch a model of "good neighborliness with the Jews." This is the classic foreign view: Holland was the country that saved Anne Frank, or nearly. But it is contradicted by Philo Bregstein's chapter on the Netherlands in the same book, chiefly on the basis of Dutch soccer slogans.

Foreigners know little about the Netherlands, and nothing about what is sung at its soccer matches. A little country like the Netherlands, whose language is not spoken abroad, can tell all sorts of lies about itself in the world. Not many people can check them. I have often sat on Dutch trains listening to Dutch people telling foreign tourists in fluent English how good the Dutch are at languages, how relaxed about drugs, how much they hate Germans because the Germans were bad in the war—in short, how wonderful Holland is.

Certainly until the attacks of 9/11 changed everything, the Dutch tended to believe this themselves. It was virtually a land without dissidents, which is why the anti-immigrant populist Pim Fortuyn caused such excitement when he suddenly began saying in the autumn of 2001 that there were too many foreigners in Holland and that the government had left the country in "ruins."

In most other countries, both these claims would have been commonplaces. In the United States, for instance, politicians are always pontificating about immigrants, and whichever party is out of power accuses the other of ruining the country. But the Dutch had never seen anything like Fortuyn. The giant, bald, flamboyantly gay magazine columnist was just about the first angry populist the country had ever produced. Other Dutch politicians never said anything very nasty about the parties in government, because they always hoped to rule with them after the next election, and before 2001 no one played the race card, because the Dutch thought their voters were above that. Then for a few months after the attacks of 9/11, Fortuyn became a popular sensation. He did a new line in camp immigrant-bashing. Calling Islam "a backward religion," and saying that he not only knew "Moroccans" but slept with them, he tapped a Dutch racism that was not supposed to exist. On May 6, 2002, he was murdered (bizarrely, by a Green activist), and at the general election nine days later his three-month-old party came second. It turned out the Dutch were not so pure after all.

Before Fortuyn, the Dutch had always been happy with the smug technocrats who ruled them. No Dutch prime minister was voted out of office from 1973 until 2010. There have been Communist dictatorships offering less job security. In 2002 the Social Democrat Wim Kok became the third Dutch prime minister in a row to step down entirely voluntarily. Like his predecessor Ruud Lubbers (who might still be in the job today had he not resigned after only twelve years in 1994) Kok was for a long time nearly universally beloved, in the way a saint-like religious leader might be in another country. Before Fortuyn came along and introduced discontent, Dutch voters almost always thought their prime minister was doing a good job.

That is no wonder, because they also seemed to believe the Netherlands was the richest country in the world. Irritated at this tenet of faith, I used to go around telling them that Switzerland or the United States or some of the Scandinavian states had far higher per-capita incomes. I could see they didn't believe me. Before Fortuyn the Dutch tended to take it almost for granted that theirs was the best organized, most tolerant (too tolerant, they often said), and generally most *relaxt* country imaginable. (The worst thing is that they had a point.)

For want of better evidence, the rest of the world tends to believe whatever the Dutch say about themselves. Recently I heard a Dutch woman who had set up a project for immigrants in the Netherlands explaining on the BBC World Service how tolerant the Dutch were. The interviewer did not question this. It was treated as a truism, like the fact that the Netherlands is largely below sea level or a member of the European Union. If the Dutch say they are tolerant, they must be tolerant. Didn't they save Anne Frank? That is why Fortuyn and later his anti-immigrant successor Geert Wilders came as such a surprise to the rest of the world.

When France tries a former Vichy collaborator it has to wash its dirty linen in front of the world. There are thousands of foreign journalists in France, and millions of people outside who speak French and care about the country. Similarly, when Rangers and Celtic fans scream sectarian rubbish at each other in Scotland, hundreds of millions of people get to hear of it because they understand English and are interested in Britain. But Holland, like Finland or Denmark or Sweden, can usually keep its domestic sores domestic. The visitor is presented with a clean and orderly country.

Of the excrescences in their collective life you will hear little. In 1992 a Dutch railway policeman named Harry Meulenbroek took two American colleagues who were preparing for the next World

Cup to see Feyenoord–Ajax. "They asked me to translate everything that was shouted," Meulenbroek told a Dutch newspaper later. "Well, I left out a lot. Like the hissing and the El Al chants. You're so ashamed in front of your colleagues."

Yet at the World Cup in the States not a hiss was heard out of the cheery, orange-clad army of Dutch fans. They were making what is known in their impenetrable language as *"Holland-propaganda."*

15

DISNEYTOWN AND
THE SECRET MONUMENTS

Every city tells a story about itself, through its streets, its monuments, and soccer clubs. In the Netherlands, the subject of these stories is very often the war. The stories told about it by Rotterdam and Amsterdam, the great Dutch rivals, are very different, and neither of them is true.

If you drive through Rotterdam along the south bank of the great Meuse River, at some point you will see on the sidewalk an old wall. From the street it appears to be just a wall. It is quite blank, without even any graffiti. However, if you get out of your car, walk around the wall, and look at it from the riverside—from behind, as it were—you will see a plaque. It reads,

HANGAR 24
Behind this wall of the former Municipal Trade Institutions stood Hangar 24. From 30 July 1942 Hangar 24 served as the first collection point for Jews called up or captured in Rotterdam and in the islands of South Holland. Stop and remember the innocent who fell prey to madness and undeserved hatred.

The people who know to look at the wall from behind probably will stop and remember. The others will pass on the street side and be spared the sight. The spot is almost as discreet today as it was in 1942, when twelve thousand Rotterdam Jews were rounded up at the hangar practically unnoticed. Leon Greenman, who with his wife and child was among them, told me, "There's nothing left there, except a bit of wall and a plaque."

If, after inspecting the wall and plaque, you walk a couple of hundred yards inland, you might find Hangar 24 Square. But you might just as well miss it. Searching for it with a friend who is a born Rotterdammer, we only chanced upon the square after a while spent going around in circles. My friend, a local history nut, had never heard of Hangar 24.

Even if you succeed in finding the square, it might take you awhile to realize that you have, because unlike every other square or street in the Netherlands this one does not appear to be marked by a street sign. Only after a long search might you spot, on a bench twenty yards from a shop called Tanja's Hair Fashion, the words "Hangar 24 Square."

Above Hangar 24 Square (or as it is locally known "that square") towers a vast, modern sculpture that seems to consist of random shapes in blue and brown. It looks nice. Only if you know what the monument is supposed to represent would you recognize in those shapes the floodlights of a concentration camp. You might then realize that the round holes in the bunker-like construction below are meant to represent murdered Jews. But if you did not know the sculpture was a Holocaust memorial, you would never guess. There is no sign, no text.

Rotterdam has built a secret monument for its murdered Jews. Yet precisely in its silence the monument is moving. It demonstrates (presumably unintentionally) that the city's Jews are not just dead but also forgotten. How many of the inhabitants of Hangar 24 Square know what the monument is? Does Tanja the hairdresser know? One thing is certain: the rage for showy Holocaust monuments that has gripped Berlin and Washington, DC, has not impressed Rotterdam.

It is a freezing day, and my friend has already fled to his car. "It's the opposite of a monument," he says. Later I phone Rotterdam Council to ask whether the monument to the city's Jews is being kept secret for fear it would otherwise be defaced. The council has no idea and refers me to the Hangar 24 Committee.

Simon Cohen, a member of the committee, says the plaque on the wall now happens to hang on the riverside because the road was moved a couple of years before. He doesn't mind. "The wall is meant to be a place of reflection. It's for people to sit on a bench and look at." However, Cohen agrees that the average passer-by will have no idea what the wall and the monument represent. "You have to know," he agrees.

Micha Gelber, chairman of the Hangar 24 Committee, concentration-camp survivor and Feyenoord season-ticket holder, says the plaque has been stolen three times so far. "This one is fixed so tightly that I think they'd have to take the whole wall with them if they wanted to remove it."

I ask Gelber whether the monuments are secret.

"We don't shout too loudly about them," he replies. That would only alert the wrong people to their existence. Gelber adds that there are another eight plaques around Rotterdam commemorating Jewish sites. These are necessary, because all that remains of centuries of Jewish life in the city are two small ruins: the riverside wall, and a gate where a Jewish hospital once stood. "Otherwise there is nothing left in Rotterdam. That's the whole point," says Gelber. The result, he adds, is that few Rotterdammers know that Jews ever lived in their city. And the consequence of that is that Feyenoord fans can sing the songs they do.

The club itself also seems to have forgotten the war. Once upon a time it remembered. On the afternoon of Saturday, May 3, 1947, a monument was unveiled beneath the grandstand of the stadium for the twenty-two club members killed in the war. Since then, however, the nine-foot-high sculpture of a figure sowing new seed has disappeared like the Maltese Falcon. No one has a clue where it is.

Henk van der Stoep, a pensioner who served as Feyenoord's unpaid archivist, did some digging in the files for me and helped solve the mystery. It seems that no one could unveil a war monument without asking permission. Feyenoord had neglected to get a permit from the appropriate ministry, and when this became apparent the club panicked. Directors begged the ministry for a permit, but were turned down. "The sculpture must now finally disappear," ordered a civil servant.

I tracked down Rie Elias, the sculptress, who had retired to a small town. Delighted that someone still remembered her monument, she sent me a long letter explaining that it had offended the standards of sober taste laid down by the ministry. She had no idea where it was now. In the Feyenoord Stadium it has been replaced by a small plaque that reads, "May you remember for a moment those loyal sporting comrades lost to the club," which Feyenoord fans do by chanting, "Hamas, Hamas, Jews to the gas chamber."

The absence of Rotterdam war monuments would seem to bear out the theory of the Dutch-Jewish author Liesbeth Levy, who says, "Because Rotterdam was bombed flat, it's a city without a memory." This is only partly true. Levy is right to suggest that the city has no memory of its lost Jews, but when it comes to the bombardment of May 14, 1940, Rotterdam is like an elephant. Everywhere are statues and plaques marking the greatest catastrophe to befall the city in the twentieth century. Over nine hundred Rotterdammers died in the bombardment. More than ten times that number were transported to their deaths from Hangar 24. Yet only the bombardment is remembered in Rotterdam.

The story that Rotterdam tells is of a city that never had anything to do with Jews but was shaped by the bombs of May 14, 1940. Central Rotterdam itself is a monument to that day: a postwar expanse of skyscrapers. Arriving here, you feel that you have been transported from the Netherlands to the American Midwest. This is a place built by square-shaped men with rolled-up sleeves, the opposite of dinky old Amsterdam.

Fans of a soccer club tend to carry in their heads an image of the territory they represent. Rotterdammers consider themselves tough, hard-working, no-frills people, and they seek those virtues in their soccer team. By contrast, they regard Amsterdammers as indolent bohemians (a view that has some justification). And so Feyenoord players have traditionally tended to be bigger than Ajax players, to have heavier beard growth, longer hair and, frequently, earrings and tattoos. They look as if they have been dug out of the ground.

So do many of their fans. Visiting the Feyenoord Stadium one morning in March 2000, the first thing I noticed was a huge advertisement just outside the ground for a company called Tattoo Bob. To judge by the fans watching that day's training session, Bob had been raking in business. Their tattoos were accompanied by long hair, beer bellies, and moustaches (or, for women, big peroxide-blonde hair). One fan had brought along his bulldog: when a player bent down to scratch its ears, the question was which of the three of them would flinch first.

Feyenoord's fans are known as "the Legion." The Legion offers total commitment. Unlike almost all other Dutch supporters, it actually makes a noise at matches. When the Legion ranges beyond songs about gas chambers this can be quite moving: one of the great sensations of Dutch soccer is the Feyenoord Stadium shaking as forty-five thousand people stamp their feet in unison. The club song, "Hand in Hand, Comrades," is sung without embarrassment.

There is a tendency among Dutchmen today to posture as postwar Resistance heroes who have never ceased fighting Germans (or at least inconveniencing them by sending them the wrong way to the train station), and this tendency is led by the Legion. Feyenoord fans dislike Germans almost as much as they do Jews. Although they would say their hatred of Germans dates back to World War II, they waited to act on this information until 1994,when five hundred of them were arrested at a game against Werder Bremen. Since then there has usually been trouble when Feyenoord has played a German team, most spectacularly at a friendly in Leverkusen in January 1999.

The Legion bizarrely shouted, "Jews!" at the Leverkusen crowd and police, threw stones and iron bars at parked cars, burned down a ticket office and ended up engaging almost the entire police force of the German state of North Rhine Westphalia. The fans were offering the resistance the Dutch had neglected to give in the war.

The Dutch often refer to Feyenoord as a "*volksclub*"—literally, "people's club." In the old days, when the Netherlands was still divided into those separate "pillars," a *volksclub* meant a working-class club. Now that almost the whole country lives in a middle-class terraced house, "*volksclub*" has acquired a different meaning: it stands for something simple, genuine, "*Hollands*," the opposite of the official cosmopolitan bullshit that for many Feyenoord fans is summed up by the word "Jews."

Feyenoord wasn't always an anti-establishment volksclub. Bennie Muller, half-Jewish captain of Ajax in the 1960s, told me that in his day Feyenoord fans did not sing about gas chambers, and Feyenoord players were as elegant and skillful as their Ajax counterparts. He himself had once nearly joined Feyenoord. "Now they've begun to play in the English way, with strength. Now they're a bone-hard club," he grumbled in the flat above his cigar shop. In other words, in the last few decades Feyenoord fans and players seem to have reinvented themselves to match the new, tough, functional city that has risen around them.

———

Amsterdam tells a very different story about its past. In the city's Dutch Resistance Museum, around the corner from my friend's art gallery in the Jewish Quarter, there is a short color film of Amsterdam in the summer of 1940. It is spooky to watch. We are used to seeing World War

II in black and white, but with color restored to the city's markets, cyclists, cobblestone streets, and big Dutch faces, Amsterdam looks almost exactly as it does today. This film does not show the Jewish Quarter, but I recognized many streets, and buildings from other parts of town, and the trams pulling into Central Station. So little has changed that if Ajax's dead prewar outside-right Eddy Hamel were to return today he could get on a bike and find his way around town, shop at the same shops, walk into the same old cafés.

That Amsterdam has barely changed is thanks mainly to what you might call the "Young Left" of the 1960s: a mixed bunch that included the students of '68, the hippies, the Marxists, and a peculiar Amsterdam tribe that called itself the Gnomes. Postwar city councils wanted to tear down the remnants of the deserted Jewish Quarter and build a four-lane highway through it to the Central Station, and later to construct a proper metro like the ones in London and New York. Dinky canal streets were out of fashion. The Young Left spent years protesting. Their final victory came around midnight on January 5, 1972, when the final plan for the four-lane highway was defeated at a council meeting by twenty-two votes to twenty-one.

So the Amsterdam of Rembrandt and Hamel has been preserved. The British author David Winner, who lived for years on a very dinky Amsterdam street indeed, calls the present city "a Disney version of itself." I think he means that Amsterdam is always doing its utmost to look old, like a Hollywood film star in reverse. The city's canal-ring district has been placed on Unesco's list of protected World Heritage Sites, which could mean Amsterdam remaining the same forever. A city that never changes, it is the opposite of Rotterdam.

Every seventeenth-century canal house is a monument to dead Amsterdammers, to Rembrandt as much as to the people killed in World War II. But the city center is also full of actual monuments. And the story they tell is from Disney too.

Imagine a city tour that starts at the Anne Frank house. Every day from 9 a.m. this building tells hundreds of tourists the following story: the Germans wanted to kill the Frank family, so the Dutch hid them, but in the end the Germans killed them after all. So sad are the Dutch about this that they have dedicated this large house in the center of their capital city to Anne's memory.

Another version of the story is that the Franks were among the lucky few Jews in the Netherlands able to find a hiding place, but were probably betrayed by a Dutch person and seized from their hiding place by a German and three Dutch policemen, one of whom was still working for the Amsterdam force in 1980.

However, the exhibition at the Secret Annexe barely touches on the betrayal, merely stating in passing that no one knows who the culprit was. The exhibition jumps from the Jews in the annex and their many Dutch helpers to the concentration camps, with barely a word in between.

I discussed this in Haifa with Shmu'el Hacohen, the Amsterdam Holocaust survivor who was campaigning against the myth of Dutch tolerance. He told me, "All that fuss about the Anne Frank house—it makes me vomit!" Hacohen said the Dutch had built a monument to themselves. He had once asked a Dutchman queuing with his family in front of the Anne Frank house, "What is Anne Frank the symbol of? Of Dutch resistance or Dutch betrayal?" The man had thought for a long time and then said, "I fear it's the latter."

The Amsterdam tour proceeds eastward along the city's beautiful canal streets, barely changed since the seventeenth century, until it reaches the old Jewish Quarter. Bits of it have gone, but the Amsterdammers have preserved an astounding amount. There are façades with Hebrew letters, and the great Portuguese synagogue (more a monument than a place of worship these days, as it is barely used except on high holidays). This city has welcomed Jews for hundreds of years and is sorry that it now has almost none left.

The goodness of Amsterdam is advertised by the whole Jewish Quarter, but it is embodied in the statue of the Dockworker on the square in front of the synagogue. The Dockworker honors the

Amsterdam proletariat, which protested against the first German raids on the Jewish Quarter by staging the general strike of February 1941. Every February there is a march past the Dockworker.

Hacohen once stood before the statue and told him, "If only you knew what they had made of you, you'd be amazed!" All that fuss over a two-day strike that was put down simply, with little violence.

The last stop on our tour is the white stucco Hollandsche Schouwburg Theater on the pretty Plantage Middenlaan. The building where Amsterdam's Jews were rounded up is now no longer a theatre but a monument. On its façade a verse (helpfully printed in English as well as Dutch) informs tourists:

> *at home in gathering isolation*
> *waiting at night in fear*
> *rounded up by soldiers*
> *caught in a trap . . .*

But the verse is a lie. Most Amsterdam Jews did not sit at home waiting for soldiers. Instead they were collected by Dutch policemen, who were coerced by the Germans with the harshest sanctions imaginable: they could lose their Whitsun leave. "Concerning the Jewish Question, the Dutch police behave outstandingly and catch hundreds of Jews, day and night," wrote Hanns Albin Rauter, the senior German police officer in Amsterdam, to Heinrich Himmler in September 1942. After the war Rauter's colleague Willy Lages would add, "We would not have been able to arrest 10 percent of the Jews without their help." The rigor of the Dutch police, and of the Dutch state generally, was matched in western Europe not even by Vichy France.

Smaller monuments around Amsterdam repeat the Disney story of the little city that resisted so bravely. Cycling each day to my friend's gallery, I used to pass a brick wall that impressed the following message on me:

A people that bows before tyrants
Will lose more than body and goods,
Then the light goes out . . .

The wall's message is that the Dutch people did not bow before tyrants. I would like to read the verse as an admonition ("You should not have bowed before tyrants"), but it makes no sense that way. Amsterdammers did bow before tyrants yet lost neither body nor goods and now live in a beautiful Disneytown where the light has not gone out. In fact, had they offered widespread resistance instead of bowing before tyrants, they probably would have lost body and goods and their town would now be a lot less beautiful too.

Almost the only Amsterdam institution that does not tell a Disney story about the Jews is Ajax. Fearful of discussing the war since 1945, the club has recently become so terrified of encouraging the anti-Semitic chants of opposing fans that it denies any connection with Jews. Club officials prefer to talk about the swastika that flew above the stadium in 1938, or the German soldiers barracked there during the war. There is no monument at the Amsterdam Arena to the club's murdered Jews. "I have asked about it at meetings," said the half-Jewish Ajax member Luc Sacksioni. "A plaque wouldn't be more than fair. Not just for the Jewish members, but for everybody. A little monument for the generality."

But Ajax's silence is the exception in Amsterdam. While Rotterdam has built a secret monument to its murdered Jews, half of Amsterdam is a mendacious monument distorting the fate of the city's Jews.

———

The Dutch as a whole have learned since the 1990s that they did not save the Jews. A barrage of television programs and books like this one has tried to debunk the myth that the Netherlands was *goed*. So frankly does the Dutch Resistance Museum deal with this issue that it might just as well be renamed the Dutch Collaboration Museum. As Renate Rubinstein phrased the country's new intellectual consensus, "Even in Germany you had slightly more chance of surviving the destruction than in the Netherlands. We were not anti-Semitic, we were just cowardly."

At the end of 1940 the future historian Lou de Jong, broadcasting from London on Radio Oranje, had said that the German anti-Semitic decrees were "in conflict with the Dutch tradition of tolerance and brotherly love." And they were. Yet only a tiny minority of Dutch people lifted a finger to combat them. Among the others there was a sense that the Jews were fated, unlucky, as if they had terminal cancer, how very sad, while oneself was fortunately spared.

Intellectually most Dutch people who think about the war know the Netherlands was cowardly and grey. Yet, as Orwell said, it is possible to know and not know at the same time. Alongside this knowledge there survives a hardy popular fantasy of a heroic little land where everyone was in the Resistance, Asterix's village writ large. This is the story the Dutch prefer to tell foreigners.

And this heroic fantasy is shaped and fed by the monuments of Amsterdam, by the Dutch pride in Anne Frank, by the harping on about every stray act of resistance, and by the fact that it is unpleasant to believe your own country was grey and cowardly even if you know it to have been so. The Dutch prefer to think of themselves as a nation of Resistance heroes.

What the Netherlands did in the war used to matter because the people who had done it were still running the country. Now it matters (if somewhat less) because people often think of a country as having an unchanging nature. If Holland was good in the past (and World War II *is*, to many Dutch people, the Dutch past) then Holland must always have been good and must be good today. If the Dutch of 1940–1945 were brave, tolerant, freethinking types who stood up to Hitler, then it follows that the Dutch today are brave, tolerant, and freethinking too. The myth of Dutch tolerance is stretched to cover past and present.

Yet the streets, cafés, and main soccer stadium of Amsterdam tell a different story about Dutch tolerance than the war monuments. Almost half of the city's inhabitants today are immigrants or the children of immigrants: black and brown people mainly from Morocco, Turkey, and the former Dutch South American colony of Surinam. But in the nicer parts of the city center you would never guess it. Almost every Amsterdam café is either almost entirely nonwhite or almost entirely white.

"The Netherlands is a country of apartheid," said Fortuyn, and he had a point. In the past few years the country has ceased to boast so much about its tolerance, and in the process it has become less tolerant. When Fortuyn first popped up in the still life that is Dutch politics, few people would admit to supporting him. By the time he was murdered six months later that stigma had vanished, and after his death it took some courage to say a word against him. The Netherlands is now a country with a large and semi-respectable racist party, led by Geert Wilders.

I often think Amsterdam is now a more segregated city than Johannesburg, where my family comes from. Some Johannesburg neighborhoods are moderately mixed, many restaurants draw a black-and-white crowd, and there are whites who drive to Soweto for an evening of jazz. In Amsterdam, a large proportion of black and brown people live in a vast ghetto outside town called the Bijlmer. The only reason many whites ever go to the Bijlmer is to watch Ajax play in the hypermodern Amsterdam Arena. Inside the arena I am always struck by the people you do not see: the dead Jews, of course, but also the Turks, Moroccans, and Surinamese, who hardly figure in the crowd. Odd, that, in the middle of the ghetto.

That Amsterdam's pre-war Jews went to watch Ajax, an institute of Dutch gentiles, suggests they felt more a part of the Netherlands than the Bijlmer's inhabitants do today. This did nothing to save them, nor would it earn them so much as a memorial plaque in the arena.

AFTERWORD TO THE U.S. EDITION

On the evening of May 6, 2002, I was sitting in a drafty Amsterdam flat editing the proofs of this book when the phone rang. It was a friend, sobbing. "Fortuyn's been shot dead," she said. It took me a moment to realize what she was saying. No Dutch politician had been assassinated since the brothers De Witt were literally torn to pieces by a mob in 1672. I switched on the TV. It turned out that an animal rights activist, who to this day is known under Dutch law only as Volkert van der G., had come to a "media park" to shoot the anti-immigrant, anti-Islam leader Pim Fortuyn. And so Fortuyn left the Dutch stage even faster than he had entered it in the autumn of 2001. A friend of mine who happened to be within earshot of the murder initially legged it after Volkert, without realizing how dangerous this was. Dutch people are not very familiar with guns.

But the Netherlands was changing. The day after the murder I had lunch in Amsterdam with two old school friends, neither of who had any sympathy with Fortuyn's racist views, but who were both shaken. One said, "I think Dutch democracy is in danger now." I was astounded. When democracy is eradicated all over the planet, it will survive longest in this staid little country. But my friend's reaction, like many in those weird days of May, helped me understand Holland better. For me, as for many Dutch people, the years since Fortuyn's death have been a sort of accelerated education in Dutchness.

The Netherlands has for centuries been one of the safest countries on earth (probably only Switzerland and Norway can compete) where as long as you weren't Jewish during World War II, nothing very bad ever happens. It is hard to explain to a foreigner just how much Fortuyn and his murder changed the Dutch atmosphere. Volkert's gunshots initiated an era of turmoil like none I have known in the country, and as I write, in spring 2012, the turmoil continues. The current leader of the anti-Islamic Dutch is the send-'em-back-home-and-ban-the-Koran man Geert Wilders, who looks rather like Mozart would have done if the composer had dyed his hair platinum blond. Wilders gets frequent death threats. His party has 16 percent of the seats in parliament. From 2010 until 2012 a Dutch minority government survives only with his support. The Netherlands has ceased to be the dull place where I grew up. And the turmoil of the last few years has been strangely echoed in Dutch soccer.

Two days after Fortuyn was murdered, Feyenoord played Borussia Dortmund in the UEFA Cup final at home in Rotterdam. I traveled down from Amsterdam. On the tram to "The Tub" stadium, Feyenoord fans sang their traditional, "Whoever doesn't jump is a Jew," and in The Tub itself fans behind the goal jumped up and down to the tune.

But Feyenoord's identity took on a new facet that evening. The Feyenoord players were wearing black armbands to mourn Fortuyn, and when the Dortmund fans sang through the minute silence, unaware that it was happening, the home crowd was incensed. In the early minutes of the game the crowd chanted, "Pim Fortuyn, Pim Fortuyn, Pim Fortuyn!" with the familiar cadences of the terraces, as if the dead man had been a soccer player. Feyenoord won the game. Afterward, as hundreds of people boarded dangerously crammed trams outside the stadium, one man leaned out of the tram window and shouted, "Auschwitz!" It was a Feyenoord joke.

That night there was the ritual fighting in downtown Rotterdam to celebrate Feyenoord's victory, but commentators later noted that the fans did not touch the flowers laid for Fortuyn outside the town hall. On a leafy patrician square just behind Rotterdam's train station, several Feyenoord flags were tied to the railings of Fortuyn's villa, his "Palazzo di Pietro."

Ian Buruma, in his wonderful book *Murder in Amsterdam,* described Fortuyn's Princess Dianaesque funeral, a high-camp affair befitting the flamboyantly gay victim, with his pet spaniels Kenneth and Carla as guests of honor. "Some [in the crowd] began to sing the English soccer anthem, 'You'll Never Walk Alone,'" writes Buruma. "They also sang the supporters' anthems to the local soccer team, Feyenoord."

As Buruma noted, "Soccer anthems might seem out of place at the funeral of a politician who never showed the slightest interest in sports. *Aïda* was much more his thing." Yet there was a primal link between Fortuyn and Feyenoord. The politician had grown up in a small town north of Amsterdam, but Rotterdam became his adopted city and the capital of his movement. Fortuyn didn't merely divide Holland between white people and immigrants. Over and above that, he split what had always been an almost classless society into two more camps: the educated versus the lesser educated. Amsterdam was mostly on the educated side of the divide, and Rotterdam on the other.

Most educated Dutch people have always been quite happy to welcome immigrants. Pre-Fortuyn they still ran the country largely under the motto of "Never again Auschwitz," and treated anything that reeked of racism as taboo. Anyway, the immigrants didn't tend to buy houses in their neighborhoods.

Many lesser-educated Dutch people, by contrast, had become very anti-immigrant, and after the 9/11 attacks in the United States, anti-Muslim. This divide between educated and lesser-educated on immigration exists in every country in the European Union, but Euromonitor polls for the European Commission suggest it is starkest in Holland. After 9/11, many lesser-educated Dutch people backed Fortuyn. Over the next few years, a sort of cultural civil war raged in the Netherlands. When a television vote was held to choose the Greatest Dutchman in 2004, the lesser educated largely championed Fortuyn, while the educated went for William of Orange, the sixteenth-century father of the nation. Fortuyn was proclaimed the winner on the night, even though William got more votes (which were discounted because they arrived after the deadline). But the Netherlands was fighting over its identity, and it wasn't a pretty sight.

The working-class harbor town of Rotterdam was the first big city where Fortuyn's people entered local government. Amsterdam, by contrast, home of the Dutch cultural elite who cycle through the cute streets to their favorite cafés, barely voted for Fortuyn. The great Dutch soccer rivalry had always been Feyenoord vs. Ajax. After Fortuyn, their two cities found themselves in opposition too.

Buruma writes, "Rotterdammers pride themselves on being hard workers, the salt of the earth, tough guys. Amsterdam, to them, has a namby-pamby image of city slickers, snobs, and cosmopolitan weirdos." Many Feyenoord fans have come to sum up these slickers, snobs, and weirdos with the word "Jews." (Probably a couple of million Dutch people have fond feelings for Feyenoord, and of course the vast majority of these people are not anti-Semites, but the most vocal Feyenoord fans are the ones who are most likely to use anti-Semitic language.)

Wouter Bos, who for much of the post-Fortuyn era was deputy prime minister and leader of the Dutch Labor Party, told me, "Rotterdammers have an enormous sense of inferiority vis-à-vis Amsterdammers. Rotterdam is much less successful than Amsterdam on all relevant indicators of social success: unemployment, crime, housing, and all those sorts of things. Unfortunately, in soccer too." Bos supports Feyenoord.

It was therefore natural that in the civil war between educated and lesser-educated Dutch people, Feyenoord should become one of the chief champions of the lesser educated. Every year a well-known Dutch comedian holds a soccer quiz in his very cute Amsterdam canal apartment. The attendees are journalists and ex-soccer players. Previous winners include the Ajax players Danny Blind and Jari Litmanen, and the non-Ajax player Simon Kuper (winner in 2001 and 2007).

Anyway, one year a Feyenoord official who shall remain nameless attended the quiz. Most of his conversation consisted of rants at Ajax and at Amsterdam, which most of the Amsterdammers present found quaintly amusing. After he had revealed the pro-Ajax conspiracy mounted by Amsterdammers in the Dutch media, he turned to another guest, PSV Eindhoven's then manager, Guus Hiddink and said, "Doesn't it drive you crazy, too?"

Nothing drives Hiddink crazy. Hiddink replied, soothingly, "Let them do what they want." This sent the Feyenoord official into a paroxysm about how unfairly the media reported the anti-Semitic chanting by his club's fans. "We shout 'Jews!' at them, and Ajax fans shout 'Farmers!' at us. It's both wrong," he allowed, "but the press only ever talks about us."

He had forgotten to mention the Feyenoord fans' hissing to imitate the sound of escaping gas, and many other Shoah references, but in fact he was sticking closely to the club line. When Feyenoord's open day in 2002 was disfigured by anti-Semitic chants—increasingly considered something of a yawn in the Netherlands—the club's chairman chastised a member of parliament for daring to complain about the sing-along, and attacked Dutch TV for broadcasting it.

As the quiz night went on, the official went into a rant about the best player Feyenoord has produced in decades, Robin van Persie. "He was unmanageable, because he has Moroccan friends," explained the official. In many Fortuynesque Rotterdam circles, this might have been considered an unremarkable comment. In that Amsterdam apartment, the racism was greeted with silence and some embarrassed giggles.

But you heard this sort of thing more and more often in Dutch settings, on TV talk shows and downwards. In most of the Netherlands, the tone of debate about immigration had hardened. Fortuyn had started it, calling Islam "a backward religion." After he was killed, people commonly said they valued his "frankness." "Murdered because you dared to say what you think," said a typical condolence card outside his villa after the murder.

"Saying what you think" came to be regarded as the highest virtue in Dutch public life. If you were angry, you said so. Opponents were treated as enemies. Dutch politicians who had traditionally spoken a convoluted technocratic language now tried to sound like Fortuyn. In 2002 Rob Oudkerk, a Social Democratic, Jewish alderman in Amsterdam, was caught on camera using the phrase *kutmarokkanen* (literally, "cunt Moroccans") while talking to the city's mayor, Job Cohen. Oudkerk wasn't made to resign. There is some debate among the Dutch about whether such harsh language is acceptable. However, those who object to it are commonly dismissed as "PC," a terrible insult in contemporary Holland.

In no sphere was the hardening more obvious than in soccer. When I was a kid, Ajax–Feyenoord matches were fairly sedate affairs. Most of my friends had sympathies for both clubs and occasionally players transferred from one to the other, Johan Cruijff himself doing so in 1983. But in the new, post-Fortuyn Holland, even the match between Ajax and Feyenoord's reserve teams became dangerous. On a Tuesday night in Amsterdam in 2004, Ajax fans invaded the field and began attacking the young Feyenoord reserves. Ajax players had to defend their opponents with their own bodies. The one happy image of that night was Ajax's Daniel de Ridder, son of an Israeli mother, using his body to shield his friend, the Feyenoord player Van Persie. (It is a sign of how badly Feyenoord misjudged Van Persie, incidentally, that he was in the reserves that night. Soon afterwards the club offloaded him to Arsenal for £3 million.)

The fight at the reserve game, unthinkable once, was no longer exceptional. Just as Dutch politicians, who had traditionally cycled to work from their terraced houses, were suddenly getting death threats, so were soccer managers and chairmen. Usually these notes would make it clear that the writer knew where the recipient lived, or where his children went to school. Chairmen often refused to expel troublemakers from stadiums because the troublemakers knew where to find them. Michael van Praag, the half-Jewish former Ajax chairman, said he wouldn't risk his life that way. A drunk Feyenoord fan once threw a punch at Van Praag in The Tub during a Feyenoord–Ajax game after the chairman had cheered an Ajax goal. The punch missed Van Praag, but knocked out a woman sitting a row in front of him. A senior security official with UEFA, a Dutchman, who witnessed the scene, told me, "The more I travel, the more I think things are very bad in Holland."

For all the anti-Jewish chants, the main victims of racism in post-Fortuyn Dutch soccer (as in Dutch politics) were Dutch Moroccans. The trendy chants for Dutch-Moroccan players were "bag snatcher" and "goat fucker." Blaise Nkufo, a black Swiss forward playing for Twente Enschede, experienced a more traditional form of terrace abuse in October 2004. Playing away at ADO Den Haag, he endured the home fans calling him a "cancer ape" for most of the match. After his team won, Nkufo gave his tormentors an ironic ovation. His own coach condemned him, a Den Haag player called him "the dumbest soccer player I have ever experienced," and the Dutch FA gave him an official rebuke.

In other words, in the early twenty-first century many Dutch people were ceasing to worry about racism. This was partly because World War II was finally ending in the Netherlands, as across much of Europe. A telling moment of closure was the death in 2004, aged 93, of the Dutch Prince Bernhard, husband of the former queen Juliana. Born a German, Bernhard had joined Hitler's SA as a young man. He had met Hitler and sent him sycophantic letters. When Bernhard married Juliana in 1937, the wedding guests politely gave the Hitler salute. Yet Bernhard went on to become a symbol of Dutch Resistance. During the war, in London, he climbed the Dutch military hierarchy to become head of the "Dutch and internal forces." Every year after the war on May 5, the day the Dutch commemorated the liberation, Bernhard inspected the veterans' parade. He embodied the supposed unity of nation, royal family, and Resistance. His death closed a murky, mythical era.

The war no longer meant quite so much anymore. Around the sixtieth commemorations of the Allied victory in 2005 French schoolchildren had a snowball fight at Auschwitz, a poll showed that most young Britons didn't know that "VE Day" stands for "Victory in Europe," and Dutch kids played soccer with the wreaths laid for the war dead. World War II was becoming like the American Civil War: remembered by history buffs, only vaguely by the public, and hardly ever studied by policymakers for its lessons. In many countries, the war had once changed everything: the landscape itself, the country's borders, its goals, its attitudes to foreigners, the subject matter of its TV programs and books and movies. Auschwitz had left the Dutch and most Westerners with a horror of racist parties. The war was "a traumatic page that we find it difficult to turn," as Fortuyn once said.

But by the 2000s, the memory of all this was crumbling. Dutch people could vote for Fortuyn or Wilders, or make jokes about Jews or Moroccans, or chant abuse at a black soccer player, because they (rightly) didn't think any of this would bring back Auschwitz. The war was over, and so Holland became a rougher place. No government in Western Europe except perhaps Denmark took a tougher stance against Muslim immigrants.

One morning in 2004, a week after Nkufo's ovation, the Dutch filmmaker Theo van Gogh was cycling through Amsterdam-East when he was shot several times. He fell, and according to an eyewitness, begged his assassin, Mohammed Bouyeri, for mercy. Instead the Dutch-Moroccan Islamic fundamentalist cut his throat. Bouyeri was arrested in a shoot-out with police minutes later.

Van Gogh, a fan and friend of Fortuyn, had thrived amid the new Dutch frankness. In the wake of Fortuyn's rise, he had turned his attention from Jews to Muslims, whom he called "goat fuckers." This made him one of many Dutch people debating Islam after 9/11 un-hindered by any knowledge of the religion. In September 2004 Van Gogh's film *Submission*, showing abused female bodies superimposed with misogynist texts from the Koran, had been broadcast on Dutch television. That was why Bouyeri killed him. The murderer also pinned a note on Van Gogh's body threatening to kill the film's author, the politician Ayaan Hirsi Ali.

Dutch gentiles have so little experience with violence that the murder caused mass panic. Gerrit Zalm, the deputy prime minister at the time, said the Netherlands was "at war." There were tit-for-tat arsons of mosques and churches. A Muslim school was burned down. Dutch pundits began comparing the situation to the last days of Weimar Germany. The staid country had grown hysterical.

———

It was in this atmosphere of turmoil and licensed racism that John Jaakke, the then Ajax chairman, called on his club's supporters at Ajax's New Year's reception of 2005 to stop calling themselves "Jews" and waving "Mogen David" symbols in the stadium. Jaakke said "current tensions" in society made it unwise.

He seemed to be subscribing to the curious strain in Dutch thought that holds that when Feyenoord or Den Haag fans shout anti-Semitic abuse, the real culprits are Ajax fans. Because they encourage their team with chants of "Jews!" or "Superjews!" the reasoning goes, they are provoking their rivals, who then have no choice but to sing about the Holocaust.

But there was more to Jaakke's appeal than this. As I argue in this book, some Ajax officials are ashamed of the club's mild Jewish heritage. In the world they work in, after all, "Jew" is a word of abuse.

Of course the club didn't want to know anything about my book on the taboo topic. One day the Dutch-Jewish youth group Moos invited me to a debate about Ajax and the Jews at the Amsterdam Arena. We had been scheduled to meet in a conference room inside the Arena, but when we arrived we were told we had to sit in a draughty container outside the stadium instead. No Ajax official was found willing to attend the event. The main speaker, Salo Muller, Jewish masseur of the "Golden Ajax" team of the 1970s, recalled that in his day there had been the same shame within Ajax about Jews. Referring to the legendary club chairman Jaap van Praag, he said, "Mr. Van Praag, as a Jew, was a little ashamed of openly associating with me as a Jew."

We asked Muller why in the 1960s he hadn't made a fuss when thugs like the Van der Meijden brothers, who had built bunkers for the Germans in the war, were welcomed at post-Holocaust Ajax. Muller replied, "Who at Ajax could I tell my story to?" He said that whenever he asked Van Praag about one of the brothers, the chairman would tell him, "That man is as kosher as I don't know what," and would order him to drop the subject.

So Jaakke's speech in 2005 appears in part to have been an attempt to shed Ajax's embarrassing Jewish image. Club officials had made the same appeal before, but Jaakke's comments made news around the world. Within a week I received three different French journalists in my living room in Paris, all looking for Dutch contacts to interview about Ajax and the Jews. All three were going on to Amsterdam, the man from *Le Monde* and the delectable freelance journalist in each other's company. The *New York Times* phoned, a Swiss magazine, and Irish radio. To them it was an exciting story—the Holocaust plus soccer—that fit perfectly onto the index card they carried in their heads about Holland. Until 2002, that index card had said something like this: Netherlands—tolerance, drugs, Amsterdam red-light district, good soccer players, hatred of Germans. Now, after Fortuyn, Van Gogh, and Wilders, the word "tolerance" had been replaced by "intolerance."

Holland's international image had changed, the then Deputy Prime Minister Bos told me. It hurt, he said, that President Bush in a speech in Brussels in 2005 had mentioned only one European country by name, condemning, "Violence such as we have witnessed in the Netherlands," or that Australia's foreign ministry had advised its citizens against visiting Holland because of street crime. "It's not at all Holland as 'guide land,' which we always used to think we were," sighed Bos. From 2010, when a coalition government backed by Wilders's anti-immigrant party took office, nobody talked about "Netherlands guide land" anymore.

WHERE ARE THEY NOW?

Most of the old men I interviewed for this book have died since: Herman Menco, who as a Jew in hiding had gone to watch Feyenoord on Sundays, died in 2002, aged 77. Hans Sonneveld, who failed to bring Diego Maradona to Sparta, went in 2004, aged 81. Oscar Heisserer, the captain of France who refused to play for Nazi Germany, died the same year, aged 90. Meijer Stad, who survived his execution at Buchenwald, died in 2005, aged 85.

Leon Greenman, the only English Jew to be sent to Auschwitz, and Albert Sing, who played soccer for Nazi Germany, both died in 2008, aged 97 and 91 respectively. Maup Caransa, Jewish sponsor of the Diamond Ajax, died in 2009, aged 93.

One of the men I've written about, who died decades too young, has been remembered since. I'm proud to have played a small role in that. Thomas Schnitzler, a German historian who teaches at the *Deutsche Sporthochschule* in Cologne, read about the murdered Dutch radio broadcaster Han Hollander in this book. In May 2009, Schnitzler arranged for memorial stones to be laid outside Amstelkade 118 in Amsterdam, the house where Hollander and his wife had lived. The stone was made and laid by the German artist Gunter Demnig, who said, "A person is only forgotten when his name has been forgotten."

Happily, as of spring 2012, some of the characters in this book are still with us. Wim Schoevaart is 94, still busy at work as Ajax's archivist. He recently celebrated eighty years as a club member. "No cross beside my name yet," he chuckles. Salo Muller is 76 and still a cheery physio in Amsterdam. He has written two books lately, both of which sold out. Abraham Klein, the Israeli referee, is 78 and recently published his autobiography in Hebrew. (If any foreign publishers are interested in translating Muller's or Klein's books, I can put them in touch with the authors.)

The Israeli kid who once flopped in Ajax's youth academy, Yossi Benayoun, has come a long way since I saw him do almost nothing for Maccabi Haifa in January 2000. He is now wrapping up a mostly successful career in English soccer at Arsenal.

Bennie Muller, the half-Jewish former captain of Ajax and Holland, has sold his cigar shop and retired, but when I last saw him he still lived with his wife in the flat above the shop. He liked the way I wrote about him in this book, and once invited me to pop round. We had a nice chat over coffee. He seemed cheerful, but of course his war trauma will never go away.

For although the war is finally over for most people in Holland, it never will be for most of the people in this book. I realized this again when reading the excellent Dutch book by Bram de Graaf, *Voetbalvrouwen* ("Football Wives"), published in 2008.

The book's chapter about Bennie Muller's wife starts with the infamous incident in 1965 when Jan Jongbloed (who was to become Holland's ill-starred keeper in two World Cup finals) called Muller a "pleurisy Jew" during a Dutch league match. One of Jongbloed's former teammates, André Pijlman, explains to De Graaf that Ajax players like Muller were "crybabies." Here is Pijlman's analysis of the Jongbloed incident: "Nothing was up, was there? I thought Jew was a 'badge of honor.'" So far, so typical of post-Fortuyn Holland. Pijlman wasn't to know that Muller lost about 150 relatives in the war.

Sjaak Swart's lost relatives aren't mentioned in De Graaf's chapter about Swart's wife, because at Swart's request his Jewish past was omitted from the book.

But De Graaf's most moving chapter features Maja Suurbier, ex-wife of the great Ajax and Holland full-back Wim Suurbier. Growing up in a household of traumatized Jewish survivors of the war, she had spent much of her childhood avoiding all the fighting around her by playing in a corner with a box of buttons. (Even Dutch-Jewish families who got through the war were often driven mad by it.) When her very old grandmother died, Maja finally stopped repressing her war traumas and began exploring them. She visited the Dutch transit camp of Westerbork, and found that 139 of her relatives had been put on trains from there to the death camps. She visited Yad Vashem, the memorial to the Jewish victims of the Holocaust in Israel. "And who did I meet there? Bennie [Muller]!" she told De Graaf. "There's only one person who walks like that, I thought, when I spotted him." I would like to think the visit helped them both, but I doubt that anything ever will.

SOURCES

BOOKS

Andrews, Gordon. *The Datasport Book of Wartime Football 1939–1946.*

Anderiesen, Wim. *Voetbalherinneringen* (Schiedam: De Boekerij, 1944).

Anon., *Cinquantenaire de la Coupe de France* (Paris: Editions Amphora, 1967).

Arendt, Hannah. *Eichmann in Jerusalem: A Report on the Banality of Evil* (London: Penguin, 1983).

Austrian Football Association, *Geschichte des österreichischen Fussballsports* (Vienna: Wilhelm Limpert-Verlag, 1964).

Bailey, John. *Not Just on Christmas Day: An Overview of Association Football in the First World War* (Upminster: 3–2 Books, 1999).

Barend, Frits, and Henk van Dorp. *Bezet Nederland in de greep van het bruine monster* (*Vrij Nederland* magazine, number 17, 1979).

Benima, Tamarah. *Een schaap vangen* (Amsterdam/Antwerp: Contact, 1999).

Blom, J. C. H. *Burgerlijk en Beheerst: Over Nederland in de twintigste eeuw* (Balans, 1996).

Boin, Victor. *Livre d'or jubilaire de l'U.R.B.S.F.A. 1895–1945* (Brussels: Leclercq & De Haas, 1945).

Bregstein, Philo. *Op zoek naar joods Amsterdam* (Amsterdam: Meulenhoff, 1981).

Cate, Flip ten. *Dit volckje zeer verwoet: Een geschiedenis van de Sint Antoniesbreestraat* (Amsterdam: Pantheon, 1988).

Chamberlin, E. R. *Life in Wartime Britain* (London: B. T. Batsford, 1985).

Cruijff, Johan and Danny, with Jaap ter Haar. *Boem* (Bussum: De Gooise Uitgeverij, 1975).

Das, H., and L. A. Heesakker (eds). *Feijenoord's Gedenkboek: Sportclub Feijenoord 1908–1958* (Rotterdam: "De Maasstad," 1958).

Derks, Frans, and Wil van der Smagt. *Frans Derks ziet het anders* (Baarn: De Boekerij, 1973).

Düblin, Dr. Jules (ed.). *Jubiläumsschrift: 50 Jahre Schweizerischer Fussball-und Athletik-Verband: 1895–1945* (Zurich: Neue Zürcher Zeitung, n.d.).

Finney, Tom. *Tom Finney's Preston North End Scrapbook* (London: Souvenir Press, 1982).

Fischer, Gerhard, and Ulrich Lindner. *Stürmer für Hitler: Vom Zusammenspiel zwischen Fussball und Nationalsozialismus* (Göttingen: Die Werkstatt, 1999).

Gans, Evelien. *Gojse nijd & joods narcisme: De verhouding tussen joden en niet-joden in Nederland* (Amsterdam: Arena, 1994).

Gans, Mozes Heiman. *Memorboek: Platenatlas van het leven der Joden in Nederland van de middeleeuwen tot 1940* (Baarn: Bosch en Keuning, 1988).

Gelder, Henk van (ed.). *Mei '45: Reconstructie van 31 unieke dagen* (Bussum: De Gooise Uitgeverij/Unieboek, 1980).

Giltay Veth, D., and A. J. van der Leeuw. *Het Weinrebrapport* (The Hague: Staatsuitgeverij, 1976).

Gjelsvik, Tore. *Norwegian Resistance 1940–1945* (London: C. Hurst & Co., 1979).

Greenman, Leon. *An Englishman in Auschwitz* (London, and Portland, OR: Valentine Mitchell, OR, 2001).

Guldemont, Henry and Bob Deps. *100 Ans de Football en Belgique 1895–1995* (Brussels: VIF Editions, 1995).

Haar, Carel ter, and Edward van Voolen (eds). *Verhalen uit joods Amsterdam* (Amsterdam: Meulenhoff, 1998).

Haarke, Karl-Heinz, and Georg Kachel. *Die Lebensgeschichte des Fussball-Altnationalspielers Ernst Willimowski* (Dülmen: Laumann-Verlagsgesellschaft, 1996).

Hapgood, Eddie. *Football Ambassador* (London: Sporting Handbooks, 1946).

Heijden, Chris van der. *Grijs verleden: Nederland en de Tweede Wereldoorlog* (Amsterdam/Antwerp: Contact, 2001).

Jakob, Hans. *Durch ganz Europa von Tor zu Tor* (Nuremberg: Olympia-Verlag, 1949).

Janes, Paul. *Ein Leben für den Fussball* (Offenbach am Main: Bollwerk-Verlag Karl Drott, 1948).

Jewish Museum London, *Leon Greenman, Auschwitz Survivor 98288* (London: The Jewish Museum, 1996).

Johnson, Amanda. *Norway, Her Invasion and Occupation* (Decatur, GA: Bowen Press, 1948).

Jong, Dr. L. de. *Herinneringen I* (The Hague: SDU, 1993).

—————. *Het Koninkrijk der Nederlanden in de Tweede Wereldoorlog. Deel 4, mei '40 –maart '41* (The Hague: Staatsuitgeverij, 1972).

Keifu, R. *Die Trainerlegende: Auf den Spuren Béla Guttmanns* (Kassel: AGON Sportartikel catalogue, 2001).

Kuper, Simon. *Football Against the Enemy* (London: Orion, 1994).

Lanfranchi, Pierre, and Matthew Taylor. "Professional Football in World War Two Britain," in Pat Kirkham and David Thoms (eds), *War Culture: Social Change and Changing Experience in World War Two Britain* (London: Lawrence & Wishart, 1995).

Lans, Jos van der, and Herman Vuijsje. *Lage landen, hoge sprongen: Nederland in beweging 1898/1998* (Wormer: Inmerc, 1998).

Liber, Jan. *Het voetballeven van Faas Wilkes* (Amsterdam: De Arbeiderspers, 1962).

Mak, Geert. *Amsterdam: A Brief Life of the City* (London: Harvill Press, 1999).

Mason, Tim. *Nazism, Fascism and the Working Class* (Cambridge: Cambridge University Press, 1995).

Murray, Bill. *The World's Game: A History of Soccer* (Champaign: University of Illinois Press, 1998).

Nyquist, R. B. *Sons of the Vikings* (London: Hutchinson, ca. 1943).

Osley, Anthony. *Persuading the People: Government Publicity in the Second World War* (London: Central Office of Information, 1995).

Peeters, Frans. *Gezworen vrienden: Het geheime bondgenootschap tussen Nederland en Israël* (Amsterdam/Antwerp: L. J. Veen, 1997).

Red Cross & St. John Fund, *Sport Scores a Million* (Red Cross & St John Fund, Sports Committee, n. p., December 1943).

Ribbens, Kees. *Bewogen jaren: Zwolle in de Tweede Wereldoorlog* (Zwolle: Waanders Uitgevers, 1995).

Riste, Olav, and Berit Nökleby. *Norway 1940–1945: The Resistance Movement* (Oslo: Johan Grundt Tanum Forlag, 1970).

Rollin, Jack. *Soccer at War 1939–1945* (London: Willow Books, 1985).

Schama, Simon. *The Embarrassment of Riches: An Interpretation of Dutch Culture in the Golden Age* (Berkeley/Los Angeles/London: University of California Press, 1988).

Scheepmaker, Nico (ed.). *Het krankzinnige kwartiertje* (Bussum: De Gooise Uitgeverij, ca. 1978).

Schleppi, John Ross. *A History of Professional Association Football in England During the Second World War* (Ohio State University, unpublished Ph.D. thesis, 1972).

Schwarz-Pich, Karl-Heinz. *Der DFB im Dritten Reich: Eine Legende auf der Spur* (Kassel: AGON, 2000).

———. *Otto Stiffling: Der SV Waldhof und die deutsche Fussball-Nationalmannschaft im dritten Reich* (Kassel: AGON Sportverlag, 1999).

Sdu Publishers, *In Memoriam* (The Hague: Sdu, 1995).

Sluyser, Meyer. *Als de dag van gisteren . . .* (Parool/Def Nieuwe Pers, n.p., n.d.).

———. *Er groeit gras in de Weesperstraat* (Amsterdam: Het Parool, n.d.)

Smit, Susan. "De bal bleef rollen: Ajax binnen voetballend Amsterdam tijdens de Tweede Wereldoorlog" (University of Amsterdam, unpublished thesis, 1997).

Stad, M. I. *Uit de dood herrezen, oorlogsherinneringen* (Amsterdam: Bataffsche Leeuw, 1995).

Straede, Therkel. *October 1943: The Rescue of the Danish Jews from Annihilation* (Copenhagen: Royal Danish Ministry of Foreign Affairs/The Museum of Danish Resistance 1940–1945, n.d.).

Swijtink, André. *In de pas, sport en lichamelijke opvoeding in Nederland tijdens de Tweede Wereldoorlog* (Haarlem: De Vrieseborch, 1992).

Ticher, Michael. "Jews and Football in Berlin, 1890–1933: A Case Study of Identity and Continuity in German Sport" (University of New South Wales, unpublished bachelor's thesis, 1994).

Verkamman, Matty, Henri van der Steen, and John Volkers. *De internationals, de historie van Oranje* (Turnhout: Thomas Rap/ Weekbladpers/Voetbal International, 1999).

Vermeer, Evert. *95 Jaar Ajax: 1900–1995* (Amsterdam: Luitingh-Sijthoff, 1996).

Vogt, Willem, and others. *Holland-België, 11 maart 1928–7 april 1968* (Hilversum: C. de Boer jr, 1968).

Volkers, Kees. *Het verzwegen Oranje: Nederlandse internationals in oorlogstijd* (Amsterdam: Thomas Rap, 1996).

Vooren, Jurryt van de. "Dienaren van het rood-witte koninkrijk, het dagelijkse leven van Feyenoord van 1933 tot en met mei 1948" (University of Amsterdam, unpublished thesis, 1996).

Vos, Evert de. "Verliest den moed toch niet: Joodse voetbalclubs in Amsterdam 1908–1948" (University of Leiden, unpublished thesis, 1999).

Walker, Roy. *A People Who Loved Peace* (London: Victor Gollancz, 1946).

Walter, Fritz. *11 rote Jäger: Nationalspieler im Kriege* (Munich: Copress, 1959).

Ward, Andrew. *Armed with a Football: A Memoir of Tim Ward, Footballer and Father* (Oxford: Crowberry, 1994).

Wilson, Jonathan. *Inverting the Pyramid: A History of Football Tactics* (London: Orion, 2008).

Winter, Leon de. *Serenade* (Zwolle: Stitching Collective Propaganda van het Nederlandse Boek, 1995).

———. *Supertex* (Amsterdam: De Bezige Bij, 1994).

Zalsman, G. *Karel Lotsy en het Nederlandsche Voetbal* (Baarn: De Boekerij, 1946).

Zanten, Gerth van. *Ajax, een klasse apart* (Amsterdam: H. J. W. Becht, n.d.).

Zevenbergen, Cees. *Rotterdams Voetbalglorie 1886–1986: Kroniek van een eeuw voetbalhistorie* (Rijswijk: Sijthoff Handelsdrukkerijen, 1986).

Zoest (ed.), Rob van. *Ajax 1900–2000* (Bussum: THOTH, 2000).

ARCHIVES

Archive of the Jewish Historical Museum, Amsterdam

Archive of the Koninklijke Nederlandse Voetbalbond, the Dutch Football Association

Archive of the *Nieuw Israelietisch Weekblad*

Archive of *Het Parool* newspaper, particularly for chapter 8, "Strange Lies: Ajax, World War II and P. G. Wodehouse," and chapter 13, "The Holocaust and the Making of the Great Ajax"

Archive of Sparta Rotterdam in the Rotterdam Municipal Archive, including many issues of the club journal *De Spartaan*

Football Association minutes 1937–1945

Football League minutes 1940–1945

OTHER MAGAZINES AND NEWSPAPERS

Ajax-Nieuws (1939–1945)

NRC Handelsblad

Sport in en om Amsterdam (1940–1942)

Vrij Nederland

INDEX